Memoir of the Rev. Elijah P. Lovejoy
Who was murdered in Defense of the liberty of the press at Alton, Illinois, November 7. 1837

By
Joseph C. Lovejoy & Owen Lovejoy

Digital Ninjas Media, Inc.

Memoir of the Reverend Elijah P. Lovejoy: Published by Digital Ninjas Media, Inc. Printed in the United States of America. Originally published by John S. Taylor, New York, in 1838. This book is understood to reside in the public domain, as its legal copyright terms have expired, for open & free use in the United States of America. For further information, please address Digital Ninjas Media, Inc. [www.digitalninjasmedia.com].

Digital Ninjas Logos Copyright 2010-2016 Digital Ninjas Media, Inc. All Rights Reserved. Cover design by Heath D. Alberts

ISBN-13: 978-153007491
ISBN-10: 1530072492

FIRST DIGITAL NINJAS MEDIA EDITION – Published In The United States – 02/15/16

16 17 18 19 20 21 ❖ 10 9 8 7 6 5 4 3 2 1

Original Works By Heath D. Alberts

Fiction
Terminal Beginning
Last Rights
The Battery Man
Deeper
Photographic Memory
Not On The List
A Twist Of Fate
Rockford Writes (Contributor & Editor)
The Meaning of Light

Non-fiction
Guerrilla Business
Guerrilla Business 2.0
Dave's Not Here

The DNM Historic Revival Collection

Fiction
The Sock Stories Omnibus
Tamerlane & Other Poems
Tales of Terror
Cab & Caboose

Non-Fiction
Fasting For the Cure of Disease
Army Life of an Illinois Soldier
The Great Book Collectors
Memoir of the Rev. Elijah P. Lovejoy

Memoir of the Rev. Elijah P. Lovejoy

Who Was Murdered in Defense of the Liberty of the Press At Alton, Illinois, November 7, 1837

INTRODUCTION

TO THE MEMOIR OF THE LIFE OF THE REV. ELIJAH P. LOVEJOY, MURDERED IN THE DEFENSE OF THE LIBERTY OF THE PRESS AT ALTON, IN THE STATE OF ILLINOIS, ON THE 7TH NOVEMBER, 1837.

In the biographical narratives of the Founder of the Christian religion, and of his primitive disciples, there is an internal evidence of truth, not less conclusive than that of the miracles which they performed. The miracles were the evidence necessary to prove the authenticity of his mission to his contemporaries, to whom he was accredited, to whom he revealed the hidden mystery of their own immortality, and to whom he proclaimed the laws of their own nature, the obligations of mutual benevolence and charity: - *love* upon earth – and *life* hereafter, were the everlasting pillars of his system of religion and of morals. So congenial to the nature of man are this precept, and this promise, that on presenting them in their simplicity to the mind, it would seem as if they must meet the universal acquiescence and assent of every intelligent human being. But before the precept of brotherly love, as the universal law of human kind, carried out to its logical conclusions, empires and kingdoms, principalities and powers. War and Slavery, were destined to fall prostrate, to crumble into dust, and to be extinguished on the surface of the globe.

The first extensive operation of the Christian system of religion and morals, was to demolish the religion of Rome, the mistress of the world, and at the same time, to abolish the ritual portion of the Jewish religion - systems of government as well as systems of religion, were to be overthrown, subdued, annihilated by this simple ray of supernatural light, and with those systems were to be overcome and vanquished all the selfish and sordid passions of man's nature, and all the aggregations of physical human power.

In the progressive revolutions effected by the Christian system of religion and morals, it was in the order of Providence that its operations should be slow and gradual, embracing a period of many thousand years.

Its first converts were among the humble and the lowly - the diseased who had no physician; and the vicious who had no friend. Its first apostles were fishermen, publicans, and tent-makers. The earthly condition of the Messiah was to be the son of a carpenter, and the first of his disciples above the rank of a centurion, is known only as having offered a sepulcher for his grave.

For the propagation of his doctrines he disclaimed once and again, with undeviating perseverance all recourse to an arm of flesh. He declared that his kingdom was not of this world. He declared that he came not to destroy, but to fulfil. He commanded his disciples to render to Caesar the things that were Caesar's, and he paid for his own person the tribute to Rome.

Yet no sooner was his system of morals disclosed than the Scribes and Pharisees, the Priests and the Rulers of the Synagogue, discovered in it the inevitable downfall of the Levitical Law. They accordingly seized, condemned, and executed him as a malefactor.

That the religion of the Roman empire was also to be exterminated by this kingdom of Heaven, the denomination given by the Savior to his new system of doctrines, was not so soon discovered, but could not long be concealed. The ignominious death of the teacher was in the ways of Providence, the most effective means of spreading abroad his faith. The apostles, to whom he had left the charge of preaching the gospel to all nations, encountered wherever they went, the persecution of the multitude, and of their rulers, and as the Baptist's head had fallen at the mandate of a king to satiate the vengeance of a rebuked adulteress, his accomplice Stephen became the victim of a lawless rabble, for proclaiming to them the doctrines of universal love and eternal life.

In those doctrines, however, there was a principle of vitality, destined to survive all persecution, and to triumph over all human power. The moral precepts of the Levitical Law, purified and refined, shone with un- dying luster in the new dispensation - its rites and ceremonies, its Priests and Levites, its sacrifices of blood, its visions, and its dreams, gave way to a simple and spiritual form of worship, the working of miracles, no longer necessary for the authentication of faith, was withdrawn from the disciples of the cross, and the new system of religion and morals was left to make its way in the world by the perpetual miracle of its celestial origin, self-evident by the internal demonstration of its irresistible power, and its superhuman perfection.

In the space of three hundred years it accomplished the annihilation of Rome's three hundred thousand gods. The beautiful and stupendous system of the Heathen Mythology, melted before its effulgence into air. The Caesars of imperial Rome bowed the knee to the name of Jesus, and Constantine, the master of the world, was taught by better proof than the visions of the night, that the cross of Christ was the sign by which he was to conquer.

It was not only over the false gods of paganism, that the religious and moral system of Christ was to prevail - nor was it only the cumbrous and sanguinary ritual of the Jewish dispensation that it was to supersede. The Christian system, meddles not directly with the organization of human government. It commands obedience to the laws. It enjoins reverence to the powers that be - but it lays down first principles, before which, carried to their unavoidable conclusions, all oppression, tyranny and wrong must vanish from the face of the earth.

That all mankind are of one blood, and that the relation between them is that of brothers. That the rule of social intercourse between them is that each should do to all, as he would that all should do to him. This is Christianity - and this is the whole duty of man to man.

The conflict of Christianity is with all the evil passions, aided by all the physical and all the intellectual powers of, man. The physical and intellectual powers are indeed instruments adapted equally to the use of Christianity and of its adversaries. It is by the unalterable and eternal truth of its principles, that the ultimate triumph of the kingdom of Christ must be extended throughout the habitable earth.

Its first great victory was over false religions. In the progress of ages, its slow, gradual, and progressive advancement has been over tyrannical governments. It has weaned the human mind from the toleration of governments founded only upon conquests, and acting only by arbitrary will and physical force. It has prompted the heart, and armed the hand of the Christian man to resist and overthrow them. It has taught him that the duty of obedience to government is founded upon a covenant of mutual respect for the unalienable natural rights of man: and that however this covenant may be violated by power, the rights can never be extinguished, and may always by power be resumed.

It is the pride and glory of the confederated North American Republic, that in the instrument of their first association they solemnly declared and proclaimed these truths, derived by clear unequivocal deduction, from the first principles of the Christian faith, to be self-evident - and announced them as the first principles both of their Union and of their Independence.

The second great victory of the Christian system of morals was over oppressive governments - and that victory has not yet been consummated. The absolute despotisms of antiquity, under which the lives, persons, and property of the subject were utterly unprotected from the will of the despot, vanished very early by the adoption of the Christian faith as the religion of the Roman empire. But that life, liberty, and pursuit of happiness were inextinguishable rights of all mankind, had never been proclaimed as the only rightful foundation of human association and government, until the Declaration of Independence, laid it down, as the corner stone of the North American Union.

It was a discovery in the combined science of morals and politics. It was an electrical spark which passed invisibly through the whole chain of the Christian nations, seen only at the instant of its emission - felt at once, though unseen by all - and from that day throughout the whole circle of the Christian nations, a simultaneous struggle has been in constant operation, though in forms infinitely diversified, to new model their governments and political institutions, to approximate the practical realization of those self-evident elementary principles.

But *Government*, whether civil, ecclesiastical, or military, is not the only nor the most pernicious agent of tyranny and oppression. The laws of war, and the institutions of domestic Slavery, have been far more effective instruments for converting the bounties of the Creator to the race of man into a curse, than all the tyrannies of emperors and kings that ever existed upon earth. War is a perpetual violation of the right of human beings to life, liberty, and the pursuit of happiness, and Slavery is no more than the base-born progeny of war. The Christian system of morals, as delivered by its Founder, prohibits war not in direct, but in implied, unqualified terms. This prohibition has not yet had its full development, among the nations which profess the Christian faith. They receive the law, and acknowledge its obligations, without yielding obedience to its precepts. But the Christian nations, in their practice among themselves, have in many important respects, mitigated, and in others, wholly abolished the most cruel usages and established laws of ancient war, among which hereditary Slavery was by far the most oppressive. In the wars of Christian nations between themselves, it has long since been totally abolished. The Mahometan and Heathen nations still continue to make slaves of their prisoners of war, and Christians, after discarding forever the practice of enslaving one another, have but recently begun to reflect upon the necessary consequence in the reasoning of moral principle, that the same precept which forbids them from holding as a slave their Christian brother, equally interdicts them from defiling themselves with the pollution of Heathen or Mahometan bondage.

The first cries of conscience against the engraftment of African Slavery, upon the Christian communities of the European colonies in America, were heard precisely at the time when the contest of liberty began between Great Britain and her own colonists in North America. They were raised by Anthony Benezet, a native of France, who had become an inhabitant of Pennsylvania. From him they passed to Granville Sharpe in England.

The labors of these two humble, obscure, powerless Christian philanthropists, first awakened the civilized world to the atrocious immorality of Slavery and the slave trade. Little less than a century has elapsed since this struggle of right against oppression commenced, and it has resulted in a conventional agreement of all the Christian nations, identifying the African slave trade with the crime of piracy.

But if the African Slavery be piracy, human reason cannot resist, nor can human sophistry refute the conclusion, that the essence of the crime consists not in the trade, but in the Slavery. Trade has nothing in itself criminal by the law of nature, or that can be made so by any law or compact of nations. It is one of the natural rights flowing from the condition of man; from reciprocal wants and reciprocal good will. Trade, therefore, can be made criminal only by the nature of the article in which it is carried on. It is the Slavery, and not the purchase and sale, or the transportation of the slave, which constitutes the iniquity of the African slave trade. The moral principle then, which dictated the interdict of the African slave trade, pronounced at once the sentence of condemnation upon Slavery.

Slavery had from an early period been introduced into the colonies of all the European powers of the western hemisphere. It existed in all the English colonies, though by one of those unaccountable inconsistencies which mark the imperfection of all human institutions, the mother country spurned from her own soil the Slavery which she established and supported in her colonies. It was even during the progress of the war for American Independence, solemnly settled by the decision of England's highest judicial court, that the slave of an English West Indian, if brought by his master to England, no sooner set his foot on English ground than he became a freeman. The same decision was made by the Supreme Court of the Commonwealth of Massachusetts, as a necessary consequence from the principles of the Declaration of Independence, repeated in the Declaration of Rights forming part of her State Constitution.

The subject of the ensuing memoir, the Rev. Elijah P. Lovejoy, was a native of the Commonwealth of Massachusetts - born in a state where the abjuration of the authority of Great Britain, and of the institution of Slavery, had been universally held to have been consummated by one and the same act, he had like all the citizens of that State, born since the Declaration of Independence, been bred and nurtured in the belief that Slavery was an institution, politically incompatible with a free Constitution, and religiously incompatible with the laws of God. Led by his destiny, in the pursuit of happiness, and in the fulfilment of his religious and moral duties, to the western region of his country, the fundamental condition of whose political existence was the exclusion of all Slavery and involuntary servitude, he there fell a victim to the fury of a band of ruffians, stung to madness, and driven to despair, for the fate of their darling Slavery, by the terrors of a printing press.

That an American citizen, in a state whose Constitution repudiates all Slavery, should die a martyr in defense of the freedom of the press, is a phenomenon in the history of this Union. It forms an era, in the progress of mankind towards universal emancipation. Martyrdom was said by Dr. Johnson to be the only test of sincerity in religious belief. It is also the ordeal through which all great improvements in the condition of men, are doomed to pass. The incidents which preceded and accompanied, and followed the catastrophe of Mr. Lovejoy's death, point it out as an epoch in the annals of human liberty. They have given a shock as of an earthquake throughout this continent, which will be felt in the most distant regions of the earth. They have inspired an interest in the public mind, which extends already to the life and character of the sufferer, and which it is believed will abide while ages pass away. To record and preserve for posterity the most interesting occurrences of his life has been considered an obligation of duty, specially incumbent upon the surviving members of his family, and in the effusions of his own mind, and the characteristic features of his familiar correspondence, the reader will find the most effective portraiture of the first American Martyr to the freedom of the press, AND THE FREEDOM OF THE SLAVE.

CHAPTER I

When the prophet Elijah was taken up beyond the gaze of his companions, it was but natural that the heir of his mantle should cherish his memory, and record the more important incidents of his life. So would we now trace the history of our brother Elijah Parish Lovejoy, dear indeed in life, but more beloved in death.

In the year 1790, our grandfather, Francis Lovejoy, removed from Amherst, N. H., to the town of Albion, Kennebec County, Maine. This region was then an uncultivated, indeed an almost unbroken wilderness. Only here and there, at great intervals, could the eye catch the lonely column of smoke curling up through the thick and rich foliage. With all this extended forest before him, in which to choose a home, our ancestor selected a beautiful eastern slope, terminating by the shore of a small lake, about five miles in circumference. Around its shores he set his traps, and over its surface dragged his lines. For these were favorite amusements, even at that season when desire fails. He died October 11th, 1818, aged eighty-five.

In the severe labors incident to an early settlement, among the dense forests of Maine, our father, the late Rev. Daniel Lovejoy, passed his early years. His mother was a truly devout woman, whose memory he ever cherished with lively and grateful recollections. Guided solely by her instructions, and assisted by her prayers, at the age of seventeen, after a season of deep mental distress, he gave himself to the covenant God of his mother. Two years after this, relying upon his own re- sources, and the never-failing energy of his character, he left the cleared spot of his father's farm, in order to obtain an education preparatory to the work of the ministry. He became a resident in the family of the late Rev. Elijah Parish, of Byfield, Mass. In the academy at that place he received a respectable education, and in the person of his benefactor, acquired a warm friend, faithful unto death.

He commenced the work of the ministry in 1805, and continued to labor in this, to him, delightful employment, with zeal and general acceptance until his death, August 11th, 1833, aged fifty-eight. His character is briefly, but correctly given in the following extract from a sermon preached at his funeral by the Rev. Thomas Adams, of Waterville, Maine.

"It will be interesting to dwell for a moment on the character of our departed friend, though this can hardly be necessary, speaking as I do to those who knew him well. I regret that my memory has not more faithfully retained the circumstances I have heard him relate, concerning his early religious history. The impression of deep interest it excited remains, though the detail has escaped me. He was not brought into, the kingdom of Christ, borne, as it were, on the tide of excitement, but it was when all was dark and cold around him, when professing Christians of any denomination were exceedingly rare, when there was almost every influence, but that of the word and the spirit of God to oppose, it was in circumstances like these, that he came forth, and took, it may almost be said, a solitary stand as a disciple of Christ, and, as is generally the case, with those who, in such circumstances, espouse the cause of Christ, he firmly maintained his stand. To this, I cannot doubt, you will all bear witness. Whatever imperfections you may have discovered in his character, and there are none without imperfections, - you never, I will venture to say, you never suspected that he was ashamed of Christ, or that he was unwilling, in any circumstances or in any society, to be known as a follower of Jesus. Never was he moved either by the sneers or frowns of an unbelieving world. His principles he was ever ready to avow without palliation or concealment. As he was ardent and decided in his feelings, he did not always, perhaps, exert that conciliating influence which one of a different temperament would have done. Peter had not all the softness and tenderness of John, but he was, nevertheless, a disciple, and perhaps the peculiar energy of his character, might render him the more extensively useful. As a minister of Christ he was highly valued. The native vigor of his mind, and the ardor of his feelings, overcame, in a great degree, the want of that early culture, which he ever considered important and desirable, as a preparation for the sacred office, and threw entirely into the shade those minor deficiencies which the more critical hearer might, perhaps, generally discover. The character of his devotional services showed that he had much intercourse with heaven. His mind was evidently habitually imbued with the spirit of devotion. As he was subject to an unnatural elevation and depression of spirits, this would of course occasion an inequality in the character of his public performances; but they were generally such as those of cultivated minds, would listen to with interest and profit, and he often rose to a high degree of excellence. To his brethren in the ministry he has ever been an interesting, as well as highly valued and profitable associate. His labors as a minister have been much with our feeble and destitute churches, and to them his services have been uniformly and highly acceptable. To the people of God throughout our land, he has ever been a welcome guest, and the number is great of those to whom his memory will be precious."

Our mother, who survives the tragic death of her son, was born at Winslow, Maine, February 1772. Her father, the late Ebenezer Pattee, Esq. of Unity, and her mother, Mary Stinson, were both from Georgetown, Maine. Their ancestors originated in Scotland. And here we cannot forbear to give this public testimony to the faithful instruction, and pious example of both our beloved and honored parents. They not only dedicated their children to God, but with great diligence labored to train them up in the fear of the Lord. And if any of them have done, or shall do anything worthy and good, it is but the reflection of that excellence which always shone bright before them, in the example of their parents.

CHAPTER II

Our eldest brother, Elijah Parish Lovejoy, was born at Albion, November 9th, 1802, just thirty-five years previous to the day of his burial. Three brothers preceded him to the grave; three yet live and two sisters. In childhood and youth he manifested the elements of character, which were fully developed in the trials of his last years. He was courageous, firm, and persevering.

When he had once taken a stand, he was sure to maintain it to the utmost of his power. Less than four years were numbered, when he began to exhibit his ruling passion, - an ardent desire for knowledge. At this age he read with fluency in his Bible. His letters were all learned, by his own solicitation, from his mother. He would take his book, go to her, and ask the name of a letter, and then retire to his seat, until he had marked its form, and indelibly fixed it in his memory; and then again to his mother for the name of a new letter. In the same way, he not only learned to read, but acquired much, and varied knowledge. Throughout his youth, the ends of the day saved from the axe, the plough, and the scythe, were all employed in the diligent use of books. When the small theological library of his father was exhausted, he had recourse to a public one, of a more varied character, in the vicinity. The stores of this also by weekly visits, were very soon transferred to his own mind. His memory was uncommonly retentive. While at the Sabbath school, his teacher one day remarked to the class, that they might increase their lessons for the next Sabbath. In the leisure hours of the following week, he committed the 119th Psalm, and some twenty or more hymns to go with it. Poetry he drank in like water. By reading any piece of one or two pages twice, he could accurately rehearse it. The writer has heard him repeat one hundred and fifty Hymns from Watts at a single recitation. In all the exercises of the district school of which he was a member, he evinced decided superiority. One of his mates lately remarked, that it was impossible to do more than gain a place next the head, for he that was there could not only spell the words, but also pronounce them in their order without the book. When the school was divided by what is called "choosing sides," his name was always first heard.

Nor was he first in the school-room only. He engaged with great zest in all the sports of his early companions. Swimming was our weekly, and almost daily amusement. A very considerable portion of the bottom of the lake, we have before mentioned was visited, in a competition to see who should dive the greatest number of feet. Mud or clams was the only evidence admitted as proof that the effort had been successful. A depth of twelve or fifteen feet was often reached in this dangerous, exhilarating sport. Elijah being once bantered fey his companions, swam the v/hole width of the lake, three fourths of a mile, and back again without stopping.

Under the forming hand of his assiduous mother, with a few months in each year at the district school, the first eighteen years of his life were passed. At this time he set his heart strongly upon obtaining a public education. He spent a single quarter in the Academy at Monmouth; during which he read thoroughly Virgil entire, Cicero, and Sallust. He had studied Latin but two or three weeks previous to this. His preparatory studies were continued at intervals in China Academy; and he entered a sophomore, in Waterville College, September, 1823. He was assisted in defraying the expenses of his education by one whose gifts are in every department of benevolence, the Rev. Dr. Tappan of Augusta. The writer pursued his studies preparatory to entering college with his elder brother; and he can truly say, he has not since met with a scholar, to whom the ancient authors appeared so nearly vernacular.

Occasionally he employed a leisure hour in the writing of poetry. One specimen is given, written previous to his entering college. With the allowance for youth, and limited advantages, which the indulgent will make, it may be read with some interest. The Poem is entitled "Europe." Having painted some of the revolutions of that continent, he now speaks of one to come still more overwhelming:

> "But Europe's fields were drunk with blood,
> Drawn from the martyrs of their God;
> The sword of vengeance long had slept, -
> But justice still its vigils kept:
> Heaven guarded with a jealous eye,
> The day of retribution nigh.
> 'Twas come! then fell the awful blow,
> And Europe drank the cup of woe,
> Till Heaven, appeased, withdrew its hand,
> And mercy saved the sinking land.
> Back to a state of bondage turned.
> Yet Freedom in their bosoms burned;
> And still they wish, in slavery bound,
> The prize oft sought but never found.
> An awful calm has filled their sky;
> Presage of some convulsion nigh;
> Like the low vapors deep, and still,
> That hang around the sunny hill, -
> Ere some dread tumult shake the skies,
> And all the heavens in anger rise.
> The wild, dark murmurings of despair
> Are kindling into madness there;
> Tyrants combined must try in vain,
> Its bursting fury to restrain;
> The spark of Freedom, Nature gives,
> Oppressive bondage but revives.

Taught by the errors of the past.
Their arms shall meet success at last.
Ah, who can view the fearful sight,
When Europe rises in its might!
In frenzied madness flies to arms,
And sounds aloud death's deep alarms!
O the dread scene that meets the eye,
As wistful fancy passes by.
Where the vast plain its surface wends,
Far as the level sight extends!
Whole nations in collected might,
Fierce for the onset join the fight.
With beaming helmets nodding high,
And broad swords flashing to the sky,
With vengeful hearts, that scorn to yield,
They stain with blood the verdant field.
In battle's fiercest, wild array.
Rise the dread tumults of that day,
Fresh slaughter bathes th' ensanguined ground,
Heaps fall on heaps and groans resound;
Fell Fury wantons o'er the plain!
Death riots on its thousands slain!
Nature alarmed, her voice awakes,
Earth to her inmost center shakes.
Terror aloft its banners spreads,
Death's angel hovers o'er their heads!
From Etna livid flashes fly.
And gleam along the blackened sky,
Heaven from on high its fury pours,
And ocean beats its sounding shores; -
Hell's blackest furies urge the fight,
Despair, wild rage, and dread affright;
Discord, the worst of all the train,
Swells the red horrors of the plain!
Fierce and more fierce the combat grows.
And loud resound the hostile blows;
Like hons rushing for the prey.
Thro' heaps of slain their urge their way,
Promiscuous mighty chiefs are killed,
Rage, death, and carnage load the field!'
Oh! tell not half the horrid tale,
'Twould make the firmest spirit quail.
Nations inhumed, unhonored lie,
And dim the warrior's flashing eye I
Lo! hovering clouds obscure the sight,
And hide the scene in sable night.
Turn where the pleasing theme would lead,
Where Freedom claims her dear bought meed;
Fell tyrants from their thrones are hurled.

Justice shall renovate the world!
Its even balance hold secure.
And anarchy shall rule no more:
No more Oppression's cruel hand
Spread devastation o'er the land;
No more beneath a tyrant's frown
Virtue shall cast her honors down.
But white rob'd peace her arms extend.
And millions in her temple bend;
From orient beams to western skies,
Sweet incense from her shrine arise.
O'er Nature's face new beauties spread,
And skies their softest influence shed;
No blasting star's malignant breath,
Shall scatter wide contagious death;
The scorching sun its beams restrain,
Nor billows toss the unruffled main.
Light playful zephyrs fan the trees,
Sweet odors rise on every breeze,
Heaven with its gifts descend to men.
And Eden bloom on earth again."

The following, written while in college, unless we are very partial judges, contains poetic merit.

THE LITTLE STAR

"I would I were on yonder little star,
  That looks so modest in the silver sky,
Removed in boundless space so very far,
  That scarce its rays can meet the gazer's eye.
Yet there it hangs all lonely bright and high.

O could I mount where fancy leads the way.
How soon would I look down upon the sun.
Rest my tired wing upon his upward ray.
And go where never yet his beams have shone,
Light on that little star and make it all my own.

I'm tired of earth, 'tis nought but care and pain.
Where misery riots on its helpless prey;
Small joy, at least that I can find, therein.

But constant grief and gloom - without a single ray,
That points the wearied soul to a more genial day.
There is no faith on earth, and truth has fled,
Man's heart is steel, unmoved at pity's tear.
And justice has on her own altar bled -

Love dwells not with us, in some happier sphere.
It makes its angel heaven to innocence so dear.

Oh! there are moments when the trembling soul
Feels its own ruins, scathed, and scarred, and torn,
And gazes wildly as the tempests howl -
Thus have I felt - Oh God! why was I born,
A wretch all friendless, hopeless, and forlorn.

And yet I am, there is a spark within,
Time cannot quench, nor yet eternity;
A boundless, countless space to kindle in, -
An emanation from the Deity, -
And while He shines it cannot cease to be.

But how or where - 'tis doubt and darkness all,
Or oft times seems so, yet full well I know.
There is beyond this sublunary ball,
A land of souls, a heaven of peace and joy,
Whose skies are always bright, whose pleasures never cloy

And if to souls released from earth 'tis given,
To choose their home thro' bright infinity.
Then yonder star shall be my happy heaven,
And I will live unknown, for I would be
The lonely hermit of Eternity."

He graduated, receiving the first honors of his class, in September, 1826. On that occasion he pronounced a poem, entitled the "Inspirations of the Muse."

"Who has not felt, when life's dull stream was low,
 When hope had fled, and pleasure waned to woe;
 When all within was dreary, dark, and wild -
 On feeling's ruins sat despair, and smiled -
 And like the shadows by the moonbeams thrown
 On chilly waters, faint and cold it shone;
 Who has not felt the melting charm that stole
 Like healing virtue o'er the stricken soul,
 When some fair hand the trembling lyre had swept,
 And waked the Muse, that lingered there and slept;
 Her magic charms, her tones so sweetly given,
 They tell like dreams which Gabriel brings from heaven,
 And, on the cold, cold regions of the breast.
 Come warm with life in visions of the blest.
 The frozen heart which never felt before,
 Dissolves in grief and smiles its mis'ry o'er,
 And as it weeps the obscuring clouds away,

Hope gilds the tears with sunshine's softest ray;
Peace o'er the tempest throws its rainbow charms,
Sure pledge of joy, yet timid from alarms:
The enchanting prospect opens wide and clear.
When Beauty blushes where the loves appear!

O who that has not proudly counted o'er
Such hours enshrined in Mem'ry's choicest store,
When, as the dream of life was flitting by,
They flashed in brightness on the suff"rer's eye;
And left their marks transcribed upon his soul,
Unsullied pages in life's gloomy scroll:
Gently they spoke in silver notes of bliss,
As if heav'n stooped to whisper words of peace.

So can the Muse enchant the yielding heart.
New hopes, new pleasures, and new joys impart;
When meek and mild, she comes in tenderness,
To sooth our sorrows, and our comforts bless.
And smiles as love smiles o'er the bed of death,
Or bends like hope to catch the parting breath;
But if, with all her gorgeous drap'ry on.
She strikes the note that glory rides upon -
With hues of grandeur deep around her thrown,
And stately mien that Virtue's self might own -
'Tis then she kindles in th' expanding soul
Desires immortal, thoughts above control.
She chants her death song o'er the hero's grave,
Each arm is mighty and each coward brave;
And when the untamed victor of the fight.
Prepared to use the vengeance of his might,
Witness, Euripides, and Homer, thou,
How oft her strains have smoothed the angry brow;
Loosed from his hands the pris'ner's slavish chain.
And bade the captive be a man again.
She strikes the chords that round her heart entwine,
And warm responses breath on ev'ry line.
The mind, awakened by the burning strain,
Starts in a flight which seraph scarce can gain:
Bursts from its mortal shroud and soars away.
And basks and revels in unclouded day;
Leaves earth's dull scenes with all its cares and woes,
Mounts into light, and kindles as it goes!

Oh! there are moments when the winged mind,
Free and unshackled as the viewless wind,
In full poetic pride goes gloriously
With cherubim in concert up the sky;
Counts ev'ry planet as it rolls away

In bold relief into eternity!
Joins the full choir which sings along the spheres,
Among the star-crowned circles of the years!
In strains that e'en the Eternal stoops and hears!
Or vent'rous soars above the thrice-arched sky.
And bends exulting through infinity.
In that vast space where unknown sunbeams sleep,
Or hidden stars their glorious night-watch keep;
Whose light still trav'ling since time first began.
Through the immense, has n-ever shone on man -
In those far regions, where no baleful beam
Shoots on the soul its dark and vap'ry gleam;
Where sinless angels play along the air.
And hymn their loves, or bend in holy pray'r;
Here can the mind expatiate unrestrained
O'er beauties such as fancy never feigned;
Or higher still, bow at th' Eternal shrine,
Where seraphim with veiled faces shine!
Nay lift the curtain from before the throne,
And gaze with wondering awe upon the Great Unknown!
So once in Eden's ground, that blissful scene.
Where fear was not, for guilt had not yet been,
Man sought the temple where his Maker trod,
And fearless held communion with his God.
Surely, if heav'nly wisdom e'er designed
One peerless gift in mercy to mankind,
One noble proof in the creative plan,
Which stamps his high original on man;
'Tis that poetic fire which bids him rise,
And claim his home, his kindred in the skies;
Which rides in safety o'er life's troublous storms,
And smiles on death in all its untried forms.
'Tis a mysterious ardor none can tell,
And which but few of favored mortals feel;
An enamation from the Deity,
That claims and proves its immortality;
A part of being subtle and refined.
The pure and hallowed element of mind;
A flame which burns amidst the darkest gloom,
Shines round the grave, and kindles in the tomb.
When fainting nature trembles on her throne.
And the last spirit to the heav'ns has flown;
In that dread hour, when hushed in deep repose,
The prelude of creation's dying throes -
The dead lie slumb'ring shrouded in their pall.
And wait unconscious for the angel's call;
'Tis this shall sound the vivifying strain,
And wake mortality to life again;
Shall snatch her harp, when circling flames arise,

And soar and sing eternal in the skies!"

CHAPTER III

For several months after leaving college, he was engaged in teaching an academy. In May, 1827, he left his friends and native state, with his eye fixed upon the inviting and youthful West. Its valleys and rivers are not graduated upon a broader scale, than were his ambition and his hopes at this period. Yet it was with great reluctance that he left the social circle, of which he was often the enchanting spirit, to make his home among strangers. On his departure, he addressed his native land in the following lines.

THE FAREWELL

"Land of my birth! my natal soil farewell:
  The winds and waves are bearing me away
  Fast from thy shores; and I would offer thee
  This sincere tribute of a swelling heart.
  I love thee: witness that I do, my tears,
  Which gushingly do flow, and will not be restrained
  At thought of seeing thee, perchance no more.
  Yes, I do love thee; though thy hills are- bleak.
  And piercing cold thy winds; though winter blasts
  Howl long and dreary o'er thoe; and thy skies
  Frown oftener than they smile; though thine is not
  The rich profusion that adorns the year in sunnier climes;
  Though spicy gales blow not in incense from thy groves:
  For thou hast that, far more than worth them all.
  Health sits upon thy rugged hills, and blooms in all thy vales;
  Thy laws are just, or if they ever lean,
  'Tis to sweet mercy's side at pity's call.
  Thy sons are noble in whose veins there runs
  A richer tide than Europe's kings can boast,
  The blood of freemen: blood which oft has flowed
  In freedom's holiest cause; and ready yet to flow,
  If need should be; ere it would curdle down
  To the slow sluggish stream of slavery.
  Thy daughters too are fair, and beauty's mien
  Looks still the lovelier, graced with purity.
  For these I love thee; and if these were all,
  Good reason were there, that thou shouldst, be loved.
  But other ties, and dearer far than all,
  Bind fast my heart to thee.
  Who can forget the scenes, in which the doubtful ray
  Of reason, first dawned o'er him? Can memory e'er
  Forsake the home where friends, where parents dwell?
  Close by the mansion where I first drew breath,
  There stands a tree, beneath whose branching shade

I've sported oft in childhood's sunny hours; -
A lofty elm; - I've carved my name thereon;
There let it grow, a still increasing proof,
That time cannot efface, nor distance dim
The recollection of those halcyon days.
My father too; I've grieved his manly heart,
Full many a time, by heedless waywardness;
While he was laboring with a parent's care.
To feed and clothe his thoughtless, thankless boy.
And I have trembled as with frown severe
He oft has checked me, when perhaps I meant
To do him pleasure, with my childish mirth;
And thought how strange it was, he would not smile.
But Oh! my mother! she whose every look
Was love and tenderness, that knew no check;
Who joyed with me; whose fond maternal eye
Grew dim, when pain or sorrow faded mine.
My mother! thou art thinking now of me.
And tears are thine that I have left thee so:
Oh do not grieve, for God will hear those prayers,
Which, constantly, are going up to heaven,
For blessings on thy lone, and wandering son.
But time is speeding-; and the billowy waves
Are hurrying me away. Thy misty shores
Grow dim in distance; while yon setting sun
Seems lingering fondly on them, as 'twould take
Like me, a last adieu. I go to tread
The western vales, whose gloomy cypress tree
Shall haply soon be wreathed upon my bier:
Land of my birth! my natal soil, Farewell."

The "Wanderer" was written while on his way to the West, after a season of sickness, followed as it will show by mental depression.

(Written on the shore of Lake Erie.)

"Cam volet ilia dies, quse nil nisi corporis hujiis
Jus habit, incerti spatium mihi finiat aevi:
Parte tamen meliore mei super altaperennis
Astra ferar."
- Ovid.

"The sun was set, and that dim twilight hour.
   Which shrouds in gloom whatever it looks upon.
Was o'er the world: stern desolation lay
   In her own ruins; every mark was gone,
Save one tall, beetling monumental stone.

Amid a sandy waste it reared its head,

All scathed and blackened by the lightning shock.
That many a scar and many a seam had made,
   E'en to its base; and there with thundering stroke,
Erie's wild waves in ceaseless clamors broke.

And on its rifted top the wanderer stood,
   And bared his head beneath the cold night air,
And wistfully he gazed upon the flood:
   It were a boon to him (so thought he there)
Beneath that tide to rest from every care.

And might it be, and not his own rash hand
   Have done the deed, (for yet he dared not brave.
All reckless as he was, the high command,
   Do thou thyself no harm,) adown the wave
And in the tall lake-grass that night had been his grave.

Oh! you may tell of that philosophy.
   Which steels the heart 'gainst every bitter woe:
'Tis not in nature, and it cannot be;
   You cannot rend young hearts, and not a throe
Of agony tell how they feel the blow.

He was a lone and solitary one,
   With none to love, and pity he disdained:
His hopes were wrecked, and all his joys were gone;
   But his dark eye blanched not; his pride remained:
And if he deeply felt, to none had he complained.

Of all that knew him few but judged him wrong:
   He was of silent and unsocial mood:
Unloving and unloved he passed along:
   His chosen path with steadfast aim he trod.
Nor asked nor wished applause, save only of his God.

Oh! how preposterous 'tis for man to claim
   In his own strength to chain the human soul!
Go, first, and learn the elements to tame,
   Ere you would exercise your vain control
O'er that which pants and strives for an immortal goal.

Yet oft a young and generous heart has been
   By cruel keepers trampled on and torn;
And all the worst and wildest passions in
   The human breast have roused themselves in scorn,
That else had dormant slept, or never had been born.

Take heed ye guardians of the youthful mind,
   That facile grows beneath your kindly care:

'Tis of elastic mold, and, if confined
   With too much stress, ' shoots madly from its sphere,'
Unswayed by love, and unrestrained by fear.

Oh! 'tis a fearful blasting sight to see
   The soul in rums, withered, rived, and wrung,
And doomed to spend its immortality
   Darkling and hopeless, where despair has flung
Her curtains o'er the loves to which it fondly clung.

So thought the wanderer: so, perhaps, he felt:
   (But this is unrevealed): now had he come
To the far woods, and there in silence knelt
   On the sharp flint-stone in the rayless gloom,
And fervently he prayed to find an early tomb.

Weep not for him: he asks no sympathy
   From human hearts or eyes; aloof, alone,
On his own spirit let him rest, and be
   By all his kind forgotten and unknown,
And wild winds mingle with his dying groan.

And in the desert let him he and sleep,
   In that sweet rest exhausted nature gave:
Oh! make his clay-cold mansion dark and deep,
   While the tall trees their somber foliage wave,
And drop it blighted on the wanderer's grave."

CHAPTER IV

In the latter part of the year 1827, our brother arrived at St. Louis, Missouri. He immediately engaged in teaching a school. His prospects and feelings at this period are given in a letter to his parents.

Saint Louis, February l8th, 1827
Dear Parents:

Your letter of the 27th December, has just been received, and with it the most welcome intelligence that the family are all well. I cannot say that I am home-sick, but certainly there is no idea on which I so love to dwell as home, and the honored parents and the beloved brothers and sisters, whom I have left there. Fortune has, in the main, hitherto looked unfavorably upon me, since I left home; but, I begin to hope for better things. Still, in all my past distresses one thought has consoled me, - *I have learned to appreciate a parent's love.*

I am now in St. Louis, engaged in teaching a school; and the prospect is, that I shall have a very profitable one. I may be disappointed, and I do not suffer myself to be too sanguine of the future; for the lessons of the year past have taught me to distrust dame fortune, even when she smiles the sweetest. I wish I could say, I had learned to contemn alike her favors and her frowns.

I have entirely recovered my health, it was never better than at present; but I look upon its continuance in this climate as doubtful. My appetite, after recovering from the ague, was such as I never had before, and in a few weeks my weight rose to 180 lbs.; being at least as much as I could ever claim. I find here many persons from the northern states, and the number is continually increasing. It is natural that I should regard these with an eye of partiality; but after making due allowances for sectional feelings, I am sure they constitute the most orderly, most intelligent, and most valuable part of the community. At the same time, I must confess that there are some most lamentable exceptions, and doubtless many a Yankee has fled here, whose vices forbade him an asylum among the descendants of the Puritans.

My dear, dearest Mother, I am sorry I cannot say to you, for the honor of your oracular impressions, anything which will tend to strengthen their infallibility. I have taxed my memory to the utmost; but, cannot find that on either of the days you mentioned, anything happened to me, which would warrant my disturbing your slumbers; and which I am sure I respect too much, to interrupt for any, except the most urgent reasons. At the same time you will allow me to say, that were I as thoroughly convinced that your "dreams descend from heaven," as I am that your motherly kindness will never fail, there is nothing for whose fulfilment I would more willingly vouch.

My honored Father will permit the observation, that though I have not heretofore always appreciated, as I ought, the motives and the feelings of a father, I hope I have learned wisdom in that respect; and my highest earthly gratification would be, to make easy the downhill of life of those parents, to whom I owe all that I am, and most that I have.

My dear Brothers and Sisters, I often think you assembled around the family board, and in my dreams am often seated there with you; but I awake and find myself separated from you, by a distance of at least two thousand miles. But though the chain which binds us together is lengthened to such a degree, I do not believe it is weakened, and oh, may nothing but death divide it. Again, as one who knows better than you can, I most earnestly advise you, again and again, love, honor, and obey your parents. Friends like them, you need not expect to find in this world. I must conclude by giving love and affection to all.

Your most affectionate and dutiful son,

ELIJAH P. LOVEJOY.

At or about this date the following stanzas appeared in the "Republican," of St. Louis.

MY MOTHER

'Men forget, hut all shall not be forgotten.'
"There is a fire that burns on earth,
   A pure and holy flame;
It came to men from heavenly birth,
   And still it is the same,
As when it burned the chords along
That bore the first born seraph's song -
Sweet as the hymn of gratitude
That swelled to heaven when ' all was good,'
No passion in the choirs above
Is purer than a mother's love!

My Mother! how that name endears.
Through Memory's griefs and Sorrow's tears!
I see thee now as I have seen
   With thy young boy beside thee -
Thou didst not know, nor couldst thou deem
   The ills that would betide me;
For sorrow then had dimmed that eye
Which beamed with only ecstasy!
Ah! life was then a joyous thing-,
And time bore pleasure on its wing-.

How buoyant did the minutes move,
For I was hope and thou wert love.
Beneath thy smiles I closed the day
And met them at the morning ray;
My infant heart was full of glee
And every chord struck harmony.
And often as there would betide
Some little griefs my heart to gall,
I bore them to my mother's side,
And one kind kiss dispelled them all.

And I have knelt with thee - when none
   Were near but thou and I -
In trembling awe before the throne
   Of Mercy in the sky;
And when thy melted heart was poured
Before the Being thou adored;
How holy was that prayer of thine.
Fit offering for a heavenly shrine -
Not for thyself a wish - not one -
But smile upon, Lord, bless my son!
And I have risen and g-one my way.
   And seemed to have forgot;
Yet oft my wandering thoughts would stray
   Back to that hallowed spot -
While feelings new and undefined.
Would crowd upon my laboring mind.

O days of innocence and peace!
O ill exchanged for manhood's years!
When mirth that sprang from youthful bliss,
Is drowned beneath misfortune's tears.
My heart has since been sadly worn.
While wave on wave has o'er it borne;
And feelings once all fresh and green.
Are now as though they ne'er had been.
And Hope that bright and buoyant thing",
E'en hope has lent despair its wing;
And sits despoiled within my breast,
A timid, torturing, trembling guest!
I dare not look upon the past,
I care not for the future cast.
Yet o'er this darkness of the soul
   There comes one cheering beam
Pure, warm, and bright, of rapture full
   As angel visits seem -
A Mother's love, a Mother's care. -
My aching heart, there's comfort there!
   It is as if a lovely rose

Should bloom amid the icy waste;
    For while the heart's life-streams are froze,
Its fragrance o'er it still is cast.

Weary and worn my bed I've shared
    With sickness and with pain.
Nor one of all that saw me, cared
    If e'er I rose again -
Heedless and quick they past along.
With noisy mirth and ribald song.
And not a hand outstretched to give
A cordial that should bid me live.
And woman, too, that nurse of ease,
Made up of love and sympathies.
Ay, woman, she - she passed me by,
With cold, averted, careless eye;
Nor deigned to ask, nor seemed to care
If death and I were struggling there!
Ah! then I've thought and *felt* it too -
My Mother is not such as you!
How would she sit beside my bed,
And pillow up my aching head.
And then, in accents true as mild,
'Would I were suffering for thee, child!'
And try to soothe my griefs away,
And look e'en more than she could say;
And press her cheek to mine, nor fear
Though plague or fever wantoned there;
And watch through weary nights and lone,
Nor deem fatigue could be her own.
And if, perchance, I slept, the last
I saw, her eyes, were on me cast;
And when I woke, 'twould be to meet
The same kind anxious glance, so sweet.
And so endearing that it seemed
As from a seraph's eye it beamed.

My Mother! I am far away
    From home, and love, and thee:
And stranger hands may heap the clay
    That soon may cover me;
Yet we shall meet - perhaps not here -
But in yon shining, azure sphere:
And if there's aught assures me more,
    Ere yet my spirit fly.
That Heaven has mercy still in store,
    For such a wretch as I,
'Tis that a heart so good as thine,
Must bleed - must burst along with mine

> And life is short, at best, and Time
> Must soon prepare the tomb;
> And there is sure a happier clime,
> Beyond this world of gloom -
> And should it be my happy lot -
> After a life of care and pain.
> In sadness spent, or spent in vain -
> To go where sighs and sin are not;
> 'Twill make the half my heaven to be,
> My Mother, evermore with thee!"

In the course of the next year he engaged in editing and publishing a political paper advocating, the claims of Henry Clay to the presidency. His prospects of political elevation were more and more flattering, until January, 1832; when on account of a change in his religious feelings, Lis future life took an entirely new direction. Of the commencement and progress of that change, he speaks in the two letters here inserted.

St. Louis, January 24th, 1832
My dear and honored Parents:

Forgive your undutiful son that he has so long neglected writing to you. I hardly know what excuse to make, and I well know there can be none sufficient. I hope you have received the "Times" regularly; this will have kept you informed of my existence, and also of the nature of my employment. I have usually enjoyed good health - much better than I anticipated. Poor brother Daniel! he is gone, and, as I trust, to a better world. If so, his departure affords no cause of lamentation. Your letter containing the information of his death was safely received.

My dear Father and Mother, amidst all my wanderings,

> "In all my griefs, and God has given my share,"

I have never forgotten - it has been the chief source of my consolation, that day and night you have been interceding for me at a Throne of Grace. I have never, for a moment, doubted that paternal affection ceased not to plead for mercy upon the wayward and far distant son. I knew that that love was yours, which neither time nor distance could weaken, and think you, that I should forget the many earnest and agonizing petitions which I have heard ascending from the family altar. Oh, never! I will tell you all. Last spring there was a partial revival of religion in this city. I became somewhat seriously impressed, I may say considerably so. I attended the inquiry meetings, and for some time really felt a delight in religious exercises. But gradually these feelings all left me, and I returned to the world a more hardened sinner than ever. At this time the spirit of God is manifesting itself in our city in a most wonderful manner. Its effects are such as I have never before witnessed. Meetings are held almost every evening, at which individuals of all ages and characters attend, and where the power of God to salvation is manifested, so that the blindest must see and the hardest feel. I have reason to hope that the good spirit has again visited me, inviting me to forsake the world and come to Jesus. I own that I hardly dare admit such a belief, it seems to me scarcely possible that one who has so long lived in sin, who has resisted so much light, and has so often grieved away the Holy Spirit, as I have, should be again visited with its heavenly influences. But I hope it is so.

And now, my dear and honored Father and Mother, will you not pray for me- if possible, with more earnestness than you have ever yet done? Will you not plead for me the provisions of that covenant into which I have been baptized? Oh, if you knew what value I place upon your prayers, if you knew what your first-born son would give to be at this moment, kneeling between you, before the altar of mercy, while you made supplication for him to the Giver of life and death. I am sure you would pray - pray earnestly - pray unceasingly, that the long-lost wanderer might be restored to the fold from which he hath strayed. Oh, forget all my ingratitude, my un-thankfulness, and the innumerable instances of my undutiful conduct, and think only of the repentant son, who entreats, who implores your prayers, that he may not perish eternally. Oh, could I this night fall down at your feet, and ask your forgiveness and beg your blessing; I should feel that there might yet be hope even for me, vile, sinful, and disobedient as I have been, both to Heaven and to you. But you will not remember aught against me, I know you will not, I know that I have your forgiveness ere I asked it. But will God forgive me, against whom my sins have been infinitely more numerous and aggravated? Can I hope for pardon from Him - I, who have done despite to the covenant of grace, and have so long counted the blood of the covenant an unholy thing?

My Father and my Mother, my dear, dear parents, let me remind you of the obligations you assumed, when you consecrated me to God in my infancy. By the vows you then made, by the gratitude you felt that God had given you a man-child, by your love for Him who has re- deemed you, by your sense of the worth of an immortal soul, let me adjure you to pray for me, - me, the chief of sinners, - me, whom, perhaps, you will never see more till we meet at the bar of God in judgment.

I request, my dear parents, that you will call the family together, read them this letter, and then unite in prayer for him, a son and brother who dwells among strangers in a strange land. Adieu, my dear and honored parents, and may Heaven bless you for all your kindness to

Your unthankful but still dutiful son,

ELIJAH P. LOVEJOY

St. Louis, February 22, 1832
My dear and honored Parents,

After reading this letter, you will, I think, be ready to exclaim with me, "God's ways are not our ways, nor his thoughts as our thoughts." When this letter reaches you, I shall, if God spares my life and health, be on my way to Princeton, in New Jersey, for the purpose of entering upon my studies preparatory to the work of the ministry. I wrote you, four weeks since last Tuesday, and, as you will have learned from that letter, was then in a state of deep distress. Sorrow had taken hold upon me, and a sense of my long career in sin and rebellion against God, lay heavy upon my soul. But it pleased God, and blessed be his holy name, to grant me, as I humbly hope, that very night, joy and peace in believing. I was, by divine grace, enabled to bring all my sins and all my sorrows, and lay them at the feet of Jesus, and to receive the blessed assurance that He had accepted me, all sinful and polluted as I was.

My dear parents, I can see you now, after having read thus far, shedding tears of joy over the return of your prodigal son; but oh! forget not to return thanks to that God of the promises, who, as I humbly hope, has at length heard your prayers in behalf of one, for whom, at times, you were ready to say there remaineth no longer any hope.. And surely, you may well join with me in saying, that nothing but a miracle of sovereign mercy could have arrested and saved me, from eternal perdition. How I could have so long resisted the entreaties, the prayers, and the tears of my dear parents, and the influences of the Holy Spirit, is, to me, a wonder entirely incomprehensible; and still greater is my astonishment, and my admiration, that God has still borne with me, still continued unto me the influences of his spirit, and at last brought me to submit myself to Him. I think I can now have some faint conceptions of boundless, infinite mercy. I look back upon my past life, and am lost in utter amazement at the perfect folly, and madness of my conduct. Why, my dear parents, it is the easiest thing in the world to become a Christian - ten thousand times easier than it is to hold out un-repenting against the motives which God presents to the mind, to induce it to forsake its evil thoughts and turn unto Him. If I could forget what I have been and what I have done, I should certainly say it was impossible that anyone could read of a Savior, and not love him with their whole heart. The eternal God - the infinite Jehovah - has done all he could do - even to the sacrificing his own Son - to provide a way for man's happiness, and yet they reject him, hate him, and laugh him to scorn! How God could suffer me to live so long as I have lived, is more than I can understand. Well may He call upon the heavens to be astonished both at His own forbearance, and the unnatural rebellion of his creatures. Do Christians ever feel oppressed, as it were, with the debt of gratitude which they owe to their Redeemer. Why, it seems to me, sometimes, as if I could not bear up under the weight of my obligations to God in Christ, as if they would press me to the very earth. And I am only relieved by the reflection that I have an eternity in which I may praise and magnify the riches of his grace.

And now, my dear and honored parents, how shall I express my sense of the gratitude I owe to you - how shall I ask pardon for all the undutiful conduct, of which I have been guilty towards you? I want words to do either; but I can pray to God to forgive me, and to reward you, and this I do daily. Oh, how much do I owe you for your kindness to me in everything, but chiefly for the religious instruction you bestowed upon me from my earliest youth; for your affectionate warnings and continued entreaties that I would attend to the welfare of my own soul; and for your prayers, without ceasing, to God that he would have mercy upon me, while I had no mercy on myself. For all these may Heaven return upon your own heads, a seven-fold blessing.

I made a public profession of religion, and joined the church in this city, on the Sabbath before the last, the 12th of the present month. With me joined also thirty-five others by profession, and four by letter. There are, probably, as many more prepared to join as soon as the next communion shall arrive. You will see by these facts that an unusual attention to religion exists in this place. God is doing wonders here. The revival still continues, and day after tomorrow will commence a four days' meeting. How long this state of things will continue is known only to God; but we know that he can work, and none can hinder.

After much prayer and consultation with my pastor, the Rev. William S. Potts, and other Christian friends, I have felt it my duty to turn my immediate attention to the work of the ministry, and shall on the first of the week start for Princeton, with a view of entering upon the necessary studies. If God shall spare my hitherto unprofitable life, I hope to be enabled to spend the remainder of it in some measure, to his glory. Time now with me is precious, and every day seems an age, till I can be at work in the vineyard of the Lord. Oh, my dear parents, are not the ways of Providence inscrutable. How long and how often did you pray that your first-born son might succeed his father in preaching the gospel, and after you had doubtless given over all such hopes, then the Lord displays his power in calling in the wanderer.

I hope to see you in the course of the summer face to face; for if practicable, and within the reach of my means, I shall take time enough in a vacation to make a visit to my dear loved home. Oh, how I long to embrace my parents, and brothers, and sisters, and tell them what God has done for me. But I feel that I ought to say, and I trust He will enable them to say, "His will be done." Surely after all his goodness unto us, we should no longer indulge in one murmuring thought.

Brother Owen and brother John, you are now the only members of the family who have not professed to hope in Christ - to have made your peace with God. Oh, let me entreat you, beseech you, not to put it off a moment longer. Tempt not God, as I have done. Think of poor brother Daniel, and make your peace with a Savior before you sleep, after reading this.

    Your dutiful and grateful son,
        ELIJAH P. LOVEJOY

It may be easily imagined that the above letters gave great joy to his parents and friends. The following is the joint reply of father and mother.

Albion, March 19, 1832
My dear first-born, and long absent Son,

You perhaps may better conceive, than I can express the sensations your two last letters have excited in my mind. Your first, found me in a state of deep mental debility, to which as you know I have always been more or less subject. But I am now better - to which your letter has contributed much. There is no other way, in which you could have given us so much joy, as you have done in the full account of your conversion, and of the intended change of your pursuits. It is just what we could have wished, had it been left to us to dictate in every particular. Let all the praise and glory be given to God through Jesus Christ, I am glad you have made haste to keep His commandments. You gave us much more credit than we think we deserve. Our faith has been wavering, and our desires far less ardent than they should have been. Our attachment to the blessed covenant has not been in proportion to its value; yet no day has passed when you have been forgotten at the throne of grace; and the blessed promises of the covenant have tended more than anything else to keep alive my hope.

Your last letter produced sensations not unlike those, which I presume Jacob felt, when he saw the wagons sent from Egypt by his long-absent son. Do not think of deferring your visit a moment longer than is absolutely necessary. Returning from Washington, I found your letter upon a generous sheet - I read and read it, and then we sang the 101st hymn, first book. We then bowed and gave thanks to the God of heaven, who hath mercy on whom he will have mercy. Thanks to his name that he has brought our dear son to the arms of the Savior, and rescued him from the wrath to come. Oh, blessed be the Lord God of Abraham, and let all flesh bless his holy name. You can but know that you are greatly beloved by all the family, and no one could diffuse more happiness among us. Your mother wishes to fill the remainder.

    As ever, your affectionate father,
        DANIEL LOVEJOY

My dear Son,

I wrote you in answer to yours of January 22d, giving you an account of our health and circumstances. I cannot say that the contents of your last letter were more than I expected; for I did really believe that God had given you a broken and contrite heart; and that is where the Holy Spirit delights to dwell. Neither can I say it is more than I have asked. It is just what I have prayed for, as I have thought, with all my heart. But I can say it is more than I deserved. But God is a sovereign; He does not deal with us according to our deserts, nor reward us according to our iniquities. For as far as the heavens are above the earth, so far are his thoughts above our thoughts.

The death of your dear brother Daniel, was a dark and mysterious providence. It almost overwhelmed me with gloom and despondency; and I thought it could never be explained to me, till I arrived at the heavenly world. But I think I can now see why it must be so. I was not sufficiently humble, nor prepared to receive the blessings, which God had in store for me. Oh, that the blessed God would keep me at his feet in the very dust before Him. I never had so clear a view of the evil nature of sin, and of the glorious plan of salvation by Jesus Christ, as I have had since the death of my dear child. God has made me feel that it is an evil and bitter thing to sin against Him - that his ways are equal. And now my dear child, I hope you will follow on to know the Lord, that you may find your going forth prepared as the morning - that His spirit may come unto you as the rain, as the latter and the former rain unto the earth.

So prays your rejoicing,
Affectionate, mother,
ELIZABETH LOVEJOY

CHAPTER V

The following letters were written soon after arriving at Princeton.

Theological Seminary, Princeton, N. J. April 2d, 1832
My dear and honored Parents,

Through the great and most undeserved goodness of God unto me, I arrived here on the 24th ult. in good health, and on the same day was admitted as a member of this institution. And so I am here preparing to become a minister of the everlasting gospel! When I review my past life, I am astonished and confounded, and hardly know which most to wonder at, my own stupidity, and blindness, and guilt, or the long-suffering and compassion of God. That He should have blessed me with such opportunities of becoming acquainted with His holy word - should have given me parents who, in the arms of their faith, dedicated me to Him, according to His gracious covenant, and who early, and constantly, and faithfully, and with many tears, warned and entreated me to embrace the offers of salvation, through Jesus Christ; and notwithstanding all this, when He saw me hardening my heart, resisting the prayers of my parents and friends, grieving His holy spirit, and counting the blood of the covenant into which I had been baptized an unholy thing, that He should have still borne with me, should have suffered me to live, and at last given me reason to hope that I have by his grace been enabled to return to my Father's house, all this seems to me a miracle of goodness, such as a God alone could perform, and far too wonderful for me to comprehend. I can only bow down my head and adore. How often do I ask myself, why have I been thus favored? why was I made to hear the invitation of the Blessed Spirit? "Return unto the Lord, and he will have mercy on you." Oh, here is love and wisdom united in a degree beyond our highest conceptions. I think I said in my last, that no part of the revealed will of God appeared more precious to me, than that which reveals to man the gracious covenant which Jesus Christ made with Abraham, and to fulfil the stipulations of which on His part, in process of time he came into the world, expiated our sins in his own body on the tree. The more I reflect upon the subject, the more reason do I see for thankfulness and gratitude to God, for his condescension in entering into such a covenant, and for his sovereign mercy in giving me parents who acknowledged its obligations, and in the arms of faith brought me before His altar, and consecrated me to God. I think I can see plainly that the Holy Spirit has made this a means of keeping the truth before my mind, when to everything else I was insensible. Oh, my dear parents, join with me in adoring and magnifying the name of the Lord God of our salvation.

   Your affectionate son,

ELIJAH P. LOVEJOY

Theological Seminary, Princeton, N. J., April 2ith, 1832
My Dear Sister Sibyl,

Your letter gave me both pleasure and pain. I was very glad to hear from you, directly, to see your hand-writing, but it grieved me much to hear of the state of our dear father's health. It is the more distressing to me, that it is altogether unexpected. I had thought that he had, at last, succeeded in banishing from his mind those fits of morbid melancholy which so entirely unman whomsoever they take possession of. Too well, do I know, by experience, that there is no remedy for a state of mind like this; none, at least, to be found on earth - neither my staying away or coming home, will have the least effect. But there is One who can minister to a mind diseased - One in whose hand are all the issues of life and death. How strange, then, my dear sister, that I, who had so often seen and so deeply felt the insufficiency of all created help, should so long have neglected not only my duty but my highest privilege, of applying to that great Physician! How depraved must be that understanding, and how perverted that intellect, which thus knows its disease, yet seeks not, nay, refuses to be healed. I hope I shall never again be at a loss for a source of consolation, let what may betide. I am sure I ought not to be, but I have great reason to tremble lest Satan and my own wicked heart get the better of me. It is no easy matter to fight such enemies as these, but with Christ strengthening me, I know I shall come off more than conqueror.

How does our dear mother do? You say in your letter, that she enjoys good health. For this, the Lord be thanked. She is a wonderful woman. You know this already, but you do not know it so well as I do - I have never seen her equal, take all her qualities together. So pure, so disinterestedly benevolent a heart, seldom lodges in a house of clay, and never, save in the bosom of a mother. Great, I doubt not will be her reward in heaven, for there is nothing here which can compensate for such love.

I have written back to Owen and to John, since I came here - having had a letter from John, but not from Owen. It is of them that I think more than of any of the rest of the family. I have, sometimes, enjoyed great confidence in the mercies and faithfulness of God, in relation to their case. If He has had mercy on me, the oldest and most guilty sinner of you all, why should I despair, or even doubt of his willingness to receive them also. I have thus far made it a rule to pray specially for them, every night and morning, and, if God will, I intend to continue this practice until my prayers shall have been answered, or my voice shall have been "lost in death." It seems to me as if they could not remain insensible, could I but see them, and tell them how unspeakably precious is Christ to the penitent soul.

Your affectionate brother,

ELIJAH P. LOVEJOY

The latter part of May, and the month of June, were spent in a visit to his friends in Maine. During this period, our beloved father was suffering under deep mental despondency. Allusion has been made to his case in the letters which have been inserted. It is again mentioned, in others which succeed. One is given also, written, as it will show, on another subject.

Theological Seminary, Princeton, N. J, Aug. 21, 1832
My dear and honored Father,

I have this day received a letter from mother, containing news, for which, I trust, I do in some measure feel thankful to God. I can hardly allow myself to credit it, and yet it is no more than I have prayed for, daily, since I left home, and no more than I have, in a good measure, believed would take place.

Mother says your health is "almost perfectly re-established." I have tried to thank a merciful God for suffering my heart to be gladdened with such blessed news. I am sure that I am thankful to him, but oh, not as I ought. Oh father! is he not a God that showeth mercy and keepeth covenant? Of all sins, it seems to me, that the sin of unbelief is the most dishonoring to God. What abundant reason have we, as a family, to praise and adore the riches of sovereign love and mercy? And what reason have all the children, and I, above all the rest, to humble ourselves, because, of our hardness of heart and blindness of mind, so that all the goodness of God could not lead us to repentance? If I am saved well do I know it can only be by sovereign love alone.

I have reason to bless God, who gave me parents, that faithfully instructed me in the knowledge of His holy word from my earliest years, who prayed for me, with many tears and strong cries unto heaven, and who gave me away in covenant to God. All these things are blessings too great to be expressed, and to them, under God, do I feel that I owe all my hopes of salvation.

I do not, my dear father, enjoy that lively sense of forgiving love, that communion with God, that I could wish. Sin has yet dominion over me, and its power is terrible. I used to think that when the heart was once renewed, it was no longer subject to the temptations of sin, and that it was as easy then to keep the commandments, as it had been to disobey them. But, either I was mistaken then, or I deceive myself now; for so far from finding it an easy matter to keep the law, I cannot, or at least I do not, do it at all. It seems almost impossible to break away from my old habits of sin, and one temptation returns upon another, until sometimes I give up in despair. My heart appears an inexhaustible fountain of sin; for no sooner is one subdued than another takes its place, no sooner is one train of evil thoughts banished, than another succeeds; and every day, and a hundred times a day, do I think that I am growing worse and worse, instead of increasing in holiness. It is at such times that I am beset with unbelief; seeing my sins so great and numerous, I doubt that the blood of Christ is sufficient to cleanse me from them. And this is the sorest trial of all; for when this hope fails me then all is gone. And thus I live, hoping, doubting, fearing, ashamed of myself, and of my own unworthiness, and yet not daring to trust unhesitatingly in the merits of Christ. Do write me, my dear father, a long letter, and deal faithfully with me. You know the trials that await the Christian, and you know me and my weak points, and those where Satan will be most likely to assault me. Where else can I look for such faithful, disinterested counsel, as from a father.

I spent nearly a week in Bath, at Mr. Ellingwood's. He was very kind and friendly; and, it seemed to me, especially interested in your case. He spoke of the missionary meeting at Fryeburg, and of the part which you took, saying, that your remarks at the administration of the sacrament, were the best he ever heard in his life.

Your affectionate son,
ELIJAH P. LOVEJOY

Theological Seminary, Princeton, N. J., Sept. 15th. 1832
My Dear And Honored Father,

Your letter of August 26th, was received with emotions such as I cannot, and I need not attempt to describe. I think I did, in some measure feel thankful to the Disposer of events; but, oh, not as I ought. How-strange that ingratitude and distrust, and cold affections should ever find place in the hearts of Christians! Is not, my dear father, the sin of unbelief one of the most heinous of all sins?

I have never, since I have been old enough to think and judge of such things, doubted that my father was a Christian, and although all my notions on this subject have been wretchedly crude, yet I could always understand the declaration of the Savior, - " All that my Father hath given unto me, I will keep;" and have, therefore, ever supposed that my father's case illustrated the truth of the declaration, - "Whom the Lord loveth he chasteneth."

Do you not recollect father, when I was at home, that I quoted to you the words of Manoah's wife, (my father, as well as Manoah, knows what a blessing it is to have a wife who can cheer and animate his drooping faith,) that "If the Lord were pleased to kill us, he would not have showed us all these things." It seems to me, if there be a family in the world who ought to adopt these words, it is ours. Sure I am, that it is not seemingly possible, that any individual can do more to provoke the Holy Spirit to leave him to his destruction, than I have done. I cannot conceive of a person more likely to resist all heavenly influences, than I was, when, as I trust, I was found by a compassionate Savior and constrained to come in. Grace, sovereign grace, nothing else, I am sure, could ever have rescued me.

And now, my dear father, I have to say, that under God, I feel myself indebted for my hopes to the faithfulness and the prayers of my parents. Never can I enough acknowledge my obligations to them, for dedicating me to God in the blessed covenant, for their religious instructions so faithfully repeated, and for that example of Christian conversation which I witnessed for more than twenty years. I am sure, that when you saw your children growing up around you, and no appearance of any effects of your long-continued labors, your faith must have been severely tried. I was about to say, that I do not see how you could thus have persevered; but, I will not say so, because, you had a covenant keeping God, in whom to trust. What an unspeakably precious thing is the covenant made with "Abraham and his seed." I cannot, and I will not doubt that my dear brothers Owen and John will yet be given to the prayer of their parents. All in the Lord's own time.

The 12th of the month, I endeavored to observe as a day of thanksgiving to Almighty God; and through his grace, I was enabled to feel a good degree of thankfulness and some humility. It was a precious thought that I was joining with my parents, and brothers and sisters in the delightful work of prayer and praise. The 30th, 103d, and 104th Psalms I read and meditated upon with a great deal of delight.

You remember, father, that I told you I should expect to see you here next spring; Sibyl's letter, just received, tells me you contemplate, the Lord willing, to take the trip then. Come here, and I will introduce you to one of the best men in the world, - Dr. Alexander. He has few equals that I have ever seen. Do write me a long letter. Give me the advice, the counsel I need so much. May the Lord God Almighty bless you, my dear father, and reward you a hundred-fold for all your goodness to me.

Mother, - It seems to me there is no need of dear before that word, for it includes within itself all of endearment that we can conceive. I have just left room enough to tell you that my health is good, my situation agreeable, and as for progress in my studies, you know that I should not do justice to either father or mother, if I did not make good progress in them. (This will do to tell a mother.) Where is John? I do not hear from him at all. Brother Owen, I suppose, is now at home. Tell him to love the Lord Jesus Christ.

      Your affectionate son,
      ELIJAH P. LOVEJOY

Theological Seminary, Princeton, N. J., Feb. 12th, 1833
My dear brother Joseph,

Your letter, filled indeed with tidings of woe, was received this morning. To the heart of a parent, the loss of a beloved child gives a pang which, I suppose, none but a parent can feel. Yet I most sincerely condole with you on the affliction which it has pleased God to send you. She was a pretty child, and one in whom I felt much interest, when at home last summer. Her age, too, was precisely that when children are to me most interesting, and I doubt not, you found her every day twining some new cord of affliction about your heart; but death, alas! has at once rudely snapped them all. Yet let this comfort you, that the hand of the Lord has commissioned him to do this thing, and, if you are his, it has been done in mercy. Reflect that if you could, at the present moment, take in all the bearings of the whole subject, if you could see what God sees, you would plainly discern, that what has been done is best both for you and the child; and instead of shedding tears of regret and unavailing grief, you would be pouring forth from a full heart and streaming eyes, tears of joy and thankfulness. When we have learned to have no will, but the will of our heavenly Father, then we shall never be disappointed: of this we are sure, because He doeth all his will, and none can stay him. Some things we can see here, and what we know not now, we shall know hereafter. "I shall go to him, but he shall not return to me," said David, and therefore he arose and was comforted. God has been pleased to give to little Sarah a short, and comparatively, an easy journey through this land of afflictions. How fast her little capacities are expanding we cannot tell; but I have little doubt, that she is drinking in full measures of happiness in the presence of her Savior, to a degree that we do not conceive of. Besides, if rightly improved, this event will make you a better man and a more successful minister, than you would otherwise have been

My dear sister Sarah,

You weep for your child, and I would not ask you to refrain from weeping; for nature will assert its supremacy in the bosom of a mother. The cords which bind a child to a mother's heart are strangely intertwined with her being; and every nerve and every affection vibrates to the blow which tears them asunder. It was your first-born, too. When your eyes first looked upon the dear, departed little one, then was opened in your heart a new fountain of feeling, sweeter and more delicious, a thousand times, than you had ever before tasted. Alas! and that fountain must now again be closed.

True, my dear sister, but do you not know where to go for consolation? There is a fountain whose streams are never dry; and though one source after another of earthly happiness may be cut off, yet this never fails. And the less we drink from the polluted fountains of earth, the sweeter will the waters taste.

What a beautiful and touching scene is that exhibited to us in the Bible, in the case of the Shunamite woman. She had left her child lying dead at home, and gone out to meet the prophet. When he asked her, "Is it well with the child?" she answered "It is well." She knew that her child was in the hands of the Lord who doeth all things well. Now, if your little Sarah were still living, and you were convinced that you ought to leave her for a while, and entrust it to the care of its father, you would leave it with regret, but still entirely satisfied that nothing would be left undone to secure its happiness; and this, together with the hope and expectation of rejoining it, in a few days or weeks, would make you comparatively resigned. Now are you not as willing to trust its Heavenly Parent? The child was his. He gave it to you for a short space, and has only taken it again. He is not only more disposed than its earthly parent to take good care of the child, but he is infinitely more able. Whatever is best for its welfare he certainly knows and will certainly do. And however long the separation may now seem to you, when you rejoin your child in heaven, it will appear to have been very short. I remember to have read, and greatly admired, a piece of poetry on this subject, when a very small boy. It was called "The Gardiner and the Rose Tree," and written by a Mr. Pierce, a Baptist minister of England. It began:

'In a sweet spot, which wisdom chose
Grew a unique and lovely Rose," etc.

I read it in an old magazine, but afterwards saw it in the "Memoirs of Mr. Pierce." I think if you will get it, you will find it affording you much consolation in the perusal. The "Memoirs" may be found, I should suppose, with almost any well-informed Baptist minister, but if not, I suspect mother knows the piece by memory, and can write it down for you. Or, perhaps, you are already acquainted with it. But, my dear sister, the best source to look for assistance to enable us to bear up under our bereavements, is an Almighty Savior. When he afflicts it is for our good, and to prepare us the better for his presence in eternity. When you shall have arrived at heaven, you will then find this very stroke under which you mourn, was necessary to prepare you for your present enjoyment. Say, then, and say from the heart, "It is well with the child," "It is well with the mother." Do write to me when your husband next writes; not in the same sheet I do not mean. May an Almighty Savior comfort and console you in this, your day of affliction.

Your affectionate brother,
ELIJAH P. LOVEJOY

Theological Seminary, Princeton, N. J., Feb. 20, 1833
My dear sisters Sibyl and Elizabeth,

It will, indeed, be a mysterious Providence, if Satan is so soon again permitted to triumph over our beloved father; but we know that, though mysterious, it is all done in wisdom. Those that will inherit the kingdom, must do it through much tribulation. All these things shall work together for good to them that believe. If father is to be so severely tried, the rest of heaven will be the sweeter. If God now hides his face, his presence will appear the more glorious in heaven. And let us all, my dear sisters, profit by the visitation of judgment. Let us humble ourselves before our Heavenly Father as he chastiseth us. How much lighter are his strokes than our guilt! And in the midst of afflictions how many blessings does he bestow!

For myself, I would record it to the praise and the glory of my Redeemer, that for the last month, or more, I have been favored with much of his presence; his loving kindness has been most abundant towards me. When I think of his surpassing goodness, and of my continual ingratitude, I am astonished and confounded. Though I find myself every day and every hour grieving his spirit and provoking him to anger, yet I find him still pursuing me with mercies. When I have provoked him to hide his face from me, as soon as I humble myself before him, he smiles and forgives. Oh, what a Savior! And what a vile, ungrateful wretch am I that can ever treat him with neglect.

I hope, my dear sisters, you find yourselves making constant advances in a holy life. You have seen but little of this world, but you have seen all. It has no good to bestow. Delusive, vain, and transitory, it cheats the soul that fastens upon it, of real and permanent enjoyment in heavenly places in Christ Jesus. Let us forsake it then, ere it forsakes us, and garner up our affections where they will be secure.

Nor yet do I mean that we should indulge in despondency. Even this world, if rightly used, can minister happiness to the mind. It is the "handy work" of God. It is a glorious manifestation of his wisdom and goodness. As such, the Christian should view it. It is not his home, it was not meant for such; but, it is a tarrying place, where many refreshments abound, until we reach our home in the skies. "Rejoice in the Lord always," said David: and why should not the Christian rejoice? Let him keep humble, as it respects himself; but let him triumph and make his boast in God his Savior. Cheerful and contented let him live in the performance of every duty, singing, as he journeys through life,

> "We'll praise thee for thy mercies past
> And humbly hope for more."

The way for the ransomed of the Lord to come to Zion, is "with songs and everlasting joy upon their heads."
Your affectionate brother,
ELIJAH P. LOVEJOY

In April of this year he received license to preach the gospel, from the second Presbytery of Philadelphia. Some months of the summer were passed in preaching at Newport, Rhode Island, and as a temporary supply at the Spring Street Church, New York. While at the latter place, the tidings of the death of his father reached him. On that occasion he wrote to the several members of the family, as follows.

New York, August 19th, 1833
My dear, dear Mother,

What shall I say to you? How shall I attempt to console you, under the afflicting hand of Providence? - Dear mother, "It is the Lord - let Him do what seemeth Him good." Mother, cannot you say so? Even now, when the hand of God is most heavily laid upon you, cannot you kiss the hand that smites? Your husband sleeps the sleep of death, but mother, your Redeemer liveth, and has he not said to your dear departed husband, and is he not saying to you, "Because I live, ye shall live also." For my dear father, I have no doubt that it is well with him. He was a Christian - his whole life, but especially the last ten years of his life, evinced it. God has dealt mysteriously with him - but I doubt not he is now singing, a glorified spirit before His throne. And why, then, should you mourn? Mother, can't you trust God? Blessed be His name, that you have long since learned to trust Him, and He has never disappointed you. He has been your Friend, and now He will enter into a still more endearing relation towards you. Thy Maker shall be thy Husband.

Had God taken your husband from you, without leaving you any hope of his future blessedness, how much more cause for grief would you have had then, than now. And so I might find ten thousand reasons why you should not mourn the exit of your husband; but these and such like, would rather convince the judgment, than affect the heart. After all, the gospel, the gospel of the Son of God, with all its glorious hopes, its rich promises, and its bright anticipations, can alone minister true consolation under circumstances such as yours. To these consolations, my dear mother, you are no stranger. He has delivered thee in six troubles, and now, in this seventh and greatest, he will not forsake thee.

And, mother, the time is short. You will soon join your husband in Heaven - your three sons you will meet there too. It may be that more of your children may precede you - and it matters not - so that they are prepared to go, the sooner God takes them from an evil world, the better for them. But for you, dear mother, I cannot doubt that a bright crown awaits you, when you shall enter the gates of the New Jerusalem. And in the midst of your bereavements, let it console you, that you have faithfully performed the part of a wife and a mother. How often have I heard my dear father say, "Never had a man such a wife as I have;" and I am sure all your children will unite with me, in saying, never had children a better mother. From my heart do I feel this; and now I have to say, that I hold myself bound to devote my life to minister to the comfort of my dear, dear widowed mother. I shall write to Joseph more particularly on this subject. May God comfort you, my mother, may His grace console you in your afflictions, and may He a thousand-fold compensate your loss in the more abundant enjoyment of Himself.

>Your most affectionate son,
>ELIJAH P. LOVEJOY

New York, August 19th, 1833
My dear sisters Sibyl and Elizabeth, and my dear brother John.

Dear Sisters and Brother,

We are orphans. God has taken from us, and, I doubt not, to himself, our dear and honored father. After a life of many vicissitudes, and much and varied suffering, he has laid down to rest in the tomb. It is a heavy stroke to us all - but to him, as we hope and believe, the end of all his sorrows, and all his pains. A sweet release from care and disquietude, and an introduction to mansions of blessedness. Why, then, should we mourn? Rather let us give God thanks that He so long continued to us the example and the prayers of such a father. To you, my dear sisters, I can speak of the consolations and the promises of the gospel, under our present afflictions. I can bid you listen to the voice of the compassionate Savior, as he says, "Mourners, dry your tears. It is I, be not afraid. What I have done is all for your good. Though you see it not now, yet you shall hereafter." If our faith, my dear sisters, is of the right kind, we shall not only know that for this very dispensation of God's providence, we shall hereafter praise him, but we shall begin our song of assured gratitude even now. We shall not only yield a cold assent to the words of David, but we shall adopt them from the heart, "Before I was afflicted, I went astray, but now I learn to keep thy law - it is good for me to be afflicted."

A letter from brother Joseph informed me of the sad breach made in the family, and also that my two dear sisters are much affected by it. My dear sisters, I sympathize with you, in all your griefs; I, too, have lost a father - a dear, an honored father; one to whom I am indebted more than I shall ever know, till I stand with him at the judgment seat of Christ. His prayers, his faithful warnings and reproofs we have together shared, and together are we deprived of them. But it is wrong to mourn excessively. And I would not, if I could, this day, recall our dear departed father. No; let him sleep in peace, in the tomb where his Savior laid before him; a tomb, in whose dark vault the lamp of Christian hope shines brightly. There let him sleep - the servant of God who has finished his work - until the God whom, in his life he served, shall come to waken him, and call him to the skies. Weep not then, my sisters, weep not, for it is well with our father. Blessed be God, we can say and believe, it is well.

For you, my dear brother John, you would not hear our father while living, will you not hear him, as he speaks from the grave, "My son, give God thine heart." Oh, my dear brother, live no longer without an interest in Christ, for fear that the separation which has now taken place between you and your father, shall be eternal. You will no longer share in his prayers - the last prayer of your father for your soul has gone up to heaven, and yet you are not converted. My brother, I tremble for the fate of your immortal soul. Oh, hear the voice of our dear father, as it cries to you from the ground, "Behold, now is the accepted time, behold, now is the day of salvation." If I have not forgotten, you may read these words on the tombstone of our dear grandfather. He was buried the day you were a year old. There lie father, son, and how soon another grandson, even you, my brother, may sleep by their side, God only knows. Be ready, I entreat you.

I commend you, my dear sisters and brother, to God, and to his grace, who can do for you all that you need in your present afflictions. Write to me, all of you, as soon as you receive this.

    Your affectionate brother,
    ELIJAH P. LOVEJOY

New York, August 26th, 1833
My Dear Brother Owen,

I had intended to write you sooner, but circumstances have prevented. Nor do I now know where to direct my letter, but shall, at a venture, send it to China.

It was indeed, my dear brother, sad news that awaited you on your return home. How little did we anticipate such an event when we parted. The ways of Providence are, truly, most inscrutable, but they are, nevertheless, all wrought in infinite wisdom. It is well, my dear brother, for God doeth all things well. And what we know not now, we shall know hereafter.

The day is soon coming, when we shall stand, along with our dear, departed father, at the judgment seat of Christ; and then shall we learn why we have been thus dealt with, in this afflictive dispensation of Providence.

But my dear brother, there is one improvement we ought to make of it, that must appear obvious to us all. And that is, to consider it as a loud call to each one of us, to be ready. Our work must be finished - our souls must be saved - since the night soon cometh when no man can work. Our dear father has finished his, and gone to his rest. One brother - nay three, and one of them by the name of Owen - went before him; and now, brother, can you tell when you and I shall be called to follow him?

My dear brother, permit me most earnestly and affectionately, to exhort you to give good heed to the warning voice, which now calls to you from your father's grave. Hear it saying to you, "My prayers, which have been constantly ascending for you since you was born, are now forever ceased - I cannot any more advise, instruct, exhort, or warn you, to flee from the wrath to come - I gave you to God, in covenant, according to his commands; these vows, and these obligations I have left resting upon your head. My cares, my watchings, and my labors for your soul's salvation, are now ended, and while I go to the bar of God to render up my account, I leave you unconverted." Oh, my brother, though our dear father's life failed to convert you, shall not his death accomplish it? Will you not hear him now, though you have hitherto neglected to hear him? Could I now be with you, my brother, I would take you to the tomb of our father, and there kneeling on the green sod that covers his dear remains, I would entreat you to make haste and be at peace with God, through faith and repentance, and a belief in the Lord Jesus Christ. Faith in him, can look beyond the tomb, can pierce the darkness that rests upon the grave, and behold the soul, darting upward, with the speed of light, to the throne of God, there to hear its doom, and enter upon its destined abode for eternity. Oh, my brother, my brother, prepare to meet thy God.

I greatly long to hear from my dear mother, and my sisters. I hope and pray that they have found grace equal to their day. Joseph informed me that mother was wonderfully supported; for which I thank God. Grace can accomplish anything. Even out of this most trying affliction to the family, it can create cause for thankfulness to us all, throughout eternity.

I wish that it was in my power, consistently with duty, to come down and see "home" once more, but I think the indications of Providence are such as forbid it. They are impatiently calling me to the West, and to the West I must go. I have some hopes that Joseph will come on here, so that I can see him, before long. I am tolerably well - am doing good, I hope. Give my love to dear mother and sisters, and to brother John. Finally, my dear brother, farewell; and may the grace of our Lord Jesus Christ be with your spirit.

    Your affectionate brother,
    ELIJAH P. LOVEJOY

CHAPTER VI

As intimated in the close of the letter inserted in the last chapter, our brother set his face again to the West. He had been requested, and strongly urged, by a circle of Christian friends at St. Louis, to return there and become the editor of a religious, weekly paper. The friends of the object at that place furnished a capital of twelve-hundred dollars for press, type, etc. From the instrument now before us, executed by the parties, the editor was to have the entire control of the establishment, with the right to mortgage the same, for the purpose, if necessary, of enlarging the "materials for printing." If, moreover, the net income of the establishment should exceed five hundred dollars a year, the editor was to pay the surplus to the proprietors.

In pursuance of this arrangement, on the 22nd of November, 1833, the first number of the "St. Louis Observer" was issued.

The first editorial article is here inserted.

St. Louis, Nov. 22d, 1833

"The first number of the Observer appears to day. We send it forth with our most cordial greetings to all its expecting friends, and with the hope that it will succeed in obtaining the good will of all before whom it may appear. It comes with no sinister motive, it appeals to no bad passion; and it asks a welcome in every home that in a spirit of meekness it may plead the cause of Him who came from heaven to proclaim 'peace on earth, and good will toward men.' Where it cannot be admitted on these terms, it will pass quietly by, neither feeling nor expressing aught of unkindness or reproach. And, however often, or with whatever words of contumely, it may be rejected from the door of any dwelling, it will still be ready to return upon the first appearance of more hospitable feelings, on the part of its inmates. For it will ever be ready to practice on the maxim it will unceasingly inculcate upon others; to forgive one another as our Heavenly Father has also forgiven us.

But while the Observer will thus seek to win its way to the hearts and consciences of men, by the kindness of the sentiments it breathes, it will not temporize as it goes. Truth is its object - divine truth in all its severity, as well as loveliness. To ascertain this, to free it from the glosses of men, and then press it home to the bosoms of its readers, as of practical and infinite importance, will always make a part of its weekly labors. It will seek no controversy, and it will decline none, when by so doing it might compromise the purity of that 'faith once delivered to the saints.' It will hold itself aloof from all angry discussions which may arise between brethren of the same sect, or of different sects, who can yet unite in glorying in the cross of Christ, other than to counsel peace and forbearance. But though actuated with the best feelings towards all, of whatsoever name, who love the Lord Jesus Christ, the Observer will, nevertheless, have a course of its own - a system of religious doctrines to which it will inflexibly adhere. What that is, will soon more plainly appear, in the course of its weekly visits. But we may here say, in brief, that it will be the same as that which Paul preached - the same, in substance, as that which Luther and Calvin rescued from the corruptions of men - the same as Edwards explained and defended - the same as now obtains, in all its distinctive features, among the great body of orthodox Christians in our land.

While, therefore, the Observer proffers the most cordial salutations to, and claims Christian fellowship with, all who can adopt the sentiment of its motto, as constituting their religion, and the whole of their religion, it will studiously avoid giving occasion of offence to any. Peace will be its aim, as far as that is consistent with the defense of the Truth. Yet it will never shrink from the post of duty; nor fear to speak out lest some over sensitive ears should be pained. Opinions honestly entertained will be fearlessly declared; and but little regard will be felt or expressed for any system of faith or practice, which rests mainly for its support upon the traditions of men, or upon the equally equivocal authority of long prescription.

One leading object of the Observer will be to diffuse information concerning the religious operations of the day, among Christians and other citizens of the West. In the Christian world it is a time of movement. The messenger of the Lord of Hosts has been heard as he passed along through the borders of the Church, calling upon her to come up to the help of the Lord against the mighty. Nor has the call passed unheeded. In all ranks the Church is in motion. She is mustering her hosts for the conquest, not of this or that petty kingdom or province, but of the World. Her heralds precede her, and even now they are running to and fro over all the earth, to proclaim the acceptable year of the Lord. Wherever she comes it is to set the bondman free, to break the chains of the oppressor, and to open the prison doors of the captive. She comes to dissipate the glooms of superstition, which have, for so many ages, rested upon the fairest portions of the globe, to pour in light upon the 'dark places of the earth which are full of the habitations of cruelty,' to rescue a lost race from the ruins of the fall, and restore it to the favor of its God. In this godlike enterprise the Church is now engaged - for this her prayers are ascending - to this her energies are directed, and in this she will assuredly triumph. Already her standard floats triumphantly over many a strong hold conquered from the enemies of her God. On the Isles of the Pacific - on the shores of Greenland - on the coasts of China and Siam - on the shores of Hither India, and far up into her broad interior - on the plains of Africa, the sunny isles of Greece, and the snows of Lapland and Caucasus, she has planted the Cross of her Redeemer, the sign and the instrument of salvation to the sin stricken nations. *That cross, wherever thus erected, shall never fall.* The Church is pledged to sustain it; and in fulfilling that pledge, she takes hold of the arm of her omnipotent Savior."

We shall here give large extracts from the successive numbers, that the American public, and all the world may know, what were the sentiments, and what the manner in which they were expressed, for which our brother was, in the process of lime, cruelly persecuted; and, for conscientiously holding fast to which, he was finally murdered. If, in these sentiments, or in the manner of expressing them, there is aught worthy of death, as he did not refuse to die, so we will not ask that his name and character be saved from reproach, or his memory from oblivion. If, on the other hand, these are the truths on which society is based, which God has published to the world, and which Christ has sanctioned with his own blood; if there is much of the spirit of him, "who, when he was reviled, reviled not again," in the manner in which these truths are expressed; then we ask you not to believe, in some cases his misinformed, and in others his malicious *slanderers*. Still farther, - we ask you not to cease calling for *justice*, till she return in her strength, majesty, and purity, with her robes washed from the stains of innocent blood shed at Alton.

Miscellaneous Editorial Articles from the St. Louis Observer

WHAT IS TRUTH?

"It is strange that what, more than all things else, it concerns mankind to know, what was expressly designed for their benefit, and what by their all wise Creator they were expressly fitted to receive, should yet be the very thing with which they are the least acquainted. Truth, though professedly the object of search to all, is confessedly apprehended by but few. And even these do but catch distant and uncertain views of its light; as when a star is seen through the fitful changes of the intervening cloud. Even as they behold they tremble lest it shall vanish from their sight, and be lost in the gathering gloom.

The reason of this must be, either that we have not the faculties for perceiving truth, or that having, we have perverted them. The first, as it would be a reflection upon either the goodness or wisdom of God or both, cannot for a moment be admitted, and there remains the only alternative, that we have carelessly or willfully gone wrong in our search for the truth. And this is just the ground on which the Bible places it, 'Seeing, men see not, and hearing they do not understand.'

Sometimes we make up for ourselves a system of metaphysics - we arrange to our taste or our caprice, the faculties of the mind, and the modes of its action, and whatever of divine truth does not suit our scheme

- which, as it has cost much labor of thought, is, of course, a cherished bantling - we reject, or at best, those sharp points, that interfere with the organized movements of our moral machinery, we carefully cover up. We have been sitting at the feet of Berkeley or Locke or Hume, and thence we bring our standard, by which to measure the doctrines of the Cross, and the revealed will of God. How often has Plato gotten into the sacred desk and crowded out Paul, or at most, permitted the Apostle a word of exhortation after the Metaphysician had sermonized his full hour, - Which exhortation, indeed, was about as consonant to the sermon, as the new piece of cloth sewed upon the ragged garment - in both cases the whole was made a piece of parti-colored patchwork.

Sometimes, having been educated in great reverence for the names and opinions of certain men, and an abhorrence for those of others; at every step we take in our search for truth, we tremble lest we shall have parted company from those we love and reverence, and have entered upon the premises of those we both fear and dislike. When in such a mood, it is wonderful what a magic there is in the mere sound of a name. To be told that if we go on, we shall soon cease to have a right to be distinguished by this or that appellation, will bring us to a halt at once. Then it is, too, that we apply the same concise and conclusive argument to others. You area 'Calvinist,' an 'Arminian,' or a 'Pelagian,' as the case may be; and those whom such an argument fails to convince, are indeed incorrigible - we give them over to blindness of mind.

Sometimes - and it is the last case we shall put - we are so tremblingly alive lest others may fall into error that we have no time to search out the truth for ourselves. We get up on the watch tower, and spend the whole day in casting our nervous, feverish glance around, in the eager expectation of seeing someone, whom we may warn of his fate, about to fall into the hands of the enemy; and, of course, have no time to examine whether they may not be nearer us than them, and even undermining the very pillars on which we stand. At such a time we are almost sure to see multiplied danger, either real or apparent. Either our wishes become the father to our thoughts, or as in the natural, so in the moral, our eye sight is strained till we see double; mole hills swelling into mountains, and men looking like trees walking,

'Till Birnam forest come to Dunsinane.'

Or, at best, as we are a voluntary watcher, even though we succeed in descrying no approaching evil, we shall still have a strong temptation to lift up our voices and cry aloud, lest those within the walls suspect us of sleeping at our post, or as wanting in alacrity and zeal.

Such is but a specimen of the difficulties that attend us in our search after truth. But, for these and all others we know of but one and the same remedy - a determination to think independently, untrammeled, by the dogmas of Philosophy or the logic of the Schools, and then an humble, diligent, prayerful perusal of the Word of God."

THE PAST YEAR

January 2d, 1834

"Another year has gone. Another of those periods, thirty of which mark the duration of a generation of mankind, has passed, bearing with it into eternity and to the bar of God, 30,000,000 of the human family. Could we read the private history of these thirty millions just removed to be here no more forever, what an instructive lesson would it teach. Some just opened their eyes upon the light, and then closed them forever. Some had just learned to return the maternal embrace, and to look, in their playful moods, into the mother's beaming eyes for approval, when Death came and took them to the grave. Others, for the first time, had gone out into the world, and with all the emotions that unbounded surprise and delight can give, were gazing upon the scene before them. There Hope was weaving her gayest tissues, and hanging garlands of joy on every object; there Beauty wore her brightest robes, and as she moved in conscious pride, turned often to bestow her sweetest smiles upon Love that followed in her train. Alas! 'twas but a dream, and even as he stands, the film is gathering upon his eye, that will shut the scene from his sight forever. In the greenness of his years and the first freshness of his hopes he fell, and these scenes of delight are exchanged for a vision of the charnel house and the tomb!

And even the man of middle age, whose hopes had been sobered and his anticipations chastened by unnumbered disappointments, even his path to the grave was strewed with the wrecks of many a cherished scheme of self-aggrandizement, which yet he had fondly thought would have secured to him the end of his toil. On yonder hill he sleeps, buried beneath the ruins of the temple he had erected to Pride, to Avarice, or to Vanity. And yet his posterity approve his sayings and are walk- ing in his footsteps.

He, too, whom the weight of years had bowed to the earth, whose strength had so far departed that the burden of life could scarcely be supported, he was surprised in the midst of plans that looked for their accomplishment far into the future. Though the wheel had long moved slowly at the cistern, he had not thought it would stop so soon.

Yet not such is the history of all whom the year through which we have just passed, has removed from this world. Some there were who had long waited to be gone, knowing that for them to live was Christ, but to die was gain. To some the year has brought a blessed relief from long continued sickness, from poverty, from unmerited obloquy, from oppression, and especially from their warfare with sin - the garb of poverty has been exchanged for garments of light, the 'world's dread laugh, ' for the approving smile of their Redeemer, and the darkness and doubt of earth for the full tide of light and truth that flows from the Throne of God and of the Lamb. For them Death had no terrors, the grave no gloom. They entered its gates with smiling countenances, and as they laid themselves down in Death's embrace sang with assured joy the triumphant song, 'death, where is thy sting, O grave, where is thy victory!' There let them rest. Their tomb is not dark! No; Like the Vestals of old, Faith has lit her lamp from heaven, and gone down to watch over their sleeping dust. Her light irradiates even the darkness of the tomb. Nor will she leave her post till He who once slept in the grave shall come to waken them from their repose and take them to that heaven whither he has ascended. They died the death of the righteous, and they will rise to the resurrection of the just.

Such is the lesson which the last year affords, and which we, who have lived through it, are permitted to read. It is a lesson full of instruction and practical wisdom. And how sad the reflection that few, comparatively, will profit by it - that, as in the past, so in the coming year, the multitude will still continue to pervert the right ways of the Lord, till, tired with the pursuits of shadows, the year now begun shall witness many of them end without hope, a life employed to no purpose.

Let us all, then, who would avoid a catastrophe so deplorable, adopt the prayer which the pious man of old addressed to his Maker: 'So teach us to number our days that we may apply our hearts unto wisdom.'"

FAITH

"How beautiful and how striking the expression, of the apostle, ' We walk by faith.' He is writing to the Corinthian Christians, and in order that he may persuade them not to be cast down in the midst of their trials and afflictions, he directs their attention to their 'house not made with hands eternal in the heavens.' 'Therefore,' he adds, 'We are always confident, knowing that whilst we are at home (or more properly, sojourning) in the body, we are absent from the Lord: for we walk by faith, not by sight.' This last clause is added as the reason of the confidence which the apostle professed - he walked by faith.

Had he, on the contrary, walked by sight - had he judged the Lord 'by feeble sense,' and regulated his conduct according to the maxims of worldly wisdom, how different would have been his course, and how different the result. He would have escaped 'persecutions,' the 'cruel scourgings and mockings,' the 'perils' by land and sea which he so frequently endured; he would have trimmed his sails to catch the popular breeze, and with his talents, his acquirements, and the advantages of his introduction into society, he would doubtless have lived admired and courted by the wise and the learned of the age - the Jewish scribe and the Greek philosopher. But what would the end have been? He might have died with the uncertain and unreasonable composure of a Socrates, with the brutal heroism of a Cato, or the mountebank vanity of an Augustus; but we should never have heard the triumphant exclamation of a soul longing 'to depart and be with Christ.' 'O death, where is thy sting? O grave, where is thy victory?' Like Hadrian or Hume, he might have uttered fool-hardy jests at the approach of death; but there would have been no record in heaven or on earth of a man, who, after a life of unparalleled exertion and unequalled suffering, went in calm serenity to the block, uttering the memorable words - 'I have fought a good fight, I have finished my course, I have kept the faith; henceforth there is laid up in heaven for me a crown of righteousness, which the Lord, the righteous Judge, shall give me at that day: and not to me only, but unto all them also that love his appearing.'

In view of such an exit from the world as this, who does not exclaim, 'Let me die the death of the righteous, and let my last end be like his! -' We walk by faith.' Thus did Paul. In the midst of a wicked and perverse generation, in the midst of temptations and trials; with everything that could tempt or allure him to turn aside, he 'walked by faith.' By faith he traced the footsteps of his ascended Lord and followed them with undeviating course. By faith he looked beyond the heavens and there beheld 'Jesus the Forerunner' entered into rest and waiting to welcome all his faithful followers. Upon this object as upon the guiding and illuminating star of his path through earth's wilderness, he fixed his steadfast eye ' looking unto Jesus the Author and Finisher of his faith.' It was this confidence in things unseen that enabled him to endure unto the end. And how much more good might Christians effect, how many more triumphs over the world, the flesh and the Devil might they achieve, would they cultivate more the grace of faith in their hearts. Not a dead faith, a faith speculatively correct, empty, vain, inoperative; but that true and living faith which works by love, and so purifies the heart, and by purifying the heart informs the head, and thus leads to holy, beneficial and well-sustained action.

When, oh! when will Christians learn to 'walk by faith' - to live confessing themselves 'strangers and pilgrims here' - by the exercise of faith to forsake the world and its vanities, and daily and hourly go up and hold sweet converse with saints and angels in light, who dwell in those heavenly mansions which are soon to be their own eternal home?"

CONVERSION OF THE WORLD

"We said last week that this was the most glorious enterprise in which human beings had ever been engaged. It is so,

1. Because of the extent of the enterprise. Too often it is the case that the schemes of man, even when designed for good, are limited in their operation, either from some defect in the plan, or, what indeed is pretty-nearly the same thing, want of enlarged views of duty in the designer. Thus, most or all of the benevolent efforts of the human mind have been confined to one's own kindred, or neighborhood, or city, or at most his country. But in carrying on the work of missions, the Church soars at once far above the influence of all such feelings. Attached as the Christian is, and as he ought to be, to his own countrymen, and his kindred according to the flesh; in this work he moves in a far higher sphere of action. All men are his brethren, in each he sees a soul for which Christ died; and looking to the immortal destinies of that soul, all earthly distinctions vanish. Here is neither rich nor poor, nor bond nor free, nor black nor white, but all are one in his view. When the Church commissions her missionary, it is in the words of her great Head, 'Go ye into all the world and preach the gospel to every creature.' And with his life in his hand, and the un-extinguishable love of souls in his heart, he goes. He pierces the gloomy forests of America, he treads the burning sands of Africa; his voice is heard on the mountains of Asia, and among the isles of the sea; the eternal snows of Iceland, and the burning heat of the line cannot deter him; he will not rest until to every kindred, and tribe, and people, under the whole earth he preaches a crucified Redeemer. So also at home; in all plans that are laid, and all the deliberations that are held, this is the end kept in view, the regeneration of every son and daughter of Adam. Alexander, and Caesar, and Napoleon, conquered provinces and kingdoms; but the soldier of the Cross is engaged in conquering the whole world.

2. The enterprise of converting the world is grand, because of the simplicity of the means employed. There is no mysterious, complex system of operations, constantly varying in its application, with which the church proposes to carry on this work. All is simple, sublime, efficacious. The doctrine of the Cross, ' Jesus Christ and him crucified,' is the only weapon she has, the only one she needs. With this she assaults the strong holds of infidelity, strikes down the pride of human learning, and humbles the conceit of vain philosophy; with this she enters the cottage of the poor, and the palace of the king, in spite of all that ignorance or sensuality can oppose to her progress; by this she makes her way through the prisons of superstition, and cruelty, and bigotry, setting free the captives and giving liberty to them that are bound.

3. In the dignity of the actors is seen the grandeur of the enterprise. For though apparently it is achieved by weak and erring man, yet in reality it is not so. To commence the work the Son of God came down to earth and died; to carry it on the Spirit of God is ever employed with its omnipotent energies, while God the Father directs the operations of his earthly providences to the same great end. The seat of influence lies not on earth, but in heaven. Thence come down supplies of grace and wisdom and strength for those engaged in this holy war; there was the plan conceived, the scheme devised, and there will its operations terminate. For,

4. The glory of this enterprise is seen in its grand results. And these are none other than to qualify men for heaven, and then carry them up thither. It proposes to elevate the whole human race to their original dignity, and thus qualify them for a seat at the right hand of God. Fallen and degraded as man now is, who but a God could have conceived such a plan, and who but a God could execute it? The work indeed is the Lord's, but the church is the instrument by which he executes it. And it is hastening, too, to its termination. A thousand signs indicate this.

Let the infidel scoff, let the bigot rave, let the multitude deride and contemn; but who that loves the Lord Jesus Christ, at such a time as this, will stand idly by, and will not rather take up his cross and march to the van. Cheered on by so many tokens of victory, upheld by the promises of an Almighty Redeemer, and looking forward to a crown that already glitters in his view, before whose brightness the stars of heaven are dim - where is the Christian who does not pant for action, or who fears what man can do unto him?

Now is the time, oh! Christian - Gird up your loins and go forth - Go as David went, in the name of the Lord of Hosts, and as surely as he triumphed so will you. And as surely as your Redeemer liveth, so surely will he with his own hands place the crown of victory upon your head."

EUROPE

March 27th, 1834

"The moral and political aspect of this quarter of the globe is, at the present time, peculiarly interesting. Though the smallest of the four grand divisions of the globe, it is, and for centuries has been, by far the most important. The history of civilization, the annals of literature, the record of important discoveries, the histories of the triumphs of Art and Science, over ignorance and barbarism, seldom extend beyond this favored portion of the globe. Strike from the annals of the human race the records of European mind, and the achievements of European intellect, and History - all at least that has come down to us - will be little else than the annals of barbarism. The only exception to this remark is presented by our own country; whose influence is indeed pervadingly manifest throughout the civilized world. Yet its existence is so recent, that in calculating the elements of the world's past history, it scarcely deserves to be taken into the account.

Eight hundred years ago, the darkness of midnight rested on Europe. Its inhabitants were slaves in the broadest sense of that term. Everything seemed combined to rivet the chains upon the bodies and souls of men. The feudal system everywhere prevailed according to the tenor of which the cultivators of the soil, were parceled out the property of petty chiefs, as much as if they had been mere fixtures on the land; these smaller chiefs were bound in fealty to nobles and barons of more extended sway, who again did homage to their sovereign King or Emperor, which

'Emperor, King, and Prince, and Peer,'

were alike ignominiously chained to the footstool of the Pope, whom, to the fullest extent of passive obedience they acknowledged as Lord of life and death, both in this and the other world.

It is not in language to paint, nay it is not in imagination adequately to conceive, the picture of the moral, political, and social desolation which Europe at this time presented. Over its whole extent the eye looks in vain for one spot of verdure, on which for a moment it may rest. All is blackness and ruin, varied only by the different features of repulsiveness and horror.

High on the throne of universal dominion which they had audaciously usurped, sat the Popes surrounded by a priesthood, venal, ignorant, and debauched in a degree almost exceeding belief; themselves distinguished from their spiritual vassals, only by that pre-eminence in all manner of wickedness which their power enabled them to commit; issuing their arrogant and impious decrees which were 'to bind kings with chains,' and 'nobles with fetters of iron.' Monks, friars, and nuns, mendicants without name and without degree, filled the monasteries and nunneries that everywhere abounded, with riots and debaucheries that cannot be described, or swarmed over the land, like the lice of Egypt, eating up all its fair fruits, and inspiring loathing and abhorrence by their pestilential presence. From the Pope to the sovereign, the noble, and thus down to the peasant and the serf, Superstition extended her Sybaritic and brutalizing influences. Beneath her benumbing grasp the palsied wretch sank down unnerved, unmanned; and worshipped as his gods and revered as his Savior, images of wood and stone, which his own hands did, or might make; or treasured in his bosom as the 'pearl of great price,' relics of 'every name and hue,' a lock of hair, a piece of dried skin, a thumb or a toe nail, palmed upon him by hungry and mendicant piety, were venerated as the means and the pledge of salvation. And - *horresco referens* - this diabolical superstition assumed the name and the offices of the Christian Religion.

Such was the state of Europe when the star of the 'Reformation' dawned upon it- that star of glorious promise, the harbinger of the Sun of Righteousness, whose beams are to irradiate and purify the whole earth. From that epoch to the present, the conflict between the powers of light and darkness, has continued without interruption. To the mere worldly observer, success on the part of Truth and Freedom has at times appeared more than doubtful; but in all this long period there have not been wanting, those whose vision, purified and strengthened by their communion with the Word of God, clearly saw, and whose pens have distinctly recorded, the ultimate triumph that awaited the friends of God and man. What they saw through a glass and by faith, we behold with open vision. To anyone who has taken even the most superficial view of the past history and present condition of Europe, not a doubt can remain of the speedy and utter extinction of the Papal Authority, both temporal and spiritual. The spirit of slavery, the doctrine of passive obedience, which are essential to its existence, are becoming more and more circumscribed in their influence and operations, and will soon be scouted from the earth, back to the regions of darkness, whence they ascended to enslave the world.

We have not time nor room in this article, to trace the gradual extension and progress of liberal opinions in Europe, from the period of the Reformation to the present time. Yet a single glance at the history of that era will satisfy everyone, that in proportion as Learning and Science have made progress in any country, has the influence of Pope and Priest been made to give way.

In modern times, the chief ornament and support of the Papal throne has been France. This country has long occupied a commanding position in the world, no less from her military prowess and skill, than from the literary and scientific acquirements of her scholars. - Though the mass of her inhabitants have been ignorant, yet learning has exercised a most important influence in elevating the sentiments and enlarging and liberalizing the views of many of her nobles, her prelates, and her statesmen. And the consequence has been just what might have been expected. The Galilean church has been exceedingly restive under the leaden influence of Rome, and his Holiness has found it necessary to be exceedingly wary how he touched the fiery spirit of the Gaul. The Galilean church has enjoyed immunities granted to no other, and which fear alone extorted from the Roman Pontiff. Yet enough was not conceded to satisfy the demands of the rising spirit of freedom; and chains, forged in the darkness of the pit, were wound so artfully around the giant limbs of France, that she lay a victim at the footstool of tyranny temporal and spiritual, until, at the epoch of the Revolution, with convulsive energy she burst asunder her bands, and in the first moments of her gratified hate, inflicted such vengeance upon her oppressors as made even humanity recoil with horror from the spectacle. Yet when we consider the nature of the long train of events that preceded the French Revolution, the various causes tending to produce it, and how long a high spirited and generous people had been goaded and oppressed by a sottish, venal priesthood and a debauched monarchy; it seems to us that that terrible catastrophe is rather to be deplored than wondered at.

As might have been expected, France, exulting in the first moments of her recovered freedom, went to the other extreme, and from having believed too much, refused to believe anything. She became a nation of infidels. And such, to a great extent, she remains at the present day. With her, priest is but another name for bigot, and Christianity she confounds with Superstition. The mistake is a very natural one, yet it is not the less to be deplored. Still there is hope for her, and hope which promises fruition a thousand times sooner than if she had remained a vassal of the Pope. If error is lamentably prevalent there, yet truth is, in a good degree, free to combat it. Public Sentiment is free, liberal opinions put forth their claims unchallenged, the universal education of all classes is becoming an object of paramount attention, to accomplish which the Government is directing all its energies. Such is now the state of France.

We have been thus particular in our remarks upon this country, because from her commanding position, the history of France is the history of continental Europe. We now proceed to show - and this was indeed the primary object of these remarks - what the condition of Europe, when considered in reference to its great political divisions, is. And here we must of necessity be very brief.

Looking at Europe with this object in view, we shall find the nations drawing together into two great divisions. In the south the liberalizing influences of France are seen at work in Spain and Portugal. In the latter they have driven Miguel, the sanguinary and bigoted favorite of the Pope, from the throne; and in the former banished the heir by ' divine right,' Don Carlos, and restored the Cortes and the Constitution. In both they are ferreting out the lazy monks from their cells of idleness and crime, and teaching them that ' they that will not work neither shall they eat.' The natural consequence of all this is, that these two nations should assimilate themselves in their habits of thought and action to France. And as this nation occupies a leading position, she may be considered at once as the irradiating and the attractive center of liberal opinions on the continent. England, since the days of her 'Reform,' is prepared to take ground by her side, and thus there will be seen under the banners of freedom, civil and religious, England, France, Spain, and Portugal, with some or most of the minor States of Germany; while on the side of despotism there will rally Russia - the head and soul of the confederacy - Austria, Prussia, and the

Pope in his double character of a temporal and a spiritual prince. We think the movements in Europe indicate that this union of kindred interests - which when it happens will necessarily produce hostility - is even now taking place and will soon be consummated. Then will come the war of opinion, predicted by Napoleon - a war more dreadful, and more fierce than any which Europe has yet witnessed. Yet the final result, though long suspended, cannot be doubtful. Truth will triumph; Freedom will triumph; Religion will triumph. Babylon will have fallen, have fallen; her incantations and her sorceries will no longer delude or destroy the human mind; and she will no longer present an insurmountable barrier to the progress of religion 'pure and undefiled.'

Such, if we read the signs aright, such is the present condition, such the future prospect of the European nations. If in the future there is much to excite regret, there is also much to animate and encourage the friends of God. It is plain that the reign of misrule, and despotism, and anarchy, and superstitious bigotry are soon to come to an end. True its down-fall will not probably be accomplished, except at the expense of much blood and great suffering. But though God permits the earthquake and the storm to desolate the earth, we know that they are necessary to purify a corrupted atmosphere. And as in the physical so in the moral world, though commotions, war, and carnage are painful in their operations, they may be necessary in their results. And in all events, the Christian is assured that the peaceful reign of the Redeemer is hastening onward, when there shall be no more war, nor 'rumors of wars,' but when

> 'Peace like a river from his throne,
> Shall flow to nations yet unknown.'"

May 1st, 1834

"After so long a time, we are again permitted, though still with trembling hand, to hold the Editorial pen. The interval during which our labors have been suspended, has indeed been to us one of much pain and suffering. But

> 'Sweet are the uses of adversity,'

when sanctified by the presence and teachings of the Holy Spirit. We return to our work, with accumulated motives, and, as we hope, a strengthened purpose, to be 'diligent in business, fervent in spirit, serving the Lord.'

And most earnestly and affectionately would we exhort our readers, that whatsoever their hand findeth to do, they do with all their might. Especially do we entreat those who have not yet commenced the work of their salvation, that they delay it no longer. A sick or a dying bed, when the mind is distracted with pain, or absorbed in the contemplation of the awful eternity that is opening upon its view, is no time to seek a Savior. Seek him now then, 'while he may be found, call upon him while he is near.' And remember that whether we make haste, or not, to secure an interest in his salvation, time is surely and swiftly hastening us to the grave and the Judgment. How soon will all who read this paragraph be sleeping in their tombs! Some undoubtedly - perhaps the writer among them - will be carried out in season for the flowers of the coming summer to bloom upon their graves. How solemn the reflection, and yet how little heeded."

VAIN PHILOSOPHY

August 21st, 1834

"If there ever was a sincere inquirer after truth it was Jonathan Edwards. And how few can hope to possess, in an equal degree, the advantages for pursuing the inquiry which he possessed?

Learned, pious, acute, and persevering, he was yet humble and docile as a child. In him pride of opinion was never stronger than love for the truth. And yet his great work on the Freedom of the Will is, in one respect, a signal failure. He has indeed abundantly proved that man is a free agent, as also that all his actions are foreknown and fore-determined by his Maker. But there needed no long train of philosophical reasoning to prove these doctrines - the Bible had already done it before him. Yet in his attempt to reconcile these great truths to each other he has entirely failed. And if he failed, who shall succeed? Nor is this failure to be wondered at; for this very question David had confessed himself unequal to meet: - ' Such knowledge is too wonderful for me; it is high, I cannot attain unto it.'

Now here lies the great error of too many men. - Instead of being satisfied with ascertaining the existence of a truth, they must needs determine the *mode* of its existence. But this is an abuse of their powers of reasoning, and it is of such very persons that Paul speaks, when he says, 'Professing themselves to be wise, they became fools.' The great Apostle was as prompt to rebuke the presumption of those who would have a God *too well known*, as he was to denounce the superstition of those who built altars to the Unknown God.

The Being and attributes of God may be learned from the Book of Nature, but of his purposes we can know-nothing, except by revelation. And it is equally an abuse of this revelation and our own faculties, if we seek to know farther than the simple facts revealed. Here it is that

'Men rush in where Angels fear to tread.'

It is not only vain but it is sinful, to attempt prying into the counsels of the Infinite Mind. A few, a very few of the purposes of God have been revealed to us, but beyond these few all is unknown. 'Clouds and darkness are round about his throne.' We may weary ourselves and offend God, in the attempt, but we can never penetrate them. It is, therefore, an abuse of reason, to endeavor to look into the counsels of the Most High.

But secondly, it is presumption in the highest degree, because we cannot understand the reasons of a revealed truth, therefore to reject it altogether. In very few instances, indeed, has God condescended to explain the reasons of his moral enactments, and in none have we a right to require them. 'Thus saith the Lord,' should at once put to rest the impertinent curiosity of man.

Eve could not see why she might not as well eat of the forbidden tree as of others, since it was as fair to look upon as they; and because God had not explained to her the reason <of his prohibition, she ventured to pluck the fruit

> ' whose mortal taste,
> Brought death into the world and all our woe.'

That her awful fate has not deterred her descendants from following her example, is proof enough both of their depravity and their folly.

Again. If we cannot reconcile two revealed truths, so as to make them consistent with each other, we have not, in consequence, any right to conclude that their agreement is impossible. Yet how often has this been done, to the shipwreck of faith as of souls. The doctrines of the Trinity, of Election, etc. are beyond our reason, but what right have we to say, that they are *contrary* to it? Who, of mortal man, or of created beings, is authorized to pronounce upon the possible limitations of the Uncreated One? How can we tell that as much Truth is not given as we can bear to know? Who shall say that if God had revealed to us more of his eternal purposes and Godhead, the knowledge would not have overwhelmed us? the light have been too great for our weak nerves to bear, and thus have made us altogether blind? Let these questions be satisfactorily answered, before we venture to complain of obscurity in the revelations of the Divine Mind. Let us cease, there- fore, perplexing ourselves in vain attempts to 'find out the Almighty.' We are finite, and how can we expect to fathom and comprehend the questions of Freedom, Necessity, and the Origin of Evil, which reach through Infinitude, and take hold of the very Throne of God? How can we construct a problem which shall embrace within its terms all the elements of Eternity?

Truth, as much of it as we need to know, is within us. In our soul of souls, in that consecrated region of the heart never disturbed by Argument or invaded by Doubt, lies a deep fountain of Truth, whose waters are continually welling up. Here let us drink and be refreshed, neither asking how it came there, since it comes from that stream which flows ' fast by the Throne of God,' nor seeking to fathom its depths. It is enough that its waters are sweet, and that they are perennial.

Beyond this we cannot know, and we must not seek to know.

We were sent into this world not to dispute about the next, but to prepare for it. Of the next world we can know nothing but by revelation from Him who made it. That revelation has been given us, and now let us not seek to be wise above what is written. Let us seek rather to resolve no questions which are not required of us, and whenever apparent difficulties in the Purposes and Providences of God, meet us as we journey towards our heavenly home, let us contentedly, and even cheerfully, say:

> 'God is his own interpreter,
> And He can make it plain.'"

THE VANITY OF MAN

August 28, 1834

"It was a beautiful thought of the Greek philosopher, when he compared the life of man to a bubble. Along the stormy ocean of life the different generations of men arise like bubbles on a stream - at best a teardrop inflated with air. Some of these bubbles sink at once into the mass of waters whence they came; others float up and down for a turn or two upon the tops of the restless weaves, and also disappear; and even those which remain the longest are in perpetual agitation and restlessness, the sport of every breeze and every tide, until they too are swallowed up.

It is even so with man. Some are born only that they may die - like the bubble blown up and destroyed by the same breath of air. Some abide a little longer, to bear the peltings of the storm, but their fragile forms are soon broken by the violence of the tempest. And those that endure for a season, what are their lives but one continued scene of disquietude, disappointment and doubt; while like the bubble tossed upon the unquiet waters, they find no resting place for a moment, until they sink back into the earth from whence they were taken.

The Bible abounds with the most impressive figures to teach us the vanity of human life. 'For what is your life?' says James, ' It is even a vapor that appeareth for a little time and then vanisheth away.' 'We spend our years,' says Moses, ' as a tale that is told.' 'Behold,' says the plaintive David, ' behold, thou hast made my days as an handbreadth, and mine age is as nothing before thee; verily every man at his best state is altogether vanity.'

Can any thing be more affecting than this? It is the language of a king-of one who had passed through many vicissitudes in life, having ascended from the occupation of a shepherd, to the station of king over all Israel. He had reached the summit, the world had nothing more to give; yet looking back upon the past, and round upon the present scenes of his life, he sighs at the reflection, which is forced upon his mind, that they are 'altogether vanity.' Alas! the man has never lived, whether king or peasant, whose breast has not been heaved by the same sigh, whose heart has not been saddened by the same reflection.

The causes that conspire to make the life of man on earth a 'vanity,' and even a vexation of spirit are many.

1. He is a stranger here - he is not at home. His company, the scenes around him, everything he sees, all he hears, are not adapted to his tastes, not fitted for his capacities. Like the caged bird his food is insipid, his vision confined, and he cannot choose but pine in his solitude, as he thinks of the purer light, the brighter scenes, and the boundless glory, among which he would fain, with unfettered wing, expatiate. But he is bound to earth; clogged with clay; and he who is fitted to soar and sing in the heavens, must grovel in the dust. And here feeding on ashes, he lives among the dead till Time can dig his grave also, into which he creeps and is seen no more.

2. The vicissitudes of life are nothing but a series of disappointments. Whether for good or for ill, none of all our ten thousand cherished plans have succeeded exactly to our wish. The catastrophe came too soon or too late; the scheme failed altogether, or its result was different from what we desired or expected. And if no present evils press upon us, we are distressed with the apprehensions of future, or disquieted with the remembrance of past misfortunes; and at best our hopes do but struggle with our fears, while we are left desolate. We are always either troubled or dissatisfied; and if nothing else makes us uneasy, even the very absence of our accustomed tormentors will make us so. And herein appears the vanity of our state, that nothing restrains us from the madness and rioting of prosperity, but that every cup we put to our lips, is dashed with the bitterness of gall. Thus it has been well said of man that 'he is always restless and uneasy, he dwells upon the waters, and leans upon thorns, and lays his head upon a sharp stone.'

And what does the experience of every man but echo back the declaration of the prophet, 'Cursed be the man that trusteth in man, and maketh flesh his arm? He who does it leans upon a cracked reed that sooner or later will break beneath him, Nisus and Euryalus, Pylades and Orestes may live in fable and in song, but they have never lived anywhere else. For so certain as winter succeeds summer, so true is it that

'The friends who in our sunshine live,
In wintry days are flown;
And he who has but tears to give,

Must weep those tears alone.'

This is poetry, it is true; but it is not fiction, as many a deserted heart, many a desolate bosom can witness. Like motes in the sunbeams, friends gather around even to annoyance in the days of prosperity, but at the first cloud that obscures the sky, at the first sound of the distant thunder they flee away, and leave him upon whom they had fattened, to bide alone the fury of the storm. Such is human friendship; so empty, so valueless.

Whither, then, shall the heart-stricken mourner turn? In the desolateness of his misery must he die, as he has lived, without hope? No, he need not. As he flees to the grave, as to a refuge and a rest from ills he can no longer endure. Religion, heaven descended, meets him and bids him no further despair. She tells him of One whose friendship never fails, whose promises are never broken - of One who 'having loved his own loveth them unto the end.' She points him to a world where ingratitude and selfishness are unknown; where the tear of anguish never flows, the sigh of sorrow is never heaved; where no vain regrets, no anxious forebodings, intrude upon the heart overflowing with joy; and bids him lie down and rest in hope, for that world is all his own. Who, then, would wish to live? or rather, who would not wish to die? Who is not ready to say with Job, 'I would not live always? Borne down with the weight of sin, oppressed with a sense of his own unworthiness and the faithlessness of others, while the whole creation is groaning around him, being like him, ' made subject to vanity,' what would the Christian, what can he, but long to die? - to close his eyes and shut his ears upon the scenes and the discords of earth, until he can open them to the beauties and the melodies of heaven?"

SIR ISAAC NEWTON

"We have just been looking through the life of this great man, by Dr. Brewster. It is exceedingly interesting as detailing the process and the several steps by which he ascended to the visible heavens, and there walked with God with the stars beneath his feet. Yet though he ascended so high, and stood where the horizons of a thousand worlds fell within his vision, though he looked upward and around into heights and depths, where the eye of no other mortal, save that of Laplace, has pierced, he had and expressed the humblest views of his own powers and acquisitions.

To others, to the great mass of mankind, he seems to have been borne on the wings of thought, even to the utmost verge of Nature's dominions, to have explored with unerring ken her most secret chambers, and to have uncovered and brought to the light all those secret springs, that complicated machinery, by which she enforces and regulates the movements of systems and suns, with all their worlds, through the regions of space. And such is the sentiment of the poet respecting him:

> 'Nature and Nature's laws lay hid in night,
> God said, Let Newton be - and all was light.'

But hear his own estimation of all that he had achieved: - 'I do not know,' said he, 'what I may appear to the world, but to myself I seem to have been only like a boy playing on the seashore, and diverting myself in now and then finding a smoother pebble or a prettier shell than ordinary, while the great ocean of truth lay all undiscovered before me.' This is undoubtedly the true estimate, and what a lesson does it teach to the vanity of man! If Newton thus humbled himself before the Uncreated Intelligence, because, with all his efforts, he could learn so little of His ways, what room is left for others to boast? This most instructive declaration affords another proof, that the studies of the Book of Nature and of Revelation lead to the same result, though in different degrees, and that the student of each will, in reference to their Author, be ready to say, in the words of the poet,

> 'The more Thy glories strike my view,
> The humbler I shall lie.'

And who, we may ask, in the pride of human strength and wisdom will venture upon a voyage over that shadowy Ocean, from which Newton shrank back dismayed? Or, if the example of this great man will not deter us, at least let us be warned from the rash enterprise by the innumerable wrecks which strew its shore, of those who have made the attempt and perished. And yet this Ocean must be passed ere we can be at rest. It rolls between Time and Eternity, between Earth and Heaven; and it is on its outmost shores, far, far beyond all mortal ken, that the land of promise lies. There, and there only, are those ' sweet fields' that

> 'stand drest in living green;'

there the 'flowery mounts;' there Jesus, the Forerunner, and the assembly of the saints made perfect; there the River of life, and there the Paradise of God.

But let us not be dismayed. It was as a Philosopher that Newton feared to venture upon its waves, and not as a Christian. Science could not bear him over in safety; but Faith could. While even to the eagle eye of Science all was unmitigated darkness, Faith with yet keener vision could pierce the gloom, and, far above the region of the tempest, could discern the Star of Bethlehem shining mildly and tranquilly down, and guiding to the haven of peace. She, too, and she alone, though the sea and all the waves thereof roar, could hear the voice of Him who walked upon the waters, saying, ' It is I; be not afraid.' With such a guide the Christian embarked in confidence, and, we cannot doubt, landed in safety.

And this, after all, was the true glory of Newton. For while he questioned Nature with high and daring resolve, and compelled her to disclose her most hidden secrets, he never questioned Nature's God. All the paths by which he walked through her labyrinths terminated in a Great First Cause, and beyond that he would not move a step. Beyond that he knew and felt was a region of 'emptiness' and 'nothingness' where he could not stand, with 'darkness upon the face of the deep' which the Omniscient Eye alone could pierce. Hence to his own mind, his profoundest researches served but to confirm the truth revealed from heaven, - 'In the beginning God created the heaven and the earth.' And thus it was that his highest flights carried him no higher than to the feet of Jesus, where he sat down to learn the simple yet sublime doctrines of the gospel, with all the docility and single-heartedness of a child.

The whole history of human learning and science affords nothing so affectingly instructive in this respect, as the example of Newton. Not that he is the only instance where profound attainments have been made subservient to the cause of divine truth. Far from it. By much the greater number of those names, which in modern days have illustrated the circle of the sciences, are found enrolled among the humble followers of the Lamb, But as of all these names Newton's is the most illustrious, so perhaps was his humility the most sincere and unfeigned."

The Editor of the Observer frequently rode into the country around St. Louis, preaching and attending meetings of the Synod and Presbytery, as also, meetings for various benevolent objects. A Sabbath spent at Apple Creek is thus described.

Apple Creek, May 22d, 1835

"The church at Apple Creek, with the exception of the First church in your city, is the largest in the State. The number of members returned to the General Assembly of 1834, was 206. I forgot to enquire the present number. The congregation also, worshipping with this church is, I judge, much more numerous, than any other out of St, Louis. Indeed, from what I saw, I should think it would come but little short, in point of numbers, to the first society in that city. To see the congregation assemble, reminded me of the descriptions I have often read, of the gathering of the Highland clans at the muster call of their leaders. An unpracticed eye could discern not the least sign that would betoken the vicinage of human beings. But at the first sound of the bugle, every brake, and hollow, the shieling of every hill, would pour forth its tide of living beings to swell the number of the gathering multitude. Even so it was here. The meeting-house stands deeply embowered in the woods, which shut the prospect in on every side. Arriving there, a short time before the hour of worship, a person accustomed to live in cities, would conclude that few would be there to disturb his solitary meditations; but as the appointed hour approaches, an unexpected change passes over the scene. As if by magic, it becomes at once animated with the presence of living beings. From every quarter, and almost from behind every tree, the hardy yeomanry of the country come pouring in, accompanied by their wives, children, and sweethearts. Generally they come on horseback, the young men glorying in their horsemanship, as they caricole from side to side of the narrow pathway, to remove the overhanging limbs and grape vines, lest they annoy the damsels who are riding at their elbows, while the man of middle age, sobered by matrimony, comes jogging up, with his wife behind, and his child before him, on the same animal. I envy not the man his feelings, who can look upon such unsophisticated examples of domestic happiness and youthful hopes, and not find his heart pervaded with sympathizing gladness. These are the sober enjoyments of everyday life, which a benevolent God gives to everyone who has not weakly or wickedly thrown them away.

Entering the house of God, you look round upon a most interesting assembly. Nearly all but the younger part, have been gathered from distant regions; they have come to die in a land unknown to their fathers, but not so to their fathers' God. Him they still worship, as they worshipped him, in the hours of their infancy - theirs is the same Redeemer, the same promises, the same gospel, and theirs, too, the same assurance of immortality. Here, close by the pulpit, is an aged pilgrim. He has travelled seven hundred miles 'leaning upon the top of his staff ' but his journeys are now over, save the last one that all must take, and from which none return.

His head is like the almond tree, and he goes bowed down alway; but he cannot fall, for a Savior's arm upholds him. Let him go in peace; let no one seek to detain him, when his Redeemer calls him to his presence, that He may clothe that mortal with immortality.

Yonder sits a man of middle age, with his family around him, his beloved and affectionate partner and his children, the youngest now verging upon manhood and womanhood. His was a covenant, and, in his case, well has he shown himself, a covenant-keeping, God. Dedicated himself in infancy, to the God of Abraham, with a heart overflowing with gratitude for the privilege, as God gave him children, from time to time, he presented them in the arms of faith before the altar, that the name of Israel's God might be named upon them, and they too be embraced in the provisions of the same gracious and ever-abiding covenant. He brought them up in 'the nurture and admonition of the Lord,' and now God has given them all to him again, in a second birth. The world calls these children poor, and this family obscure. But is it so? Children of the covenant, the Spirit has now sealed them as heirs of God's eternal kingdom - trace their course a few years onward, and they are seen shining in that kingdom, higher and brighter than the stars forever and ever. If this be poverty and obscurity, then what are this world's riches and splendor?

There is a young woman - no father or mother has she to whom she may look for counsel and instruction, no sister into whose sympathizing bosom she might pour her joys and sorrows, no brother on whom to lean for that support, which none but a brother can give. And yet she is not alone. Daily she communes with her Saviour, and through him, with heaven and all its delights. On him she leans, from him she receives counsel and instruction, while in obedience to his commands she seeks to fulfill as an ' hireling her day,' that when it is over, she may go to rest in His bosom forever.

Such are some of the varieties of character to be met with in a congregation in Missouri. Alas! it is to be feared there are others of a different type. There may be the hoary head, with all its sins resting unforgiven upon it - there may be the apostate from the church and the altar of God, there a young man, who has broken away from the restraints of a pious home, to commence a career of vice and profligacy: and there another, who has renounced the God of his fathers, and having himself become the head of a family, is founding a new dynasty of rebels. Better had that man never been born! I rejoice to say, that I saw no indications of any such in the congregation at Apple Creek. The assembly was universally and uniformly attentive and devout."

CHAPTER VII

In this chapter several articles upon Romanism are introduced, which exhibit the arguments and the spirit, with which the Editor of the Observer combated the delusions, errors, and wickedness of the "Infallible Church."

TRANSUBSTANTIATION

"There is one plain argument against this doctrine, which can never be set aside:

1. We are required to believe that the consecrated bread and wine are really the flesh and blood of the Lord Jesus Christ, because the Bible says, or rather the Savior speaking in the Bible, 'This,' (that is, the bread,) 'is my body,' and 'This,' (that is, the wine,) 'is my blood.' Now supposing I ask how am I to know that the Bible says any such thing? The priest opens the book, and shows me the very words, 'This is my body.' But now I ask to see the bread and the wine thus metamorphosed. The priest gives me the wafer, I taste it, it tastes like bread; I smell it, it smells like bread, I handle it, it *feels* like bread. And so of the wine.

2. I therefore turn to the priest, and say here are three senses to one, in favor of these elements being bread and wine still; I am therefore bound to believe them so. I *cannot*, from the very laws of my being, believe one sense in preference to three. I am, therefore, bound to seek some other fair interpretation of the words "This is my body,' than the one you have given them, or else reject them altogether. And here I need be at no loss. Turning to John x. 9, I find Jesus saying, 'I am the door;' and in John xv. 1, he says 'I am the true vine,' yet you do not pretend to make the Savior literally say, that he was a door or a vine. Or if he had, when speaking to his disciples, intended to be understood literally, and they had so understood his meaning, they could not have believed him. They heard him say so, but they smelled, saw, and felt that he was not so; and consequently must distrust their own hearing, or his veracity. And the case would be the same when sitting with him at the supper of the passover. If he declared to them that they were eating and drinking flesh and blood, they could only know that he did so by the sense of hearing, whereas by three senses, taste, touch, and smell, they would be assured they were doing no such thing. According to the very laws of the human mind, therefore, they could not so understand him.

3. The only remark we have to make upon this argument, is, that no man, in his senses, ever believed fully and fairly, the doctrine of transubstantiation. It is impossible that he should do so. He might as well believe that fire is cold and ice is hot, or that a thing is and is not at the same time. Let us not be misunderstood; there have, doubtless, been many men who honestly thought they believed it; but owing to the

prejudice of education, their minds, in this point, was dark, and saw things that were not as though they were. So often do we see individuals afflicted with mental imbecility on some particular subject, but perfectly sane on every other. In this way we can account for the fact that many good men have unquestionably supposed they believed the doctrine of transubstantiation; a dogma which, if true, makes, as has been well said, every other truth a lie."

NUNNERIES

"That these institutions should ever have acquired any favor in a community so shrewd, sagacious, and suspicious as the American people are, is truly a wonder. And that they should have succeeded in obtaining inmates from the families of Protestants and even members of the Church, is still more astonishing. It is to be accounted for on no common principle of human action. In this, as in other things, Romanism has shown itself a 'mystery of iniquity.'

What is a Nunnery? Have the American people ever asked themselves this question? And if so, have they ever reflected long enough upon it to obtain an answer satisfactory to their own minds? What is a Nunnery, we ask again? We will tell. It is a dwelling whose inmates consist of unmarried females, of all ages, tempers, dispositions, and habits. These females have entered into voluntary vows of chastity, poverty, and obedience to the rules of their order and their spiritual superiors. They have been induced to take these vows and exclude themselves from the world, from various motives. Some whose affections were young and ardent, from disappointment of the heart; some from love of retirement; some from morbid sensitiveness to the world of society, and some others, from the blandishments of Priests and Lady Superiors. In Europe there is another cause - operating more than any other, perhaps than all others - which peoples the Convents. Unfeeling parents make them the receptacle of those daughters, who may be in the way of the aggrandizement of other members of the family, or who may be disposed to contract an alliance which, they will not approve. This, too, is probably a remote cause of many entering convents in this country.

Very well; now let us take a Convent, whose inmates have been brought together from causes like the above. There are the aged, the middle aged, the young, the ardent, the beautiful. Thus much concerning them we all know.

But one of these communities issues, through their Superior, to the community in which it is situated, proposals for taking young ladies as inmates in their dwelling, and educating them there. This is all well enough. But now suppose a Protestant parent, before committing his daughters to their guardianship, visits the Convent to learn something of its character. He finds it situated in a retired place, surrounded with a high wall, embosomed in luxurious groves. All the charms of nature and art are combined to render its retreat inviting, and its bowers alluring. Into one only room can the visitant have access. Labyrinthian passages, in various directions, lead to apartments never to be profaned by a Protestant eye. All here is seclusion and mystery. These doors are locked; and neither parent, brother, friend, nor even sister, can turn the key. Yet to this rigid exclusion there is one exception. The Catholic Priest is privileged to come at all hours, and on all occasions as may suit his convenience. He has the ' open sesame,' before which the door of every department flies open, and admits him to familiar, unrestrained intercourse with its inmates. But who is the Catholic Priest? Is he aged, venerable? Is he even a married man? No; he is (or may be) a young man, and like those whom he visits bound by his vow to a life of celibacy. And whatever his vow may have been, his looks show abundantly that fasting, penance, and mortifying of the body make no part of his practice. His is not the lean and subdued countenance of the penitent, but the jolly visage of the sensualist rather. Alas! for the ladies of the convent, if his vow of chastity is kept no better than his vow of poverty and penance. And what reason have we to suppose it is? If he violate it in one case, why not in the other? The temptation is, at least, as great.

We will present this subject in a little different light. - Suppose a dozen young ministers from the Theological Seminary of Princeton, having just been ordained, should come out and take up their abode in the city of St. Louis. Supposing some one of our wealthy citizens, or, if you please, citizens of Boston, or New York, should furnish them with the funds requisite to put up a building in some retired place in the outskirts of the town - supposing the building finished - furnished - enclosed with a high wall, evidently intended for exclusion. Suppose now the young gentlemen advertise in the newspapers of the city, that they have brought with them from Boston a dozen young ladies, who have each made a solemn promise that they will never marry, and that these ladies are now in the newly erected building, prepared to open a school, and to receive female pupils as boarders. Suppose they also should make it known that these young ladies had chosen one of their own number - or perhaps the arrangement might be that they should take turns in performing this office, but always so that but one at a time should be at the house - to be their father confessor, and that he was to have access to their dwelling at any or all times, coming and going unquestioned, and that he, or certainly his fellows, were to be the only males who should have access to, or authority in, the establishment. All this being perfectly understood, let us, for the last time, suppose that one of these young gentlemen should go round to the respectable families of our city, and solicit that their daughters might become the inmates, as pupils, of their establishment. What reception would he be likely to meet with? How many young ladies would he be likely to collect for his school?

Yet, gentle reader, suppose all the above conditions fulfilled, and you have a Protestant Convent, or Nunnery, formed, in all its essential features, on the most approved model of the Romanists. Who would trust a dozen Protestant ministers, under such circumstances as these? No one. And, indeed, the very fact, that they asked to be trusted would prove them all unworthy. But do the annals of the Church show that the Popish priesthood are more worthy of trust, purer, holier than the Protestant clergy? Read 'Scipio de Ricci,' and 'Blanco White;' read 'Secreta Monita' of the Jesuits, 'Bower's History of the Popes,' and 'Text Book of Popery,' or if these will not convince, read Hume, Gibbon, Robertson, and even Lingard himself - read Roscoe's Leo the Tenth; nay their own approved manuals of faith and practice. Read these and know that corruption, rank and foul, has always steamed and is now steaming from the thousand monasteries, convents, and nunneries, that are spread, like so many plague spots, over the surface of Europe.

We do not say, for we do not believe, that they have reached the same degree of pollution in this country. Far from it - and yet we are no advocates of, or believers in, their immaculate purity. But what we say is this, that so long as human nature remains as it is, so long will the *tendency*, the unavoidable tendency, of such institutions be to iniquity and corruption. We care not in whose hands they are, Popish or Protestant, they tempt to sin all who are connected with them. We might even admit that they were founded with good intentions - which, in many instances, we have no doubt has been the case - and still our objections to them would be no whit lessened. Talk of vows of chastity, in chambers of impenetrable seclusion, and amidst bowers of voluptuousness and beauty! 'Tis a shameful mockery, and especially with the records of history spread out before us. For that informs us that the Nunnery has generally been neither more nor less, than a seraglio for the friars of the monastery."

WHY DISCUSS THE SUBJECT OF POPERY?

June 11th, 1835

"We need not inform our readers that our columns have been, for some months past, considerably occupied with the discussion of Popery, in all its bearings, civil, and religious; social and intellectual. We now propose briefly, to state the reasons why we have thought proper to take such a course.

1. It is not to gratify any personal feelings of our own. We can truly say that there is not a single individual, a member of the Romish church, towards whom we have a single feeling of unkindness. Many of them in

this city, have been our personal friends, and for aught we know are so still - at any rate we are theirs. With the Romish clergy, we have no personal acquaintance, and towards them, as individuals, have none but the kindest feelings of good will - it being our daily prayer that they may see, and renounce, the dangerous and deadly errors of their religious creed.

2. It is not that we distrust the patriotism of the members of the Romish church in this city, that we sound the alarm of danger to our institutions from Popery. There is no more respectable or intelligent portion of our citizens, than many of those who are of French origin, and who are either nominally or really members of the Romish church. We have known them long, and bear our willing testimony to the high minded and honorable feelings which actuate them as friends, as men of business, and as American citizens. They are republicans, in the genuine sense of that term, and there is no class of our citizens to whom we would more readily or confidently entrust the guardianship of our free institutions. We do not believe they would surrender them to King, Bishop, or Pope. Many of them are among the wealthiest and m.ost influential of our citizens, distinguished for the urbanity of their manners, the hospitality of their houses, and those other social virtues that so favorably characterize the country of their ancestors. It cannot therefore be for the purpose of injuring any of this class, that we denounce the tendencies of the religion, so many of them profess.

3. It is not for the sake of acquiring popularity. With a great majority of our fellow citizens, the course we have taken, and which we intend to pursue, with unabated vigor, is a most unpopular one. So far as we know, with some few exceptions, *all* that class of our citizens who may be called *nominal* Protestants, are entirely and decidedly opposed to our course. This opposition sometimes - when there are immediate selfish purposes to be gained - assumes the character of personal hostility, and an open stand in favor of Popery. In the hearts of the ignorant, and, of course, bigoted adherents of the Romish church, and especially in those of its Priests, it has engendered, and still supplies a fountain of the bitterest and most malignant hatred, which weekly discharges itself upon our head, in an undiluted stream of vulgarity and abuse. Lastly, there are many of our brethren, who view the matter in a light different from us, and from whom we receive no aid, but discouragement rather, and cold regards. At the East it is different; but where our paper circulates, not one half of the members of the different Protestant churches, are awakened to a sense of the danger that is pressing upon us from the increase of Popery. By many of our fellow citizens, whom we respect, and whose good opinion we highly value, we are called bigot, fanatic, intolerant, quarrelsome; and besides have often to encounter the cold regrets of many of our well-meaning, but timid brethren. These things have all along been seen and felt by us; and it will therefore be readily acknowledged that in

espousing the cause we have chosen, we did it not for the sake of popularity, or of making our position as Editor, an easy one.

The question now again returns: why then choose such a position, and why maintain it? Why continue these attacks upon the tenets of Popery, when confessedly many unpleasant consequences will result? We are now prepared to give this question a short and decisive answer. It is this. We maintain our warfare against the principles and dogmas of Popery, because WE BELIEVE THE CAUSE OF HUMANITY, OF FREEDOM, OF VITAL PIETY, IN A WORD, THE CAUSE OF TRUTH, DEMANDS IT.

Such being our entire and undoubting conviction, we should be false to every sentiment we profess, a recreant coward in defense of every principle we hold most dear, should we lay down our weapons and retire, or permit ourselves to be driven from the field. The contest we admit, is an arduous one; we have to bear up against a host of opposing influences, that would long since have crushed us, had we not been upheld by an abiding and controlling sense of duty. Hitherto that has sustained us, and by the grace of God it shall still sustain us, in our conflict with the 'Man of Sin,' 'whose coming is after the working of Satan, with all power, and signs, and lying wonders,' until the Lord shall destroy him 'with the brightness of his coming.' Then - if it come in our day - will we lay down the 'weapons of our warfare;' if not we shall continue to ' fight the good light' until death, assured that others more worthy will finish, what we, in common with others, were honored to begin.

One word more. It is often said - and it constitutes the most plausible objection we have heard - that the discussion of this subject tends to introduce unkind feelings into society, to create jealousies, ill-will, and distrust among neighbors and fellow citizens. We admit, and regret, but cannot help this consequence. It proves nothing, however, either for good or for evil. 'I came not to send peace on earth,' said the Savior, 'but a sword.' Wherever Paul went, preaching the gospel, he was accused of turning society 'upside down;' and the charge, as to the mere fact, though not in the evil sense intended, was true. Whoever sets himself, firmly, to breast the current of popular sentiment, will find at once, its waves breaking around him; and in proportion to the strength of the current, will be the violence of their onset and the noise of their roaring. If frightened at the outcry and clamor of those, whose easy onward progress has been interrupted, or at the gathering fury of the waters, let him give way and turn and swim with the stream - he will soon find a perfect calm again. Neither of these is our own case. We took our stand under the firmest convictions of duty, coolly, calmly, deliberately; having counted well what it would cost to maintain it. These same convictions still fix us there - where we expect and intend to remain, until the Master we serve shall call us away, to fill our place with one more devoted to his interests, and more skilled to contend with his enemies.

P. S. We were writing the above article, in our office, on Saturday morning, and had got about two-thirds of the way through it, when a friend stepped in, saying as he entered, ' I come at the request of Mr. ----, to subscribe, in his name, for the 'Observer.' He says, that while so many of the Protestant Newspapers and Clergymen, are fearful and undetermined, he wishes to give his support and countenance to a paper that has so boldly set itself to resist the tide of Popery, which is now flowing in and threatens to overwhelm us.' Mr. ---- is a Methodist brother, and resides in Michigan Territory.

Now this incident is a small one of itself, but we notice it because of the effect it had upon our feelings, particularly in reference to the time of its occurrence. We could not but regard it as a good omen; as an indication of Providence, that our course in this matter was approved."

St. Louis, Aug. 27th, 1835

"We recommend to the 'Argus' a perusal of the following paragraph copied from the 'National Gazette,' The 'Argus' has taken the Catholics into his special keeping. Why? Simply because he wants their votes. Now we do not care on which side the Catholic votes, nor to which party he belongs. Nor do we wish to touch any of the rights belonging to any class of citizens, Catholic or Protestant, Jew or Mahometan. But what we say, and maintain, and prove by undeniable facts, is, that Popery and Freedom, whether civil or religious, are incompatible with each other - they cannot co-exist. What we warn our countrymen to be on their guard against, is, the hordes of ignorant, uneducated, vicious foreigners who are now flocking to our shores, and who, under the guidance of Jesuit Priests, are calculated, fitted and intended to subvert our liberties.

But the 'Argus' wishes us to hold our peace because it wishes religion to be kept entirely unconnected with politics.' Doubtless, doubtless it does. Its conduct shows that plain enough. But we can tell the ' Argus' that it is for this very reason that we will not hold our peace. It is because we see the 'Argus' and other similar politicians, of all political creeds and complexions, endeavoring to separate religion and politics, that we labor to prevent this divorce. We wish every man when he votes, to do it in the fear of God; and that is what we call a union of religion and politics. And it is the only union we desire.

Partisan politics - for why should we not speak out I - are operating the downfall of our country. Do we accuse one party more than another? No. We see a mournful destitution of moral principle among them all. They turn with the veering wind. Look at the New York Courier and Enquirer. Two or three years ago it was the champion of Irishmen; it would not suffer a word to be said in derogation of them or their priests. And why?

Simply because it was then attached to that party to which most of these ignorant foreigners belonged.

But the Courier has since changed its position, and is now as zealously engaged in proclaiming the dangers of Popery, as it once was in defending it from all attacks. And though we believe that it is now on the right side, so far as Popery is concerned, yet have we any confidence in such a co-adjutor? None at all. Self-interest, real or supposed, placed the Courier where it is, and at its bidding it would go back to its old position.

So here, in our own city. Unconnected with any party, but an American citizen, and as such, and especially as an American Christian, deeply interested in the perpetuity of our free institutions, our civil and religious freedom, we saw the encroachments of Popery upon both. We saw the stealthy, cat-like step, the hyena grin, with which the 'Mother of Abominations,' was approaching the Fountain of Protestant Liberty, that she might cast into it the poison of her incantations, more accursed than was ever seethed in the Caldron of Hecate. We saw, too, that as it had been with us, so it still was with most of our citizens - they were insensible to the danger awaiting them. We raised the alarm. We have continued to sound it aloud; and we have the unspeakable gratification to know that it has not been wholly in vain. In the discharge of this sacred duty, owed first to our God, and next to our country, we have had nothing but a good conscience to sustain us. Obloquy and reproach have been our portion; and who has ventured to defend us? Not a single political press of any party. Discordant as might be their voices in other matters, they chimed harmoniously in attacking us, and defending the Papists. Thus the 'Republican' and the 'Argus.' And why? Because each wanted Catholic votes. Well; the 'Argus,' it seems, has got them; and the 'Republican' now says, through its correspondents at least, the very things against Papists which it abused us for saying; while the 'Argus' redoubles its zeal and fury in their defense. We rejoice at the stand the 'Republican' has now taken. We hope it will have courage to maintain it, but we greatly fear the contrary. Let history be consulted, let the present state of the world be inspected, and the 'Republican' will find that in no way can it render so effectual a service to its country, as by opposing that tremendous tide of foreign emigration which even now threatens to sweep away all that we hold dear.

For the 'Argus,' we hope the lesson it has just received will not be lost upon it. Let it learn, henceforth, to pay some regard to principle in the selection of its leaders. The great mass of the people are of honest intentions. They may be deceived and deluded, but, in this country, they cannot well be corrupted. If no higher principle, therefore, restrain the 'Argus' from allying itself to Jesuitism, let it at least be restrained by the fear, even in this, of being thrown into a minority. And even if victorious, depend upon it, Mr. 'Argus,' the only reward which Jesuitism would give you, would be the same which Polyphemus vouchsafed to Ulysses - that of being the last devoured."

CHAPTER VIII

We come now to the subject of Slavery. Articles upon this subject were occasionally found in the "Observer" from the beginning. It did not, however, occupy a larger proportion of the entire sheet, than *two and a half millions* bear to *fifteen millions*. The Editor was, during this period, thoroughly convinced of the sin of Slavery, and, at the same time, cherished an ardent desire to see it abolished. But he was seeking a point where these views, and opposition to immediate abolition might be coincident. To discover such a point, he framed all the moral problems, and drew the figures for their illustration, which a fertile genius, extensive knowledge, and honest intentions could devise. That point, however, we hardly need say, he never found. Thousands made the same experiments before him, and many are continuing these attempts, destined, we doubt not, to the same disappointment. It is devoutly to be hoped, that with equal frankness they will acknowledge their mistake, and come forth and stand upon the immoveable basis of everlasting-Truth. One thing always gave us pleasure, while we differed in opinion from our brother upon this subject, - he ever appeared to act up to the light which shone upon his path. When, therefore, he saw that immediate abolition was the only ground on which to stand, and move the mass of cruelty, injustice, and corruption which the word Slavery imports, he placed himself upon it, and here 'he conquered, though he fell.'

We shall now give such extracts from the editorial pen as will exhibit his sentiments, and the manner in which he treated this subject.

SLAVERY

June, 1834

"This subject is one which has always, since we have known anything of the Southern and Slave-holding Western States, been regarded as exceedingly delicate and difficult of management. We feel it to be so at the moment of penning these remarks. Not because - as some of our Abolitionist brethren will charge us - we fear the truth, and are unwilling to perform our duty, but, because there is real difficulty in ascertaining what that duty is. The man who has been reared in the midst of Slavery, and acquainted with the system from his earliest infancy, who regards the colored man as part of the estate bequeathed to him .by his parents, and his right over him guaranteed by the constitution of his country, becomes excited, when any one denies this right, and lays down ethical principles for his government, that, in their operation, must beggar him. Nor is this all; he finds himself the subject of bitter invective and unmeasured denunciation. As a man, stripped of all honorable pretension, and made a participant with the heartless man-stealer, whose crime he abhors. As a Christian, denounced and accounted a profaner of the symbols of his holy religion. Held up to society as a monster in human shape, a tyrant who delights in the pangs inflicted upon his fellow-man. We have never wondered that under such circumstances, it should be an exciting subject - he must be more than human who would not be sensible of the recoil in his feelings. He may at the same time be wrong. But his early associations - his prejudices, are all upon the side of long established opinions; and hence it should hardly be expected, that at the first glance, he should see the truth as one differently situated may see it, and instantly espousing the opinion of the opposite party, give an evidence of his sincerity that the other was never called to give, by passing immediately from affluence to poverty. In all controversies there is a strong tendency in the parties to take extreme ground - so in this - and hence he finds himself charged with views and feelings, and base motives for his opposition, which he is at the moment conscious he does not possess, and which the very man who presses the charge against him, in his cooler moments, would not think of making. Certain it is, that in this controversy, no one will be persuaded by naked denunciation or misrepresentations - but cool and temperate argument, supported by facts, must perform the work.

It has been with pain that we have seen recently the heated and angry meetings and discussions, which have taken place, amongst our eastern brethren of the Abolition and Colonization parties. Though we have certainly our own preference on this subject, yet, eschewing the papacy, as we do, we are not disposed to set up our claims to infallibility in his stead, and always regret when we see good brethren take such a stand. That the recent movement in Great Britain and the West Indies, could take place and leave us unaffected, we never supposed - that it must work changes in our system, we did then and do still believe, but the danger is in the manner in which that change is to brought about. That Slavery is a curse, politically and morally, to every state where it exists, is a sentiment to which the South and West respond. And this response is given by the Slaveholder, with a deeper and more experimental conviction in the South than in the East. The great desideratum with the reflecting in both sections of the country, is to get rid of the evil. Now, starting upon the same premises, it is to be regretted that such widely different conclusions should be arrived at, and still more, that angry feelings should be elicited in the contest.

We have read the declaration of the Abolition Convention held in Philadelphia, and also of the Lane Seminary, and felt prepared to adopt, in the main, the abstract principles set forth by them. With the means by which they declare they will seek the accomplishment of their object - the dissemination of light, thereby creating a correct public opinion - we are satisfied. But the danger is, that the friends of abolition will not strictly adhere to these terms, and thereby excite prejudices and bitterness. We infer this from the overstrained and highly wrought picture that was presented at Lane Seminary by some zealous and heated young men, under the temptation that it would be popular to make a good speech, and which statements have gone the length and breadth of the land. From the examination of Thomas C. Brown, a disappointed emigrant, in New York, in which he was compelled to retract much that he had previously detailed to the injury of the Colony at Liberia - and from the heated speeches of some good men at the late anniversaries in that city. When means like these are resorted to, whatever the effect may be in the East, in the South and West they are calculated to recoil, and produce a want of confidence in the efforts of good men. Still, we believe that the Abolitionists have done good. They have aroused the country to more reflection on the subject. They have detected defects in the management of the Colonization Society - and they have, by showing that society that they will hereafter be watched with Argus eyes, secured the better conduct of its affairs. But why wage a war of extermination upon a kindred institution? Will the sending away to the land of their fathers of some hundreds of manumitted slaves and free persons of color, annually, prevent the rise of public opinion in favor of abolition? If it is said that free persons do not wish to leave the soil - it is well - let them remain. The Colonization Society compels no one to go. Admit that our laws are unjust in the heavy load of disabilities which they impose upon the colored man - and that those are the compelling power - the Society did not make the laws, but taking the statutes as they were, they provided a home where these disabilities were unknown. If it is said this Society does not provide an effectual remedy for the evil, and hence it is a waste of funds that might be better employed Why not permit it to go as far as it can? And what prospect is there that if these funds are diverted from their present channel they will flow into another that is better? Surely the Abolitionists can have no hope that their coffers would be supplied by the friends of Colonization in the South and West.

But we will not extend our remarks. Our object is peace and concert in action with every good man, in every good work. We are not sensible that we possess any prejudices upon the subject. We do not promise by any means, that we shall not become an Abolitionist, strictly, at some future day, and see the necessity of following the example of our worthy brother Cox, in forsaking the Colonization enterprise, but arguments of sufficient weight must be laid before us in order to this consummation."

SLAVERY

April 16th, 1835

"We ask from every professor of Christianity - as also from all others - a careful, candid, and *prayerful* perusal of the article on our first page on this subject. It is from the pen of one* who is entitled to be heard in the case; inasmuch as having been a slave holder once, he has ceased to be such by emancipating all his slaves. The main principles, facts and inferences stated by the writer, we are so far from questioning that we believe them entirely correct. 'How hardly shall they that have riches be saved,' said One who perfectly well knew the principles by which the human mind operated and was operated upon. For the same reason though found in the opposite extreme, we may say how hardly shall they that are slaves enter into the kingdom of heaven. In either case there is nothing which absolutely forbids heaven to either class, or which renders it of itself more difficult of attainment, yet judging from analogy and from the results of experience, we are enabled confidently to predict that not 'many wise, not many noble,' and not many ignorant slaves, will make their way through the difficulties that surround their positions, to a heaven of disinterestedness and intelligence.

While therefore we cordially adopt the main sentiments of our correspondent, and would affectionately, yet urgently, press them upon our Christian readers as a reason why they should introduce a thorough change in their manner of treating, or rather neglecting, their slaves, so far as religious instruction is concerned; we do not believe that this change ought to be immediate and unconditional emancipation. We are entirely convinced that such a course would be cruel to the slave himself, and injurious to the community at large. But something must be done and done speedily on this all-important subject. While Christians have been slumbering over it, the eye of God has not slumbered, nor has his Justice been an indifferent spectator of the scene. The groans, and sighs, and tears, and blood of the poor slave have gone up as a memorial before the throne of Heaven. In due time they will descend in awful curses upon this land, unless averted by the speedy repentance of us all.

Look at the manner in which our sister state, Louisiana, is treating her slaves! Why, as surely as there is a thunderbolt in Heaven and strength in God's right arm to launch it, so surely will it strike the authors of such cruel oppression. Look, too, at the *slave-drivers*, who go up and down our own streets, lifting their heads and moving among us unashamed, unrebuked - as if they had not forfeited all claim to the name of max. All abhor the traffic, and detest the wretch who pursues it; why then is he not driven from the face of day, and made to hide himself in some dark corner, whose murky gloom might faintly emblem the savage darkness of his own heart?

Why? simply because public sentiment has never been aroused to think on the subject. "If the laws protect the miscreant who coins his wealth out of the heart's blood of his fellow creatures, he can at least be crushed beneath the odium of public opinion.

There is another fact we wish to introduce in this place. It is this. Congress, acting only as the organ of public opinion, has pronounced the slave trade from the coast of Africa piracy. Those engaged in it are punishable with death. From a statement given in the Journal of Commerce, it appears, that last November there were no less than forty eight slave vessels on the African coast engaged in this nefarious traffic. It was supposed these vessels would carry off at least 20,000 victims - victims in every sense of the term, to tyranny, brutality, and lust. It also appears that many of these poor wretches eventually land in the United States, by way of Cuba, and other Spanish Islands. Particularly is it to be feared and supposed that many of them are smuggled into Louisiana. Now, although the system of domestic Slavery is not necessarily connected with this foreign piratical trade, yet no one can deny that it tends greatly to encourage it. And no one can deny, that if domestic Slavery should cease throughout Christendom, the slave trade from Africa would cease of course. We mention these things as affording strong incidental reasons for action among ourselves at home. Above all the rest, the same paper states that there is no doubt a slave vessel left New York a few days since.

In this connection it gives us heart-felt pleasure to introduce the following extract from the 'Republican' of Friday last. The Editors are referring to the Convention about to be called for the purpose of amending our Constitution. With the sentiments of the extract we most cordially concur, and hope the Editors will not fail to keep the subject before their readers till the time for action shall arrive. And who are the individuals or individual, who will make it their business between the present time and the time for voting, to arouse and enlighten public sentiment on this great subject? What a glorious opportunity is now offered to such a one - an opportunity such as will not be likely again to arise for centuries to come - to confer a lasting, an unspeakable benefit upon the citizens of this state, of this republic, and upon the cause of universal humanity! Is it too much to ask of Christians, that they will ask the Lord, in fervent, importunate prayer, to send such a laborer into the field of this state? We do not want a man from the northern or middle states; we want one who has himself been educated in the midst of Slavery, who has always lived in contact with it, who knows, experimentally, all its evils, and all its difficulties - one who will not lift his head up into the region of abstract speculation, and in the loftiness of his pride, in a beautiful theory, disdain alike to make acquaintance with facts and with common sense. To such a man a golden opportunity of doing good is offered. We believe the minds of the good people of this state are fully prepared to listen to him - to give a dispassionate consideration to the facts and reasonings he might present connected with the subject of Slavery. Public sentiment, amongst us, is already moving in this great matter - it now wants to be directed in some defined channel, to some definite end.

Taken all in all, there is not a state in this Union possessing superior natural advantages to our own. At present, Slavery, like an incubus, is paralyzing our energies, and like a cloud of evil portent, darkening all our prospects. Let this be removed, and Missouri would at once start forward in the race of improvement, with an energy and rapidity of movement, that would soon place her in the front rank along with the most favored of her sister stales.

But we stay too long from the extract from the 'Republican.'

'We look to the Convention as a happy means of relieving the state, at some future day, of an evil which is destroying all our wholesome energies, and leaving us, in morals, in enterprise, and in wealth, behind the neighboring states. We mean, of course, the curse of Slavery. "We are not about to make any attack upon the rights of those who at present hold this description of property. They ought to be respected to the letter. We only propose, that measures shall now be taken for the abolition OF SLAVERY, at such distant period of time as may be thought expedient, and eventually for ridding the country altogether of a colored population. The plan has been adopted in other states, and they have been effectually relieved from the incubus which, even now, is weighing us down. With no decided advantage in soil, climate, productions, or facilities, the free states have shot far ahead of those in which Slavery is tolerated. We need go no further than Ohio and Kentucky for an illustration of this assertion. For ourselves, if this one principle shall be adopted, whatever may be the errors of the Convention - no matter with how many absurdities the Constitution may abound, we shall gladly overlook them all. To secure so important a benefit, we must set about it at once. Now is the time for action. The evil of which we are speaking, may be arrested in its incipient stage. It is perhaps the last time we shall have an opportunity of attempting it. And we call upon all citizens, of whatever rank, sect, or party, to aid in this good and glorious work. It is one in which all, laying aside minor controversies and considerations, may unite, and all may exert a favorable influence. Let us to the work, then, firmly and heartily!'"

SLAVERY

April 30th, 1835

"There can be no doubt that this subject in its various bearings will occupy much of the attention of the good people of this state, the ensuing season. We take it for granted there will be a convention of the people, at the time designated by our Legislature, (next December,) for the purpose of amending our constitution. This Convention will afford an opportunity for again deciding the question whether Missouri shall hereafter be a free, or continue a slave state. We look upon this question as one of more importance than we have words to express. And in its discussion and final decision by the Convention, we feel how much need there is of mutual forbearance among all those who shall have a word to say on the subject - as well as the exercise of that calm, sagacious, patriotic foresight which looks to the good of the whole community, and consults for the good of future as of present generations.

Let an unbiased, intelligent decision of our fellow citizens in the matter be had, and we have no fears of the result. We know, very well, that a right decision of the case, will, in many instances, have to be made in the face of immediate personal interest; but we look with confidence to the intelligence, the good sense, and moral justice of our citizens, as fully adequate to the crisis.

Slavery, as it exists among us, admits of being considered in a three-fold view - in a civil, a religious, and a moral view. Considered in any of these lights, it is demonstrably an evil. In every community where it exists, it presses like a night-mare on the body politic. Or, like the vampire, it slowly and imperceptibly sucks away the life-blood of society, leaving it faint and disheartened to stagger along the road of improvement. Look at Virginia - that noble commonwealth, the mother of states and great men - how strikingly does her present condition illustrate the truth of this sentiment!

The evils of Slavery in a moral and religious point of view, need not be told; they are seen, and palpable, by all. It becomes us as a Christian people, as those who believe in the future retribution of a righteous Providence, to remove from our midst an institution, no less the cause of moral corruption to the master than to the slave. It surely cannot be thought wrong, to press such a notion as this upon the consideration of our fellow citizens.

Gradual emancipation is the remedy we propose. This we look upon as the only feasible, and indeed, the only desirable way of effecting our release from the thralldom in which we are held. In the meantime, the rights of all classes of our citizens should be respected, and the work be proposed, carried on, and finished, as one in which all classes of our citizens are alike interested, and in which all may alike be called upon to make sacrifices of individual interests to the general welfare of the community.

There is, however, another matter - and we mention it here, lest our silence may be misinterpreted - connected with this subject, which admits, nay, demands a very different mode of treatment. We mean the manner in which the relations subsisting between Christians and their slaves are fulfilled. Here the reform ought to be thorough and immediate. There is no possible plea which can afford excuse for a moment's delay. On this point, we expect to have much to say; and we hope our readers will bear in mind - and thus save themselves from confounding our arguments on the two points - that while on the general subject of Slavery we are decidedly gradual, on this part of it we are as decidedly immediate Abolitionists. It is fearfully true that many professed Christians habitually treat their slaves as though they had no immortal souls, and it is high time such a practice as this were abolished."

LETTER FROM THE EDITOR

Mississippi River, May, 21st, 1835

"We have just swung from our moorings, and are going up to the upper part of the town, to take in some passengers. What glorious prospects are opening before the city of St. Louis! The time cannot be far distant when it will be enthroned, without a rival, the Queen of the West. Already, Front Street is, I should think, more than a mile in length. Seventeen Steamboats, among which were the mammoth Mogul, and the unfortunate Majestic, line its shores this morning. The whole quay is covered with merchandize and alive with the bustle of business. One boat was discharging freight, another was receiving it; here was one with her flag floating in the wind, indicating that she was soon to depart, and there another whose bell was calling all on board, who did not choose to be left behind - here was one blowing off, and there another raising her steam. Altogether, the scene was a most animated and animating one.

One thing depressed my spirits. It was the moral condition of a large portion of those whom I saw. As I passed up and down the quay, among the busy, hurrying multitude, the drunkeries and drinking I witnessed, the oaths and the obscene blasphemies I heard, caused my spirits to sink within me. I felt assured, too, that Christians in St. Louis, were not doing enough - are they doing anything? - for the boatmen in our harbor. I fear these last may truly say, 'No man careth for our souls.'

As we rounded to, and approached the shore of our sister state, a little below the city, we saw several little children at play upon the river's bank. Someone in the company remarked, ' That is a land of liberty!' Now the subject of slavery had not been mentioned, and the fact that such a thought was suggested by the very sight of the soil of Illinois, shows that the atmosphere of slavery is an unnatural one for Americans to live in. The institution is repugnant to the very first principles of liberty. The remark was the more worthy of notice as coming from one who has for many years, even from infancy, resided in a slave state, and who is the owner of slaves? I envy not the prosperity of our sister state, Illinois: I rejoice in it the rather, and look forward with delight to the period, and that not far distant, when the busy hum of industry shall be heard over all her prairies, while schools, colleges, and religious temples, shall adorn and strengthen the institutions of two millions of freemen. Yet when contemplating this glorious and exciting spectacle, I cannot help saying, with a half suppressed sigh of despondency, 'Oh! that Missouri, my own beloved state, were in a condition to compete for the prize of such renown?' And why may she not? What nobler race of men exists in this wide world, than those who have followed Daniel Boone from the blood-bought fields of Kentucky, and pitched their tabernacles in Missouri? Alas! the single word SLAVERY, tells us why. So long as that remains amongst us, we may long for those improvements in art, science, and the habits of social life, which mark a rapidly advancing community, but they can never be ours. These are the rewards of well-directed industry alone.

I look forward to the approaching Convention in our state with more solicitude than I have words to express. It does seem to me a crisis that calls for the exercise of all the candor, enlarged patriotism, and sound judgment of all our citizens. We have it in our power to bequeath to posterity a benefit, for which all future generations shall bless us, or we may put back the hopes of humanity, and, instrumentally, the benign purposes of Heaven, a whole generation. Fearful responsibility! And will not all those who believe in the efficacy of prayer, and who know that God hath in his hands the hearts of all men, will they not cry day and night to Him, that he would graciously be pleased, by his Spirit to move upon the minds of our fellow citizens, inspiring them with right sentiments on this infinitely important subject. There is power sufficient in the church to accomplish this matter, if that power can only be brought to bear.

The more I think on this subject, the more am I penetrated with a sense of its magnitude. God and man are calling to us to be up and doing. Hayti and Southampton have written *their* lesson of warning in lines of blood. Virginia has traced hers upon many a ruined and deserted spot, once the most fertile of all her wide domains, but which has long since become as the 'plains of Sodom,' beneath the withering blight of slavery. The example of England is showing us that gradual abolition is safe, practicable and expedient. God from on high, and by his providence in making slave labor unprofitable, is commanding us to 'break every yoke, and let the oppressed go free.' It may not be, that we can slight all these warnings, exhortations, and commands, and yet prosper.

The physical and moral laws of God must both be inverted first. I could write forever on this subject but must close. Our boat is walking the water like a 'thing of life.' We are just opposite Herculaneum."

CHAPTER IX

Perhaps no other place is more appropriate in the order of events than this, to state that at the age of thirty-two he found the Scripture verified - "It is not good for man to be alone." On this subject, although so important in its consequences, there is everywhere license given to a playful mood in speaking of it. We therefore insert his own letter announcing this event to his friends. The reader will, of course, make some allowance for the partiality of a husband - his veto to the contrary notwithstanding.

St. Louis, March 10th, 1835
My dearest Mother,

I am married. So much for the first sentence, which contains the substance of the whole matter. But as I suppose you would like to have a few particulars, they follow.

I was married on Wednesday last, the 4th inst. at St. Charles, a village about twenty miles distant from this place. My wife's maiden name was Celia Ann French I thought we made a very respectable couple at the time. As for my own personal appearance, you know enough of that already. For the lady, I can tell you (she sits at my right hand while I write,) that she was twenty-one years of age last August, is tall, well-shaped, of a light, fair complexion, dark flaxen hair, large blue eyes, with features of a perfect Grecian contour. In short, she is very beautiful. This is not a mere expression of a fond husband, but just the simple truth. John will tell you if you ask him.

But the best is yet to come. I need not tell you she is pious, for I hope you knew I would marry no one who was not. She is, I know, intelligent, refined, and of agreeable manners; and unless I have entirely mistaken her character, she is also sweet-tempered, obliging, kindhearted, industrious, good-humored, and possessed alike of a sound judgment and correct taste. I am sure you will not think it the least evidence of these last - at any rate, I do not - that she has chosen your son for a husband. In addition to all this, she loves me, I think, about as much as I deserve. I shall now leave you to measure that love.

With such a wife I think I ought to be happy - I am sure I am thankful to the Lord who gave her to me.

Celia sends love to you, and to all her new sisters and brothers in Maine. She will expect a letter from sisters Sarah, Sibyl, and Elizabeth.

Pray tell me what is the reason of your long silence in Maine? I have heard nothing for a long time from a living soul in all that region. John is well, and so am I, and so is my dear wife, I have my hands full of business, but the Lord has hitherto sustained me.

Your most affectionate son,

ELIJAH P. LOVEJOY

Sun and clouds alternate in the horizon which surrounds the earth. We now pass to that period of our brother's history, when his trials and persecution commenced, and which terminated only with his death. The causes of these will be unfolded in the progress of the narration. In October, 1835, he was absent from St. Louis for several weeks. During this time, a great excitement commenced in that city upon the subject of Slavery. The proprietors of the "Observer" became alarmed at the threats of a mob, and caused the following notice to appear in that paper.

St. Louis, October 8th, 1835
"The Editor will be absent two or three weeks, in attendance on Presbytery and Synod."

"Since the Editor left, the Publishers of the Observer have received a communication from the Patrons and Owners of the property of this paper, advising an entire suspension of all controversy upon the exciting subject of Slavery. As this course is entirely agreeable to the feelings and views of the publishers, nothing upon the subject will appear in its columns, during the absence of the Editor. Upon his return the communication will be submitted to him, and the future course of the paper finally arranged in such a manner, as, we doubt not, will be consonant with the wishes of the proprietors.

The articles upon the subject of Slavery in our paper today, were prepared by the Editor before his departure, and could not have been omitted without great inconvenience."

The mob not being satisfied, and still threatening the destruction of the office of the "Observer," another concession to the "new code" " of our most respectable citizens' soon followed.

St. Louis, October 22d, 1835

"The Editor being still absent, we again issue our paper without much editorial matter. We hope it will not be the case another week."

TO THE PUBLIC

"The Proprietors of the St. Louis 'Observer' having heretofore expressed their determination that nothing should be advanced in the columns of that paper, calculated to keep up the excitement on the Slavery question; and being one and all opposed to the mad schemes of the Abolitionists, have heard with astonishment and regret, that certain evil disposed persons have threatened violence to the 'Observer Office.' We call upon all prudent men to pause and reflect upon the probable consequences of such a step - there is nothing to justify it. And it is asking too much of any set of men to stand patiently by and see their property destroyed.

We believe this to be a momentary excitement, arising out of the apprehension of the white men who stole Major Dougherty's negroes, and who having been dealt with according to the new code by several of our most respectable citizens, and that they will see that no evil arises out of that excitement.

The Proprietors of the
St. Louis Observer."

October 21st, 1835

Whether the last sentence of the above paper, does not give full sanction to the "new code," which means nothing less than mob law, the reader will judge. The acts done by this "new code" "of most respectable citizens," were, "two men had been taken up on suspicion of having decoyed away some negroes, had been brought by illegal violence from Illinois; taken about two miles back of the city, and there whipped between one and two hundred lashes, by about sixty of our most wealthy and influential citizens. They whipped by taking turns, so many lashes a piece. Before whipping, it was put to the vote, whether they should whip or hang them, and about twenty out of the sixty were given for hanging, and among them were some members of the Church."

St. Louis, October 5th, 1835
To The Rev. E. P. Lovejoy, Editor of the Observer.

Sir: The undersigned, friends and supporters of the "Observer," beg leave to suggest, that the present temper of the times require a change in the manner of conducting that print in relation to the subject of domestic Slavery.

The public mind is greatly excited, and owing to the unjustifiable interference of our northern brethren with our social relations, the community are, perhaps, not in a situation to endure sound doctrine in relation to this subject. Indeed, we have reason to believe, that violence is even now meditated against the "Observer Office," and we do believe that true policy and the interests of religion, require that the discussion of this exciting question should be at least postponed in this state.

Although we do not claim the right to prescribe your course as an Editor, we hope that the concurring opinions of so many persons, having the interests of your paper, and of religion both at heart, may induce you to distrust your own judgment, and so far change the character of the "Observer," as to pass over in silence everything connected with the subject of Slavery; we would like that you announce in your paper, your intention so to do.

We shall be glad to be informed of your determination in relation to this matter.

     Respectfully, your obedient servants,
       ARCHIBALD GAMBLE,
       NATHAN RANNEY,
       WILLIAM S. POTTS,
       JNO. KERR,
       G. W. CALL,
       H. R. GAMBLE,
       HEZEKIAH KING.

I concur in the object intended by this communication.
       BEVERLY ALLEN.

I concur in the foregoing.
       J. B. BRANT.*

*We find this document endorsed as follows:
"I did not yield to the wishes here expressed, and in consequence have been persecuted ever since. But I have kept a good conscience in the matter, and that more than repays me for all I have suffered, or can suffer. I have sworn eternal opposition to Slavery, and, by the blessing of God, I will never go back. Amen,"
 October 24lh, 1837   *E. P. L.*

The manner in which this communication was disposed of, will appear in his address to the public. That some parts of that appeal may be understood, it will be proper to insert two or three resolutions passed at a meeting of the citizens of St. Louis. The first deprecates the interference of foreign emissaries on the subject of Slavery.

2. *Resolved*, That the right of free discussion and freedom of speech exists under the constitution, but that being a conventional reservation made by the people in, their sovereign capacity, does not imply a moral right, on the part of the Abolitionists, to freely discuss the question of Slavery, either orally or through the medium of the press, It is the agitation of a question too nearly allied to the vital interests of the slave-holding states to admit of public disputation; and so far from the fact, that the movements of the Abolitionists are constitutional, they are in the greatest degree seditious, and calculated to incite insurrection and anarchy, and, ultimately, a disseverment of our prosperous Union.

3. *Resolved*, That we consider the course pursued by the Abolitionists, as one calculated to paralyze every social tie by which we are now united

to our fellow man, and that, if persisted in, it must eventually be the cause of the disseverment of these United States; and that the doctrine of amalgamation is peculiarly baneful to the interests and happiness of society. The union of black and white, in a moral point of view, we consider as the most preposterous and impudent doctrine advanced by the infatuated Abolitionists - as repugnant to judgment and science, as it is degrading to the feelings of all sensitive minds - as destructive to the intellect of after generations, as the advance of science and literature has contributed to the improvement of our own. In short, its practice would reduce the high intellectual standard of the American mind to a level with the Hottentot, and the United States, now second to no nation on earth, would in a few years, be what Europe was in the darkest ages.

4. *Resolved*, That the sacred writings furnish abundant evidence of the existence of Slavery from the earliest periods. The Patriarchs and Prophets possessed slaves - our Savior recognized the relation between master and slave, and deprecated it not: hence, we know that he did not condemn that relation; on the contrary, his disciples, in all countries, designated their respective duties to each other;

Therefore, *Resolved*, That we consider Slavery as it now exists in the United States, as sanctioned by the sacred Scriptures."

In the same number of his paper which contained these resolutions, and also the doings of another meeting, appointing committees of vigilance to look up all persons suspected of Abolitionism, appeared the following appeal.

TO MY FELLOW CITIZENS

November 5th, 1835

"Recent well-known occurrences in this city, and elsewhere have, in the opinion of some of my friends, as well as my own, made it my duty to address myself to you personally. And, in so doing, I hope to be pardoned for that apparent egotism which, in such an address, is more or less unavoidable. I hope also to write in that spirit of meekness and humility that becomes a follower of the Lamb, and, at the same time, with all that boldness and sincerity of speech, which should mark the language of a freeman and a Christian minister. It is not my design or wish to offend anyone, but simply to maintain my rights as a republican citizen, free-born, of these United States, and to defend, fearlessly, the cause of TRUTH AND RIGHTEOUSNESS."

[Here followed a statement in relation to the "Emancipators" and "Human Rights," sent to Jefferson City, also his sentiments on the subject of Slavery. These have been sufficiently indicated.]

"Let this statement, fellow citizens, show you the impropriety and the danger of putting the administration of justice into the hands of a mob. I am assured that had I been in the city, at the time when the charge here referred to, was first circulated, I should surely have suffered the penalty of the whipping-post or the tar-barrel, if not both! I understand that a Christian brother was one of those who brought the report here from Jefferson City, and was among the most active in circulating it, and declaring his belief in my criminality. If this meets his eye, he is assured that I forgive him with all my heart.

And now, fellow citizens, having made the above explanation, for the purpose of undeceiving such of you as have honestly supposed me in error; truth and candor require me to add that had I desired to send a copy of the 'Emancipator' or of any other newspaper to Jefferson City, I should not have taken the pains to box it up. I am not aware that any law of my country forbids my sending what document I please to a friend or citizen. I know, indeed, that *mob law* has decided otherwise, and that it has become fashionable in certain parts of this country, to break open the Post Office, and take from it such documents as the mob should decide, ought not to pass *unburned*. But I had never imagined there was a sufficiency of respectability attached to the proceeding, to recommend it for adoption to the good citizens of my own state. And grievously and sadly shall I be disappointed to find it otherwise.

In fine, I wish it to be distinctly understood that I have never, knowingly, to the best of my recollection, sent a single copy of the ' Emancipator' or any other Abolition publication to a single individual in Missouri, or elsewhere; while yet I claim the *right* to send ten thousand of them if I choose, to as many of my fellow citizens. Whether I will *exercise* that right or not, is for me, and not for the *mob*, to decide. The right to send publications of any sort to slaves, or in any way to communicate with them, without the express permission of their masters, I freely acknowledge that I have not. Nor do I wish to have it. It is with the master alone, that I would have to do, as one freeman with another; and who shall say me nay?

I come now to the proceedings had at the late meetings of our citizens. And in discussing them I hope not to say a single word that shall wound the feelings of a single individual concerned. It is with principles I have to do, and not with men. And in canvassing them, freely, openly, I do but exercise a right secured by the solemn sanction of the Constitution, to the humblest citizen of this republic - a right that, so long as life lasts, I do not expect to relinquish.

I freely acknowledge the respectability of the citizens who composed the meetings referred to. And were the questions under consideration, to be decided as mere matters of opinion, it would become me, however much I might differ from them, to bow in humble silence to the decisions of such a body of my fellow citizens. But I cannot surrender my principles, though the whole world besides should vote them down - I can make no compromise between truth and error, even though my life be the alternative.

Of the first resolution passed at the meeting of the 24th Oct., I have nothing to say, except that I perfectly agree with the sentiment, that the citizens of the non-slaveholding states have no right to interfere with the domestic relations between master and slave.

The second resolution, strictly speaking, neither affirms nor denies any thing in reference to the matter in hand. No man has a moral right to do anything improper. Whether, therefore, he has the moral right to discuss the question of Slavery, is a point with which human legislation or resolutions have nothing to do. The true issue to be decided is, whether he has the *civil*, the political right, to discuss it, or not. And this is a mere question of fact. In Russia, in Turkey, in Austria, nay, even in France, this right most certainly does not exist. But does it exist in Missouri? We decide this question by turning to the Constitution of the State. The sixteenth section, article thirteenth, of the Constitution of Missouri, reads as follows:

'That the free communication of thoughts and opinions is one of the invaluable rights of man, and that every person may freely speak, write, and print on any subject, being responsible for the abuse of that liberty.'

Here, then, I find my warrant for using, as Paul did, all freedom of speech. If I abuse that right I freely acknowledge myself amenable to the laws. But it is said that the right to hold slaves is a constitutional one, and therefore not to be called in question. I admit the premise, but deny the conclusion. To put a strong case by way of illustration. The Constitution declares that this shall be a perpetual republic, but has not any citizen the right to discuss, under that Constitution, the comparative merits of despotism and liberty? And if he has eloquence and force of argument sufficient, may he not persuade us all to crown him our king? Robert Dale Owen came to this city, and Fanny Wright followed him, openly proclaiming the doctrine that the institution of marriage was a curse to any community, and ought to be abolished. It was, undoubtedly, an abominable doctrine, and one which, if acted out, would speedily reduce society to the level of barbarism and the brutes; yet who thought of denying Mr. Owen and his disciple, the perfect right of avowing such doctrines, or who thought of mobbing them for the exercise of this right? And yet, most surely, the institutions of Slavery are not more interwoven with the structure of our society, than those of marriage.

See the danger, and the natural and inevitable result to which the first step here will lead. Today a public meeting declares that you shall not discuss the subject of Slavery, in any of its bearings, civil or religious. Right or wrong, the press must be silent. Tomorrow, another meeting decides that it is against the peace of society, that the principles of Popery shall be discussed, and the edict goes forth to muzzle the press. The next day, it is in a similar manner, declared that not a word must be said against distilleries, dram shops, or drunkenness. And so on to the end of the chapter. The truth is, my fellow citizens, if you give ground a single inch, there is no stopping place. I deem it, therefore, my duty to take my stand upon the Constitution. Here is firm ground - I feel it to be such. And I do most respectfully, yet decidedly, declare to you my fixed determination to maintain this ground. We have slaves, it is true, but I am not one. I am a citizen of these United States, a citizen of Missouri, free-born; and having never forfeited the inestimable privileges attached to such a condition, I cannot consent to surrender them. But while I maintain them, I hope to do it with all that meekness and humility that become a Christian, and especially a Christian minister. I am ready, not to fight, but to suffer, and if need be, to die for them. Kindred blood to that which flows in my veins, flowed freely to water the tree of Christian liberty, planted by the Puritans on the rugged soil of New England. It flowed as freely on the plains of Lexington, the heights of Bunker Hill, and fields of Saratoga. And freely, too, shall mine flow, yea, as freely as if it were so much water, ere I surrender my right to plead the cause of truth and righteousness, before my fellow citizens, and in the face of all their opposers.

Of the 3d resolution I must be allowed to say, that I have never seen the least evidence, whatever, that the Abolitionists, with all their errors, have ever desired to effect an amalgamation of the two races, black and white. I respectfully ask of the individuals composing the meeting that adopted this resolution, if they have ever seen any such evidence? They have formally, solemnly and officially denied it. It is certainly an abhorrent thing even in theory, and a thousand times more so in practice. And yet, unless my eyes deceive me as I walk the streets of our city, there are some among us who venture to put it into practice. And in the appointment of the numerous committees of vigilance, superintendence, etc., methinks that not one of them all was more needed than a Committee whose business it should be to ferret out from their secret ' chambers of iniquity,' these practical amalgamationists. If He who said to the woman taken in adultery, 'Go and sin no more,' had stood in the midst of the meeting at our Court House, I will not say that he would there have detected a single amalgamator; but I am sure that if a poor Abolitionist were to be stoned in St. Louis for holding this preposterous notion, and the same rule were to be applied that our Savior used in the case referred to, there are at least some amongst us who could not cast a pebble at the sinner's head.

What shall I, what can I, say of the 4th resolution? It was adopted, in a large assemblage of my fellow citizens, with but a few dissenting voices. Many of our most respectable citizens voted for it - Presbyterians,

Methodists, Baptists, Episcopalians, Roman Catholics; those who believe the Bible is the Word of God and those who do not, all united in voting for the resolution that the Bible sanctions Slavery as it now exists in the United States. If the sentiment had been that the Bible sanctions the continuance of the system until proper measures can be taken to remove it, I too could adopt it. If I have taken my neighbor's property and spent it, and afterwards repent of ray sin, and wish to restore what I had unjustly taken, but have not the means, the Bible no longer holds me as a thief, but sanctions my withholding the money from my neighbor, until I can, by the use of the best means in my power, obtain it and restore it. And although, meanwhile, my neighbor in consequence of my original crime, may be deprived of his rights, and his family made to suffer all the evils of poverty and shame, the Bible would still enjoin it upon him to let me alone, nay, to forgive me, and even to be content in the abject condition to which I had reduced him. Even so the Bible now says to our slaves, as it said in the days of the Apostles, 'Servants, (or slaves) obey in all things your masters according to the flesh; not with eye-service, as men-pleasers; but in singleness of heart, fearing God.' But then it also adds, 'Masters, give unto your servants that which is just and equal.' "What is meant by 'just and equal' we may learn from the Savior himself - 'All things whatsoever ye would that men should do to you, do ye even so to them: for this is the law and the prophets.' Thus far the Bible. And it will be seen, that in no case does it sanction, but the rather, absolutely forbids, all insurrectionary, all seditious, all rebellious acts on the part of the slaves. But be it remembered, that, with equal decision and authority, it says to the master, 'Undo the heavy burden, and let the oppressed go free.' If either disobey these injunctions, then it bids us leave the whole matter with that God who declares 'Vengeance is mine, I will repay, saith the Lord.'

But I am not at liberty so to understand the resolution.
From the preamble, and from conversation with several who voted for it, I am compelled to understand the meeting as voting that the Bible - the blessed Savior, and his holy Apostles - sanctions the principle of Slavery - the system itself, as such, as it now exists amongst us. Fellow citizens! I mean not to be disrespectful to you, but I declare before you all, I have not words to express my utter abhorrence of such a sentiment. My soul detests it, my heart sickens over it; my judgment, my understanding, my conscience, reject it, with loathing and horror. What is the system of Slavery ' as it now exists in the United States? It is a system of buying and selling immortal beings for the sake of gain; a system which forbids to man and woman the rights of husband and wife, sanctioning the dissolution of this tie at the mere caprice of another; a system which tolerates the existence of a class of men whose professed business it is to go about from house to house, tearing husband and wife, parent and child asunder, chaining their victims together, and then driving them with a whip, like so

many mules, to a distant market, there to be disposed of to the highest bidder. And then the nameless pollutions, the unspeakable abominations, that attend this unfortunate class in their cabins. But I spare the details. And this is the system sanctioned by the Prince of Mercy and Love, by the God of Holiness and Purity! Oh God! - In the language of one of the Patriarchs to whom the meeting in their resolution refer, I say, 'Oh my soul, come not thou into their secret, unto their assembly mine honor be not thou united!'

The fifth resolution appoints a Committee of Vigilance consisting of seven for each ward, twenty for the suburbs, and seven for each township in the county- in all EIGHTY THREE persons - whose duty it shall be to report to the Mayor or the other civil authorities, all persons suspected of preaching abolition doctrines, etc., and should the civil authorities fail to deal with them, on *suspicion*, why then the Committee are to call a meeting of the citizens and execute their decrees- in other words, to lynch the suspected persons.

Fellow citizens; where are we and in what age of the world do we live? Is this the land of Freedom or Despotism? Is it the ninth or nineteenth century? Have the principles of the Letters de Cachet, driven from Europe, crossed the Atlantic and taken up their abode in Missouri? Lewis the XIV sent men to the Bastille on suspicion; we, more humane, do but whip them to death, or nearly so. But these things cannot last long. A few may be made the innocent victims of lawless violence, yet be assured there is a moral sense in the Christendom of the nineteenth century, that will not long endure such odious transactions. A tremendous re-action will take place. And remember, I pray you, that as Phalaris was the first man roasted in the brazen bull he had constructed for the tyrant of Sicily, so the inventor of the guillotine was by no means the last, whose neck had practical experience of the keenness of its edge.

I turn, for a moment, to my fellow-Christians, of all Protestant denominations.

Respected and beloved fathers and brethren. As I address myself to you, my heart is full, well-nigh to bursting, and my eyes overflow. It is indeed a time of trial and rebuke. The enemies of the cross are numerous and bold, and malignant, in the extreme. From the situation in which the Providence of God has placed me, a large portion of their hatred, in this quarter, has concentrated itself on me. You know that, now for nearly two years, a constant stream of calumnies and personal abuse of the most viperous kind, has been poured upon me, simply because I have been your organ through which - I refer now more especially to my Presbyterian brethren - you have declared your sentiments. You know, also, that I have never, in a single instance, replied to, or otherwise noticed these attacks. And now not only is a fresh attack, of ten-fold virulence, made upon my character, but violence is threatened to my person. Think not that it is because I am an Abolitionist that I am so persecuted. They who first started this report knew and still know better. In the progress of events Slavery has doubtless contributed its share, though a very small one, to the bitterness of hatred with which the 'Observer,' and I as connected with it, are regarded. But the true cause is the open and decided stand which the paper has taken against the encroachments of Popery. This is not only my own opinion, but that of others, and indeed of nearly or quite all with whom I have conversed on the subject, and among the rest, as I learn, of a French Catholic.

I repeat it, then, the real origin of the cry, 'Down with the Observer,' is to be looked for in its opposition to Popery. The fire that is now blazing and crackling through this city, was kindled on Popish altars, and has been assiduously blown up by Jesuit breath. And now, dear brethren, the question is, shall we flee before it, or stay and abide its fury, even though we perish in the flames? For one, I cannot hesitate. The path of duty lies plain before me, and I must walk therein, even though it lead to the whipping-post, the tar-barrel, or even the stake. I was bold and dauntless in the service of sin; it is not fitting that I should be less so in the service of my Redeemer. He sought me out when there was none to help; when I was fast sinking to eternal ruin, he raised me up and placed me on the Rock of Ages; and now shall I forsake him when he has so few friends and so many enemies in St. Louis? I cannot, I dare not, and, His grace sustaining me, / will not.

Some of you I know are with me in feeling, in sympathy, and in prayer. And this knowledge is, indeed, a cordial to my heart. We have wept and prayed together in the midst of our present afflictions, and we have risen from our knees, refreshed and cheered by a sense of God's presence and his approving smile. And indeed, but for this, - but that I have felt the upholding hand of God supporting me, I had long since fallen. 'I had fainted, unless I had believed to see the goodness of the Lord in the land of the living.' And the heaviest blows have been those which I have received from the hands of some of my brethren. May the Lord forgive them, as freely and heartily as I do.

But oh, my brethren, what shall I say to those of you who recorded your votes in favor of the resolution that the Bible sanctions Slavery? It is not for me to reproach you; nor have I the least disposition to utter one unkind word. I only wish that I could make you sensible of the feelings I experienced when I first read that resolution as sanctioned by you. It did seem to me as though I could perceive a holy horror thrilling through all heaven, at such a perversion of the principles of the gospel of the Son of God. Oh, my brethren, may I not entreat you to pray over this subject, to ask for the wisdom of heaven to lead you into the truth? Depend upon it, you are wrong, fearfully wrong. Not for all the diadems of all the stars of heaven, though each were a world like this, would I have such a vote, un-repented of, to answer for at the bar of God, my Judge.

Oh, were the Church united at such a crisis as this, what a triumph we might achieve! But it never can be united, until you come over to us. Did you ever hear of a Christian, once holding the contrary doctrine, giving it up for yours? Never, I venture to say it, unless at the same time he gave up his Christianity with it. But there are instances, daily, of conversions from your side to ours. Come over then, brethren - Oh, come over. Let us unitedly take our stand upon the principles of truth and RIGHTEOUSNESS. Standing by them we cannot be moved. Even the Heathen could say of the just man, that he would remain undismayed though the heavens should fall around him. How much more, then, may it be said of the Christian? In the midst of every assault, when foes are gathered around him on every side, in the calm, yet exulting confidence of faith, he can look up- ward and exclaim - 'The Lord is my light and my salvation; whom shall I fear? the Lord is the strength of my life; of whom shall I be afraid!'

A few words more, and I have done.

Fellow citizens of St. Louis, above, you have my sentiments, fully and freely expressed, on the great subjects now agitating the public mind. Are they such as render me unworthy of that protection which regulated Society accords to the humblest of its members? , Let me ask you, why is it that this storm of persecution is directed against me? What have I done? Have I libeled any man's person or character? No. Have I been found in gambling-houses, billiard-rooms, or tippling-shops? Never. Have I ever disturbed the peace and quiet of your city by midnight revellings, or riots in the streets? It is not pretended. Have I ever, by word or deed, directly or indirectly, attempted or designed to incite your slaves to insubordination? God forbid. I would as soon be guilty of arson and murder. And here you must permit me to say that the conduct of those who so fiercely accuse me here, strongly reminds me of the scene which took place between Ahab and the prophet Elijah. You remember that in a time of great drouth, which Elijah had predicted, and which God sent upon the land for the wickedness of Ahab and Israel, when Ahab met Elijah, he said to him, in great wrath, ' Art thou he that troubleth Israel V But the prophet boldly, and in conscious innocence, replied, 'I have not troubled Israel, but thou and thy father's house,' etc. Elijah did not bring the drouth and the famine upon Israel, he simply announced what God had determined to do in punishment of their sins. The drouth would have come, though there had been no prophet to announce it. Yet so far as he had any personal agency in the matter, he may well be supposed to have been actuated by kind motives towards Ahab and his countrymen, inasmuch as by forewarning them of the evil, he gave them an opportunity to prepare for it at least, if not to avert it by a speedy repentance. Even so, my fellow citizens, is it unreasonable and unjust to charge upon those who, applying to the case the maxims of the

Bible, of experience, and history, foresee and foretell to you the evil effects of the continuance of Slavery, the crime of having introduced those very consequences. And here let me say, that in my opinion the proceedings of the late meetings in this city, and the agitation consequent upon them, have done more to disquiet and render uneasy and restless and discontented, the minds of the slaves, than all that the "Observer" could or would have said in an hundred years.

I again, therefore, ask you what I have done, that I am to be made an object of popular vengeance? From the time that I published the account of the consecration of the Cathedral, threats have been constantly coming to my ears that I was to be mobbed, and my office torn down. Is it to be borne, that a citizen in the peaceable exercise of those rights secured to him solemnly by charter, is thus to be hunted down and proscribed? If in any thing I have offended against the laws of my country, or its constitution, I stand ready to answer. If I have not, then I call upon those laws and that constitution, and those who revere them to protect me.

I *do*, therefore, as an American citizen, and Christian patriot, and in the name of Liberty, and Law, and Religion, solemnly protest against all these attempts, howsoever or by whomsoever made, to frown down the liberty of the press, and forbid the free expression of opinion. Under a deep sense of my obligations to my country, the church, and my God, I declare it to be my fixed purpose to submit to no such dictation. And I am prepared to abide the consequences. I have appealed to the constitution and laws of my country; if they fail to protect me, I appeal to God, and with Him I cheerfully rest my cause.

Fellow citizens, they told me that if I returned to the city, from my late absence, you would surely lay violent hands upon me, and many of my friends besought me not to come. I disregarded their advice, because I plainly saw, or thought I saw, that the Lord would have me come. And up to this moment that conviction of duty has continued to strengthen, until now I have not a shadow of doubt that I did right. I have appeared openly among you, in your streets and market-places, and now I openly and publicly throw myself into your hands. I can die at my post, but I cannot desert it.

I have one request to make, and but one. The original proprietors of the 'Observer,' have, as you know, disclaimed all responsibility in its publication. So far as depends upon them, nothing would appear in the paper on the subject of Slavery. I am sure, therefore, that you will see the propriety of refraining from any act which would inflict injury upon them, either in person or property. I alone am answerable and responsible for all that appears in the paper, except when absent from the city. A part of the office also belongs to the young men who print the paper: and they are in no way responsible for the matter appearing in its columns. For the sake of both these parties I do, therefore, earnestly entreat you, that whatever maybe done to me, the property of the office may be left undisturbed. If the popular vengeance needs a victim, I offer myself a willing sacrifice. To any assault that may be made upon me, I declare it my purpose to make no resistance. There is, I confess, one string tugging at my heart, that sometimes wakes it to mortal agony. And yet I cannot, dare not, yield to its influence. For my Master has said, 'If any man come to me, and hate not his father, and mother, and WIFE, and children, and brethren, and sisters, yea, and his own life also, he cannot be my disciple.'

Humbly entreating all whom I have injured, whether intentionally or otherwise, to forgive me; in charity with all men; freely forgiving my enemies, even those who thirst for my blood, and with the blest assurance, that in life or death nothing can separate me from my Redeemer, I subscribe myself.

                Your fellow citizen,
                ELIJAH P. LOVEJOY"

CHAPTER X

It will be proper here to insert several letters which show the workings of his spirit in secret, while he was thus breasting the pitiless storm without.

St. Louis, November 2d, 1835
My Dear Brother,

We have just got into the Abolition excitement here. For some days past St. Louis has been in an "uproar." The immediate cause of the excitement, was the abduction of several negroes from a town into Illinois, by some persons, it is not certainly known who. However, on the strength of *suspicion*, two men were seized by about sixty of our "*most respectable*" (so say the papers) citizens, taken above three miles back of the city, and there whipped, as near as can be ascertained, one hundred and fifty or two hundred lashes each. Some of the sixty *respectable* citizens were for hanging them up at once, but in this they were overruled. And what is more, it is now said, and I suppose correctly, that one of the men thus whipped, was, and is, totally innocent!! They whipped him on suspicion, telling him if he would confess they would let him of; and when the poor fellow could endure no longer, he accused himself.

We have had several public meetings here - the result of which you will see in the "Observer."

I was not in town during the height of the excitement, being absent as I told you. And now that I am here, it is at the daily peril of my life. I am accused of being an Abolitionist, and threatened in the newspapers of the city, and throughout the city, as well as various places in the state, with violence. *I expect it*. I expect that I shall be *lynched*, or tarred and feathered, or it may be, hung up. All are threatened. There is a burning hatred on the part of the Popish priests and their minions, which would delight to quench itself in my blood. And nothing would be more convenient for it, than to execute its purposes, under the mask of opposition to Abolition. I have known, for some months, that I was in danger from the hand of violence - but the matter is now about to come to a crisis. In the "Observer" of Thursday, I shall come out, openly, fearlessly, and as I hope, in such a manner as becomes a servant of Jesus Christ, when defending His cause. And whatever may be the consequences, I think, I trust, that through the grace of God, I am prepared to meet them - even unto death itself. My friends are trembling, my enemies - numerous and influential - are open and fierce in their threats, but I can truly say, I never was more calm. I have fasted and prayed. I have earnestly sought the path of duty, and think, I am assured, that I have found it; and now I am determined that not all the fury of men or devils shall drive me from it. Yet you need not be disappointed to hear that I have fallen a victim, at least to the lash or the tar barrel. If they content themselves with whipping, I will not run until I have been whipped as often, at least, as Paul was - eight times.

The abominable resolutions passed at the meeting were voted for by professing Christians! two or three Methodists had the courage to say no to the fourth and fifth and that was all. They were voted for by at least two Elders in the Presbyterian Church!

And yet my dear brother, I am not an Abolitionist - at least not such a one as you are. But I shall be more full in the paper.

Give my love to dear mother, sisters and brother. We are all well. My wife is just now at her mother's. My best love to Sarah. Tell mother not to be disquieted - The Lord reigneth. And let me entreat my brothers and sisters to pray for me, that I may pass through this "fiery trial," without denying my Lord and Master.

Your affectionate brother,
ELIJAH P. LOVEJOY

St. Louis, November 10th, 1835
Dear Brother,

Before this reaches you, you will have read the "Observer," containing an "appeal" to the public. I hasten to inform you, especially that dear Mother may not be kept in suspense as to my fate, that I believe the result will be for good. I do not think that I shall be mobbed - a re-action has taken place in this city. Unexpected friends have been raised up, and the truth is likely to triumph. The original proprietors of the "Observer" took it from me, but others rose up and restored it to me. The paper will not be published this week, but will be resumed the next, and go on.

I am sure it is doing good or the Devil would not be so mad about it.* But I have a hard battle of it. If you can do anything for me in Maine, I hope you will do it.

---

* Sometime after this a plain but warm friend wrote him - "It does seem as though the Devil knowing his time is short, had come down in great wrath to afflict David Nelson, George B. Cheever, and Elijah P. Lovejoy." - Eds.

I will send you some extra copies of the "Observer," which I hope you will circulate. Tell me what you think of it, and what the brethren generally think of it.

I shall lose a good many subscribers here in Missouri, but I hope to gain them elsewhere. It is important that the paper be kept up here. Thousands read it who will not subscribe for it; and they cannot say of it, that it is "foreign interference."

You see our committees of vigilance, and all that. They have whipped two men here, nearly to death, merely on suspicion, and not a single paper but the "Observer" dares to open its mouth on the subject.

There was a time when I did expect to be tarred and feathered, and probably hung. And I can truly say - and I bless God that I can say it - that never in my life did I feel so calm, so composed, and tranquil in mind. I am sure that I could have gone to the stake, as cheerful as I ever went to a bed of rest. But the crisis is now over. By the grace of God, I stood firm, and having the truth on my side, I was more than a match for my enemies. Tell mother there is no danger, not the least.

Good bye. Love to Sarah, to sisters, to Owen, to all. The Lord be with you.

Your affectionate brother,
ELIJAH P. LOVEJOY

St. Louis, November 23d, 1835
Dear Mother,

Knowing that you will feel anxious to know how matters proceed here, in St. Louis, I write to you again, by which you may, at least, know that I am not yet *hung up*. Neither have I been tarred and feathered, nor yet whipped, nor, indeed, in any way molested bodily; of slander and falsehood, and malignant abuse, I have had abundance.

We are getting quiet again. The Lynchites are getting ashamed of their doings. The Papists, the Irish, and the pro-slavery Christians finding that I am not to be driven nor frightened away, are beginning to feel and act a little more reasonably. A large majority of the Protestants in the city are decidedly with me.

I can but hope that the cause of human rights, of mercy, and of truth will be advanced in this city and state, by the late disturbances here. For this, I am sure you will pray.

Let me state to you one fact. The man who headed the whole business of the late public meetings, and who was the most active and virulent in his endeavors to excite the public mind against me, and stop the "Observer," the other night whipped his female negro slave almost to death. Her cries and screams brought a multitude around his house, and he narrowly escaped having his house broken into, and himself made the victim of mob violence. I knew that the wicked, sooner or later, fall into the pit they have digged for others; but was not this sudden retribution? And what shall we say of those professing Christians, yea, elders in the church, who follow in the wake of such a man, to stop the "Observer" because it advocates the Abolition of Slavery? *We have such elders in St. Louis* - four of them in our church. The woman was rescued from the monster by the constable and taken to jail. His name is Arthur L. McGinnis, an Irishman, and states' attorney for this district.

We have another man here, walking our streets in open day, who, about a year since, actually whipped his negro woman to death. He was tried for the murder, but as negro evidence was not admitted, he could not be convicted, or rather was not. Such men are not mobbed, but he who ventures to say that Slavery is a sin, does it at the risk of his life.

The "Observer" stopped one week, but is going again, and like to go; that is, if the Christian public will support it; if not, it must go down. Wife is well, very well for her. She sends her love to you, to sisters, and to all. Do let me hear from you soon.

Affectionately, your son,
ELIJAH P. LOVEJOY

We now insert the main part of a letter written in January following, giving a full account of his trials up to that time. His letter was nearly all copied by mother, and the original sent away, which has not been obtained. And, unfortunately, the copy does not give the date, al- though it is known to have been written in January.

St. Louis, January, 1836
My Dear Brother,

I have taken a large sheet and expect to fill it; and if you do not read it through, mother, I know, will I have thought it would be interesting to you to have a particular account of those things which have lately transpired in this city. One main reason why I write these things, is to enable you to join with me, in blessing that grace which carried me safely through all my trials. I need not say that for some time past the "Observer" has been prominent in its attacks on Slavery and Popery. In a community like this, where those institutions exercise so controlling an influence upon society, it is not at all to be wondered at, that a deep and bitter hostility should come to be fixed upon the "Observer" and its Editor. This feeling of hostility I knew existed, and it only required some plausible occasion to break out.

The mobs in Boston, Philadelphia, and New York, gave them this pretext. During the summer, an elder in the First Presbyterian Church was frequently coming to me and telling me to beware - that I was in danger - that the constant talk was about mobbing me. To this I paid no heed. The first of last September, I went to Potosi, a town about sixty miles southwest of this, to attend a camp-meeting. On my way back, I heard that two men had waited in that village, for half a day, for the purpose of tarring and feathering me. Providentially, I did not come into town till the next morning, and these men, tired of waiting, went home. On my return into the city, I found the excitement getting up, and I was informed by the elder above mentioned, that a handbill had been printed, to circulate throughout the city, for the purpose of collecting a mob to tear down the office of the "Observer." The Missouri Argus openly called upon the hurrah boys to mob me down. All these things did not change the course of the "Observer;" and under these circumstances, I left the last of September, to attend the meeting of our Presbytery and Synod at Union, a place sixty miles west of this. I expected to be absent about four or five weeks. We had a most harmonious session, and a set of resolutions passed on the subject of Slavery. They were of my drafting, and passed unanimously. From Union we went to Marion, to the meeting of the Synod. Here this same St. Louis elder appeared fresh from St. Louis, full of excitement and alarm, and fuss, about Slavery. The excitement was rising in St. Louis, and he had a thousand frightful things to tell the Synod. According to him, we must disavow and denounce Abolitionism, and everything like it, or the Presbyterian Church would be destroyed in Missouri. We had a warm debate; a majority of the ministers went with me, but the lay members turned the scale. Two ministers from New England voted against us - a fact as lamentable and disgraceful as it is true. Eastern men when they go over constitute the most ultra-defenders of Slavery. The elder above mentioned, previous to his coming up to the Synod, had written an article, published in one of the daily papers of the city, declaring that Slavery had the sanction of the Holy Scriptures, signed an elder in the Presbyterian Church.

Reports now came up thick from St. Louis, that they were whipping men almost to death, that the whole city was in commotion, that no one suspected of Abolitionism could live in it. Under these circumstances the Synod adjourned, and I started for home, I rode with a good brother about half the way - seventy miles. We talked the matter over. On the whole, he advised me not to go into St. Louis. The same advice was given me by other brethren at Marion. I had a wife; any violence done to me, of a serious nature, I feared would destroy her. Her health, at all times delicate, was peculiarly so now. The brethren told me I had no right to sacrifice her, whatever I might do with myself. I was taken exceedingly ill on the road, but managed to get on to St. Charles, a place about twenty miles from St. Louis.

I found my wife as I had left her, sick in bed - was myself detained three days by sickness. By this time I had fully made up my mind, that duty and fidelity to my Lord and Master required my presence at St. Louis. My friends advised me not to go; *all but wife - she said GO, if you think duty calls you.*

Accordingly I came into St. Louis. I found the community in a state of dreadful alarm and excitement. The press was fanning the flame - the Jesuits at the bellows, blowing it up. The "Observer" had been muzzled by the original proprietors. A communication had been sent me, signed by them, and by my friend Mr. Potts, requesting me to say no more on the subject of Slavery. I was accused by name, in one of the city papers, of being an Abolitionist, in the bitterest manner, and the public vengeance invoked upon me. The elder of whom I spake, had come back from the Synod, and in an article of the same paper, declared, that I was acting contrary to the wishes of the Synod, and of the Presbyterian Church, in the state. This was followed by a declaration of the editor of that paper, "that they would soon free the church of the rotten sheep in it;" - the very expression used. A mob had been raised to tear down the "Observer Office;" but had concluded, after assembling, to defer it a little longer. On my arrival, men came to me, and told me I could not walk the streets of St. Louis by night or by day. Men's hearts were failing them. I was the only Protestant minister in the city. The question then arose, what must I do? Earnestly I sought to avoid collision with the excited and angry community, if that might be consistent with faithfulness to God.

But daily, as I sought counsel at the Throne of Grace, my convictions strengthened, that for me to give way, would be a base desertion of duty. I was alone in St. Louis, with none but God of whom to ask counsel. But thrice blessed be his name; he did not forsake me. I was enabled, deliberately and unreservedly, to surrender myself to him - thought of mother, of brothers and sisters, and above all, of my dearest wife, and felt that I could give them all up for Jesus' sake. I think I could have gone to the stake and not a nerve have trembled, nor a lip quivered. Under the influence of these feelings, I wrote and sent forth my appeal. The effect was tremendous. I was immediately waited upon by the original proprietors, and requested to retire from the editorship of the "Observer." Even those most friendly, feared, lest in the temper of the public mind, the step was too bold. It was alike unexpected to friend and foe. For two days the result seemed altogether doubtful. But then the tide begun to turn. Friends began to rally and to increase. Men who had never taken the "Observer," even some infidels, said the stand taken must be maintained, or our liberties were gone. The pressure, which seemed as though it would crush me to the earth, began to lighten. Light began to break in upon the gloomiest day I have ever seen. I cannot think or write about it without my eyes filling with tears, to think of the deliverance which God wrought by so weak and unworthy an instrument as I am. The manner of it was as follows:

In compliance with the request of the proprietors, (they could not compel me to do it; for I had an absolute legal control of the office and materials, for the purpose of publishing a religious paper; yet I felt it my duty not to keep them contrary to their wishes,) I gave up, and thought my work done in St. Louis. But mark the sequel. I had given my note in the bank for five hundred dollars to procure money to pay the workmen. To the endorsers of this, I had mortgaged the office to secure them. The note had been due, and renewed, and was about coming due again. Of course when they took the office, they had to take the note with it. The proprietors met, and requested Mr. Moore, (the name on the note,) giving him a written request to that effect, to take possession of the office, break it up, and pay himself and the other endorsers, and they would be satisfied. He at once utterly refused to sell it at auction, whereupon they authorized him to take it and pay himself the five hundred dollars any way he chose. Upon this he took his departure, came to the office, and took possession of it; and immediately turned round to me, and offered it to me again, saying, that rather than the "Observer" should stop, he would pay the note himself. Nothing could have been more unexpected to me. It was as life from the dead, as light out of thickest darkness.

He, however, required that I should remove the paper to Alton, in the other state - thinking, that such was the excitement against me, that I could not possibly stay. I started the next day for Alton, - found the brethren there ready to receive me with open arms. But while I was making my arrangements, a letter arrived from St. Louis, from Mr. Moore and others, adjuring me by all means to come back.

Thus far the letter. He did accordingly return, and went on publishing the "Observer." In closing the account of this important period in his history, it will be proper to insert a letter addressed to one of the proprietors, at the time of the excitement and difficulties in November.

ARCHIBALD GAMBLE, Esq.

St. Louis, November 27th, 1835
Dear Brother,

In taking a course to which I was impelled by a sense of duty, I was fully aware that I was making myself liable to suffer the pains and penalties of much misrepresentation and abuse. And I had fully made up my mind to make no reply, whatever, to all that might be said of this nature, so long as it did not affect my character for veracity as a man and a Christian minister.

But an article in the last "Missouri Argus," signed "A Presbyterian," does both. I therefore take the liberty of enclosing it to you, and of respectfully asking your reply to the following questions:

1. When I became the Editor of the "St Louis Observer," did not the original proprietors, (yourself being one,) execute to me a legal instrument, whereby I became possessed of the whole, as completely, as though I had bought the materials with my own money, with the single proviso that I was not to alienate them from the business of publishing a religious newspaper, (but for this purpose I had the power of mortgaging

them,) as also that when the net profits of the office should amount to five hundred dollars, per annum, then I was to pay the surplus, (if any,) to the original purchasers, until they had received the original purchase money back, when the office was to be wholly mine?

2. Was there in this original agreement any right whatever reserved to the original proprietors, (one of whom drew up the article,) of controlling the editorial course of the "Observer?" And on the contrary, is there not, in the article an express disclaimer, on the part of the original proprietors, of all responsibilities or liabilities, as connected with the "Observer Office?"

3. Did not an article appear in the "Observer," in the absence of the Editor, signed "The Proprietors," expressly saying that nothing more on the subject of Slavery should appear in the columns of the "Observer?"

4. After the publication of my appeal to my fellow- citizens, when called upon by yourself and brother Hezekiah King, in behalf of the original proprietors, and requested, (it gives me pleasure to say in the kindest manner,) to retire from the Editorial duties of the "Observer," did I not unhesitatingly reply, that, though I certainly could with legal, and perhaps moral justice, hold the "Observer Office," yet I would not do it, a single day, against the wishes of the original proprietors; and did I not promptly surrender into your hands, (where it now is,) the legal instrument by which I held the Office?

5. When a proposition was made to me by yourself and brother King, that the materials of the "Observer Office" should be sold me, for a certain sum, provided I would obligate myself not to publish a paper in St. Louis county, did I not unhesitatingly, and at once, reject the proposition, saying I certainly would bind myself by no such pledge?

In fine, will you please to state, if in any of the transactions between yourself and brother King, as a committee of the original proprietors, and myself, I said or did anything that you considered reprehensible? As to any transactions between the two gentlemen, mortgagees of the Office, I of course, know nothing. I am sure, however, they will state that I never authorized them to make any stipulations with the original proprietors, founded on any promise of mine, that I would remove the "Observer" from St. Louis.

Your Christian brother,
ELIJAH P. LOVEJOY

On the back of this letter is found the following endorsement.

The within letter was addressed to Mr. G. that together with his answer, it might be published. He refused to answer it, though by so doing, he might have freed me from every unkind imputation under which I was then laboring. In the end, however, all proved for the best, and I received from a covenant God, that protection which I vainly sought from some of my brethren.

I have forgiven brother G. from my heart, and I doubt not he has, ere this, sincerely repented of his whole course on that eventful occasion.

ELIJAH P. LOVEJOY

February 13th, 1836

In July, 1836, as the prospect was, that the paper would be better supported at Alton he determined to remove it there. The same paper that announced this determination, contained also his remarks upon the famous charge of Judge Lawless to the Grand Jury.

The crime of which the Judge speaks in his charge, was thus recorded and noticed in the "Observer."

AWFUL MURDER AND SAVAGE BARBARITY

St. Louis, May 5th, 1835

The transactions we are about to relate, took place on Thursday, a week ago, and even yet we have not recovered from the shock they gave us. Our hand trembles as we record the story. The following are the particulars, as nearly as we have been able to ascertain them from the city papers, and from the relation of those, who were eye and ear witnesses of the termination of the awful scene.

On the afternoon of Thursday, the 28th ult., an affray between two sailors or boatmen took place on the steamboat landing. Mr. George Hammond, Deputy Sheriff, and Mr. William Mull, Deputy Constable, in the discharge of their official duty, attempted to arrest the boatmen, for a breach of the peace. In so doing they were set upon by a mulatto fellow, by the name of Francis J. McIntosh, who had just arrived in the city, as cook, on board the steamboat Flora, from Pittsburgh. In consequence the boatmen escaped, and McIntosh was arrested for his interference with the officers. He was carried before Patrick Walsh, Esq., a Justice of the Peace, for this county, and by him committed to jail, and delivered to the same officers to be taken thither. On his way he inquired what his punishment would be, and being told that it would not be less than five years' imprisonment in the State Prison, he immediately broke loose from the officers, drew a long knife and made a desperate blow at Mr. Mull, but fortunately missed him. Unfortunately, however, a second blow, aimed with the same savage violence, had belter success, and struck Mr. Mull in the right side, and wounded him severely. He was then seized, by the shoulder, by Mr. Hammond, whereat he turned and stabbed him in the neck. The knife struck the lower part of the chin and passed deeply into the neck, cutting the jugular vein and the larger arteries. Mr. H. turned from his murderer, walked about sixty steps, fell and expired! Mr. M. although dangerously wounded, was able to pursue the murderer who had fled, until his cries alarmed the people in the vicinity. They turned out, and without much difficulty secured the bloodthirsty wretch and lodged him in jail.

The bloody deeds of which McIntosh had been guilty soon became known through the city; and crowds collected at the spot, where the body of Mr. Hammond lay weltering in its blood. The excitement was intense, and soon might be heard above the tumult, the voices of a few, exhorting the multitude to take summary vengeance. The plan and process of proceeding were soon resolved on. A mob was immediately organized and went forward to the jail in search of their victim. The Sheriff, Mr. Brotherton, made some attempts to oppose their illegal violence. Apprehensive for the fate of his family, who occupied a portion of the jail building, he then retired taking them along with him to a place of safety. Another of our fellow citizens courageously attempted to reason with the angry mob, and to stay them from their fearful proceedings. When, however, 'he saw that he could prevail nothing, but that rather a tumult was made,' being himself threatened with violence, he was compel- led to retire from the place and leave the enraged multitude to do their work. All was done with the utmost deliberation and system, and an awful stillness pervaded the scene, broken only by the sound of the implements employed in demolishing the prison doors. Those who have read Scott's description of the Porteus' mob, as given in the Heart of Mid Lothian, will have an accurate idea of the manner of proceeding at the jail, on Thursday night. All was still; men spoke to each other in whispers, but it was a whisper which made the blood curdle to hear it, and indicated the awful energy of purpose, with which they were bent upon sacrificing the life of their intended victim. Armed persons were stationed as guards to protect those engaged in breaking down the doors.

At length between eight and nine o'clock at night, the cell of the wretch was reached. Loud shouts of execration and triumph rent the air, as he was dragged forth, and hurried away to the scene of the burnt-sacrifice! Some seized him by the hair, some by the arms and legs, and in this way he was carried to a large locust tree, in the rear of the town, not far from the jail. He was then chained to the tree with his back against its trunk, and facing to the south. The wood, consisting of rails, plank, etc., was then piled up before him, about as high as his knees, shavings and a brand were brought, and the fire kindled!

Up to this time, as we have been informed, McIntosh uttered not a word; but when the fire had seized upon its victim, he begged that someone in the crowd would shoot him. He then commenced singing a hymn and trying to pray. Afterwards he hung his head and suffered in silence, until roused by someone saying, that he must be already out of his misery. Upon this, though - wrapped in flames, and though the fire had obliterated the features of humanity, he raised his head, and spoke out distinctly, saying, 'No, no; I feel as much as any of you, I hear you all; shoot me, shoot me.' He was burning about twenty minutes, before life became extinct.

But the tale of depravity and woe is not yet all told. After the crowd had somewhat dispersed, a rabble of boys who had attended to witness the horrid rites, commenced amusing themselves by throwing stones at the black and disfigured corpse, as it stood chained to the tree. The object was to see who should first succeed in breaking the skull!

Such, according to the best information we have been able to obtain, is a faithful description of the scene, that has been transacted in our midst. It has given us pain to record it; but in doing so, we feel, deeply feel, that we are fulfilling a solemn duty, which as one of its members we owe to this community, and as an American citizen to our country at large. Let no one suppose that we would lightly say a word, in derogation of the character of the city in which we live: on the contrary we have, as is natural, a strong desire to sustain and vindicate its reputation. But when constitutional law and order are at stake, when the question lies between justice regularly administered or the wild vengeance of a mob, then there is but one side on which the patriot and the Christian can rally; but one course for them to pursue.

We have drawn the above gloomy and hideous picture, not for the purpose of holding it up as a fair representation of the moral condition of St. Louis - for we loudly protest against any such conclusion, and we call upon our fellow citizens to join us in such protest - but that the immediate actors in the horrid tragedy, may see the work of their hands, and shrink in horror from a repetition of it, and in humble penitence seek forgiveness of that community, whose laws they have so outraged, and of that God whose image they have, without his permission, wickedly defaced; and that we may all see, (and be warned in time,) the legitimate result of the spirit of *mobism*, and whither, unless arrested in its first out-breakings, it is sure to carry us. In Charlestown it burns a Convent over the head of defenseless women; in Baltimore it desecrates the Sabbath, and works all that day in demolishing a private citizen's house; in Vicksburg it hangs up gamblers, three or four in a row; and in St. Louis it forces a man - a hardened wretch certainly, and one that deserved to die, but not thus to die - it forces him from beneath the ægis of our constitution and laws, hurries him to the stake and burns him alive!

It is not yet five years since the first mob, within the memory of man, (for the French settlers of this city were a peaceable people, and their descendants continue so.) was organized in St. Louis. They commenced operations, by tearing down the brothels of the city; and the good citizens of the place, not aware of the danger, and in consideration of the good done, aside from the manner of doing it, rather sanctioned the proceeding, at least they did not condemn it. The next thing was to burn our Governor in effigy, because in the discharge of one of the most solemn functions belonging to his official character, he had not acted in accordance with the public sentiment, of a part, of this community. The next achievement was to tear down a gambling-house; and this was done last winter. The next and last we need not again repeat.

And now we make our appeal to the citizens of this community, and wherever else our voice can be heard, and ask, and ask with the most heart-felt anxiety, is it not time to stop? We know that in a case like the present, it is difficult to withdraw our thoughts and feelings from the great provocation to violence, to be found in the murderous atrocity of the wretch who has so fearfully atoned for his crime. But we do say, and insist, that these considerations must not be permitted to enter at all, into our reasoning and practice on this point. We must stand by the constitution and laws, or all is gone!

For ourselves, we do not hesitate to say, that we have awful forebodings on this subject. Not of St. Louis in particular, for the experience of the past year has shown, that we are 'not sinners above other' cities - but for our whole country. We have, as a nation, violated God's Holy Sabbath, profaned his Holy Name, and given ourselves up to covetousness, licentiousness, and every evil work; and He in return seems evidently to be withdrawing the influences of His Spirit from the land, and leaving us to be 'filled with our own devices.' And the consequences are plainly to be seen. Men and communities, hitherto peaceable and orderly, are breaking over all restraints of law and shame, and deeds are done amongst us which show that man is yet a fiend at heart.

We visited the scene of the burning, on the day following, about noon. We stood and gazed for a moment or two, upon the blackened and mutilated trunk - for that was all which remained - of McIntosh before us, and as we turned away, in bitterness of heart, we prayed that we might not live. The prayer, and perhaps the feeling which dictated it, might be wrong, yet still, after a week's reflection, our heart will still repeat it. For so fearful are our anticipations of the calamities that are to come upon this nation, (and which unless averted by a speedy and thorough repentance, we have no more doubt will fall upon us, than we have that a God of Holiness and Justice is our Supreme Governor,) that were our work done, and were it His will, we would gladly be ' taken away from the evil to come.' Meantime, let every Christian, and especially every Minister of the sanctuary, flee to a Throne of Grace, and standing between the porch and the altar, weeping, pray - ' Spare thy people. Oh Lord, and give not thy heritage to reproach.'"

In the No. dated July 21st, 1836, is found the following article.

THE CHARGE OF JUDGE LAWLESS

"The horrid transaction which called forth the document to which we now refer, is fresh in the minds of all our readers. A fellow-creature was torn from prison, by an infuriated mob, and burned alive in the city of St. Louis. This deed it became the duty of Judge Lawless to bring before the constituted authorities of the land, and he has done it in the charge to the Grand Jury, now lying before us. In this charge the ground is openly taken that a crime, which if committed, by one or two, would be punishable with death, may be perpetrated by the multitude with impunity!!! Says the Judge:

'If, on the other hand, the destruction of the murderer of Hammond was the act, as I have said, of the many - of the multitude, in the ordinary sense of these words - not the act of numerable and ascertainable malefactors; but of congregated thousands, seized upon and impelled by that mysterious, metaphysical, and almost electric frenzy, which, in all ages and nations, has hurried on the infuriated multitude to deeds of death and destruction - then, I say, act not at all in the matter; the case then transcends your jurisdiction - it is beyond the reach of human law!!!!!!!!!!!!

1. In this charge of Judge Lawless we see exemplified and illustrated the truth of the doctrine we have, for years, been endeavoring to impress on the minds of our countrymen, viz. that foreigners educated in the old world, never can come to have a proper understanding of American constitutional law. Judge Lawless is a foreigner - a naturalized one it is true, but still to all intents and purposes a foreigner - he was educated and received his notions of government amidst the turbulent agitations of Ireland, and at a period too, when anarchy and illegal violence prevailed to a degree unprecedented even in the annals of that wretched, and most unhappy land. Amidst the lawless and violent proceedings of those times Mr. Lawless grew up. He is next found in arms, in the service of France, fighting against the country to whom his allegiance was due. His third appearance in a public capacity, is as Judge in one of the republican states of America, where he delivers such a charge to our Grand Jury, as the one now under our consideration.

We disclaim all wish or intention to wound the feelings, or injure the personal reputation of Judge Lawless; but we do wish to disarm the monstrous doctrines he has promulgated from the bench, of their power either as a present rule, or a future precedent: and we apprehend that when the school in which the Judge was educated, is known and candidly considered, his notions of practical justice, at once so novel to Americans, so absurd and so wicked, will have little influence with our sound hearted, home educated republicans.

2. Judge Lawless is a Papist; and in his Charge we see the cloven foot of Jesuitism, peeping out from under the veil of almost every paragraph in the Charge. What is Jesuitism but another name for the doctrine that principles ought to change according to circumstances? And this is the very identical doctrine of the Charge. A horrid crime must not be • punished because, forsooth, it would be difficult perhaps to do it. The principles of Justice and of constitutional law, must yield to a doubtful question of present expediency. Doubtless the Judge is not aware whence he derived these notions; and yet it cannot be doubted that they came originally from St. Omers, where so many Irish priests are educated. So true is it, that Popery in its very essential principles is incompatible with regulated, civil or religious liberty. Our warning voice on this subject is lifted up in vain; but some of those who now hear it, will live to mourn over their present incredulity and indifference.

3. In his answer to the remarks of the New York American, Judge Lawless intimates that the safety of this office is owing to the course he took in this matter. We do not believe him; but if he says true, then what a disgraceful truth to St. Louis! What had the 'Observer' done? It had told the story of the horrid tragedy enacted here in plain, unvarnished terms, just as the affair occurred. No one pretends that our version of the affair was incorrect, and we added nothing more than in the spirit of earnest and solemn warning, to entreat our fellow citizens to stay such proceedings, or their all was lost. And for this the Judge says, but for his interposition, our office would have been destroyed. That is, a mob in St. Louis burns a man up, and then citizens tear down the office of the press, that dares to reprobate such an act. This assertion of the Judge is a gross libel upon the city, as we verily believe. We have never heard of any threats to pull down our office, which did not originate with his countrymen - mark that.

But even supposing it true, and that our office was endangered by what we wrote concerning the McIntosh tragedy, we desire no such volunteers as Judge Lawless, with such principles, to come to our rescue. We reject all such. We desire not to be saved at such an expense. To establish our institutions of civil and religious liberty, to obtain freedom of opinion and of the press, guaranteed by constitutional law, cost thousands, yea, tens of thousands of valuable lives. And let them not be parted with, at least, for less than cost. We covet not the loss of property nor the honors of martyrdom; but better, far better, that the office of the 'Observer' should be scattered in fragments to the four winds of heaven; yea, better that editor, printer, and publishers, should be chained to the same tree as McIntosh, and share his fate, than that the doctrines promulgated by Judge Lawless from the bench, should become prevalent in this community. For they are subversive of all law, and at once open the door for the perpetration, by a congregated mob, calling themselves the people, of every species of violence, and that too with perfect impunity.

Society is resolved into its first elements, and every man must hold his property and his life, at the point of the dagger.

Having travelled somewhat extensively of late, we have had opportunity of learning the impression made abroad by recent occurrences in this city. And we know that the feeling excited by this charge of Judge Lawless, is far more unfavorable than that consequent upon the burning of McIntosh. For that, say they, was the act of an excited mob, but here is the Judge on his bench, in effect sanctioning it!!

The subject grows upon our hands, but we forbear. We again repeat that we have had no wish in all we have said, to injure the reputation of Judge Lawless. The subject is one altogether too important to allow personal feelings to enter into the discussion of it, either one way or the other. For all that part of his charge where an attempt is made to identify the 'Observer' with Abolitionism, and then charge upon that the McIntosh tragedy, we can only say, that we have not the least doubt, that the Judge is perfectly sincere in the expression of this opinion. And the ignorance and prejudice which could lead to such an expression of opinion, however censurable in the Judge is still more pitiable in the man. Of this part of the charge, Charles Hammond, Esq. of the Cincinnati Gazette, says - 'It is as fanatical as the highest state of Abolition fanaticism can be.'"

In the same paper in which these criticisms appeared, he gave his reasons for removing to Alton.

THE OBSERVER- REMOVAL

June 21 St, 1836

"After much deliberation, and a consultation with a number of our friends, we have determined hereafter to issue the 'Observer' from Alton, Illinois.

In taking this step we have not been actuated solely, nor even mainly, by personal considerations. Doubtless it will be, under all circumstances, more for our personal comfort to reside at Alton, but so long as duty seemed to require our remaining here, we were determined to re- main, at whatever sacrifice of personal comfort, reputation, or safety.

The way now seems opened, in the Providence of God, to change the location of the 'Observer,' without in the least impairing its usefulness. On the contrary, we believe it" will be much more useful under the present arrangement than it has been. It will enjoy equal facilities for circulation in the two states, at Alton, as at St. Louis; and we hope to maintain the same connection with our subscribers in both the states as formerly.

The chief reason, (and without which it would not have been removed,) for removing to Alton, is, that there is no doubt the paper will be better supported there than it now is, or is likely to be, remaining in St. Louis. We hope this reason will be perfectly satisfactory to all our good friends in Missouri, who might otherwise think its removal uncalled for."

CHAPTER XI

We now come to his arrival at Alton the scene of his last sufferings and death. The causes of his removal have already been given. Speaking of the destruction of his press on its arrival at Alton, he thus writes in his paper of the 8th of September, that being the first number issued at that place.

"The real facts of the case, as we have before stated, are simply these. Contrary to our stipulation with the officer of the steamboat which brought it, the press was landed here on Sabbath morning, about daylight. We declined receiving it on that day. It lay in safety, on the bank, through the Sabbath, until two or three o'clock on Monday morning, when it was destroyed by five or six individuals. And of these much doubt exists, as we learn, in the minds of many, as to whether they were citizens of Alton or not. If to this we add that a very full meeting of the citizens, on the next day after, (July 22d, 1836,) or rather the same day of the outrage, voluntarily and unanimously pledged themselves to make good the loss occasioned by the destruction of the press, they surely must be acquitted of all participation, in thought or deed, in the disgraceful act."

At this meeting several resolutions were passed, expressing their disapprobation of Abolition, and, as the above extract intimates, condemning in severe language, the doings of the mob, and pledging themselves to make up for the loss of the press. It was at this meeting that the pledge, of which so much has been written, is said to have been given. To this we shall have occasion to recur hereafter. It should be remembered, that owing to sickness, and other "providential hindrances," the "Observer" was not issued from the middle of July to the 8th of September. During this time, the following letters were written, which, with the remarks above, will explain themselves.

Alton, (Illinois,) July 30th, 1836
Dear brother Joseph,

By the Alton Telegraph, which I send you today, you will learn that I have had the honor of being mobbed at last. I have been expecting the catastrophe for some time, and now it has come.

The "Observer" will have informed you of the immediate cause of the outrage. Because I dared to comment upon the charge of Judge Lawless - an article so fraught with mischief and falsehood; the mob, which I chose to call his officials, tore down my office. What a comment upon the freedom of our institutions!

The act was the more mean and dastardly, inasmuch as I had previously determined to remove the office of the "Observer" to this place, and had made all my arrangements accordingly, and had so stated in the number of the paper issued previous to the act of the mob.

You will also see that on my arrival here, a few miscreants undertook to follow the example of St. Louis, and so demolished what was left of the printing office. However, they met with but little countenance here. Thus the whole of the "St. Louis Observer" is destroyed. Not, however, until by the influence it has exerted, it has paid for itself, as I think. It has kindled up a fire in Missouri, that will never go out, until Popery and Slavery are extinct. And, moreover, I hope its very death will tell with effect upon the cause of human rights and religious liberty.

Tell my dear mother, that I am no whit discouraged. I feel myself standing on the broad basis of eternal justice, and so long as I stand there, full well do I know, that all the hosts of hell cannot prevail against me. I have found God a very present help in this my time of need. He has gloriously fulfilled his promises, and held me up, so that I have been astonished at the little effect produced upon my feelings by these outrages. But I determined when He carried me through last fall, that I would never again distrust Him.

Though cast down, I am not destroyed, nor in the least discouraged; and am now busily engaged in endeavoring to make arrangements for starting the "Observer" again. I think I shall succeed. I do believe the Lord has yet a work for me to do in contending with his enemies, and the enemies of humanity. I have got the harness on, and I do not intend to lay it off, except at His command.

What is said in the resolutions at the public meeting here about Abolitionism, and all that, is all for effect. I told them, and told the truth, that I did not come here to establish an Abolition paper, and that in the sense they understood it, I was no Abolitionist, but that I was the uncompromising enemy of Slavery, and so expected to live, and so to die.

My health is good, and so is John's. My dear wife is sick with a fever, but I think she is recovering. The babe is well. Give my love to all. Tell sister Sarah I wish she would write to me. Tell all to write. I am so very busy that I can write no more.

                      Your affectionate brother,
                            ELIJAH P. LOVEJOY"

Alton, August 31st, 1836
My dearest Mother,

Having a little time now, inasmuch as I am unable to do anything else, I have determined to write you a somewhat detailed account of the scenes through which I have lately been called to pass. I know you will be interested in every detail, though some of them might seem too minute for other eyes than yours.

The account of the mob in St. Louis you have had in my letter to Joseph, and in my Extra, received I presume before this time, as also of the second edition of it enacted at this place.

A few of the brethren here immediately convened after this last event, and it was determined that a new printing office should be procured without delay from Cincinnati. Accordingly I went on to procure it. On my way I became quite unwell, owing to the excitement, anxiety, and exposure of the week or two previous. By the time I reached Cincinnati I was fit only for the bed, but I could not prevail with myself to give up. I therefore kept about, finished my business, and started for home, with my materials for the office along. On my arrival at Louisville I found my illness so increasing upon me, that I was compelled to stop; and took my bed with a bilious fever deeply hold of me. I was received into the house of Rev. Mr. Banks - formerly from Connecticut - where I was treated with all the tenderness and assiduity that could have been bestowed upon a son. Providentially too I fell into the hands of a skillful physician, so that at the end of a week I found myself so far convalescent, that I ventured to pursue my journey. I continued to mend till I reached St. Charles. But riding from that place to this - a distance of twenty miles - and starting early in the morning, which was raw and chilly, by the time I arrived I found myself much chilled, and feared a relapse. However, such was the pressing need of my attention to the business of starting the "Observer," that I could not think of giving up. I accordingly kept about from Monday - the day I arrived - till Wednesday evening last, when I was again driven to my bed with a relapse of my fever, attended with cold sweats, and alternate chills and fever. I am now better, and with prudence hope to regain my health, though still very weak.

Thus you see, my dear mother, that my path through this life is not a flowery one. And to add to my difficulties, both my attacks of illness have come upon me in the absence of my dear wife. When I had determined to remove from St. Louis, she went to her mother's in St. Charles, where she still is. And what is worse, she too has been severely sick with very much such an attack as mine. Our dear babe thus far, thanks to a merciful Providence, remains well.

Why, when my services are so much needed, I should be laid up on a bed of sickness, I cannot tell; why, when God has in his wise and holy providence let loose upon me angry, and wicked men. He should also so heavily lay his own hand upon me, I cannot see, but he can, and I desire to submit without a murmur. I can now feel, as I never felt before, the wisdom of Paul's advice not to marry; and yet I would not be without the consolations, which my dear wife and child afford me, for all the world. Still I cannot but feel that it is harder to "fight valiantly" for the truth, when I risk not only my own comfort, ease, and reputation, and even life, but also that of another beloved one. But in this I am greatly favored. My dear wife is a perfect heroine. Though of delicate health, she endures affliction more calmly than I had supposed possible for a woman to do. Never has she by a single word attempted to turn me from the scene of warfare and danger - never has she whispered a feeling of discontent at the hardships to which she has been subjected in consequence of her marriage to me, and those have been neither few nor small, and some of them peculiarly calculated to wound the sensibility of a woman. She has seen me shunned, hated, and reviled, by those who were once my dearest friends - she has heard the execrations wide and deep upon my head, and she has only clung to me the more closely, and more devotedly. When I told her that the mob had destroyed a considerable part of our furniture along with their other depredations, "No matter," said she, "what they have destroyed since they have not hurt you." Such is woman! and such is the woman whom God has given me.

And now do you ask, Are you discouraged? I answer promptly, no. I have opened my mouth for the dumb, I have plead the cause of the poor and oppressed - I have maintained the rights of humanity, and of nature outraged in the person of my fellow-men around me, and I have done it, as is my nature, openly, boldly, and in the face of day, and for these things I am brought into these straits. For these things I have seen my family scattered, my office broken up, my furniture - as I was moving it to this place - destroyed - 'have been loaded with execrations, had all manner of evil spoken of me falsely, and finally had my life threatened, and laid down at night, weary and sick, with the expectation that I might be aroused by the stealthy step of the assassin. This was the case the last night I spent at St. Louis. Yet none of these things move me from my purpose; by the grace of God I will not, I will not forsake my principles; and I will maintain, and propagate them with all the means He puts into my hands. The cry of the oppressed has entered not only into my ears, but into my soul, so that while I live I cannot hold my peace.

Meanwhile, I must confess, that present prospects look somewhat dark. In the midst of so many enemies I have, it is true, a good many friends. But the evil is that Christians in this quarter, even the best of them, have become a good deal worldly minded, and are greatly engaged in speculation; so that the work of the Lord is left to languish. Insomuch that I find it extremely difficult to obtain that aid and assistance needed in my very arduous enterprise. Had I means at my own command I would not care. I should deem them well spent even though destroyed by a mob, in maintaining the cause I have espoused. But as I have them not, such as I have I give freely - my time, my energies, the best years of my life, some little ability, and a good deal of zeal - these I give, and bless God for the opportunity, to so holy a cause. I may not live to see its success - I may even die - though most unworthy - its victim and its martyr, yet, that it will ultimately succeed, and that too at no distant day, I am as well assured as I am that there is a God in Heaven, who sits on a Throne of Righteousness, Providence permitting, we shall get out a number of the "Observer" next week. It will be much enlarged, in hopes by that means to induce more to subscribe. Tell brother Joseph I wish he and his brother ministers in Maine would try and do something for me. I think I ought to get considerable aid from my native state. Mr. Adams of Brunswick, told me at the General Assembly, that he thought that I was doing more to put down Slavery than any other man in the United States. Now if half that be true, surely my paper ought to be supported.

But I shall weary you with the reading, as I am myself exhausted with the effort of writing this long letter. Give my love to sisters S. and E. Why do they not write to me? Surely, surely, they cannot wait for a letter from me, when I have hardly time, and ability even to read my Bible. From Owen I have not heard for a long time. I expect him and sister E. out here this fall. Are they not coming? I wish they would come. Wife wants Lizzy very much, and I want Owen. John enjoys excellent health and spirits, and is improving very much. Love to brother Joseph, and to all. Do write me soon.

Your most affectionate son,
ELIJAH P. LOVEJOY

After the re-establishment of the Observer at Alton, it continued to be issued regularly till the 17th of August, 1837, soon after which it again became the object of mob violence. The character of the paper, as it regards the ability and spirit with which it was conducted, may be learned from the subjoined editorial articles, that appeared in it during this time.

It may not be out of place, here to state, that the number of subscribers to the "Observer" continued to in- crease from its arrival at Alton, till it rose from less than one to more than two thousand; and would doubtless, within the year, have reached twenty-five hundred.

THE BUBBLE BURST

Alton, May 25th, 1837

"For the last three or four years the people of this nation have been pursuing after wealth, as their chief good, with an eagerness unknown before in our history. Wealth has been the god after which this nation, in the language of Scripture, has gone a whoring. And never was idol more devoutly worshipped. It has been the supreme object which has occupied our waking thoughts, and our dreaming hours. Our 'visions by night' have been of rail-roads, canals, bank stock, sections and quarter sections of land, and town lots. Speculation had become a perfect mania, and we had become a nation of gamblers. Even the steadiest minds and the firmest judgments, were carried away by the rush. We know of nothing like it, except the South sea and Mississippi schemes of England and France. The former was called the 'South Sea Bubble,' and we think that an appropriate name for ours would be the 'Town Lot Bubble.' But the bubble has burst - and all our hopes of universal wealth are dissipated into thin air. We find ourselves a nation of bankrupts instead of a nation of Croesuses. And better it should be the former than the latter.

We say better, not because we rejoice over the widespread desolation and ruin that have overtaken our citizens, God forbid that we should do that, but because we do sincerely believe that this nation cannot be trusted with riches. In the present difficulties that have come upon us, we think we see the interposition of a kind Providence in our behalf: and if the blow has been unexpected and most severe, may it not have been needed, in order that we should not, in the season of returning prosperity, forget our chastisement? The evil effects of this seemingly boundless prosperity, which for the last three or four years has attended us, uninterrupted, are many and various. We can only enumerate two or three of the most obvious, and those which alarmed all sober observers of the times.

1. The moral sense of the nation has become awfully blunted and obtuse. The love of money is an earth-born, groveling propensity, and it debases proverbially all whom it influences, in the precise proportion as they are under its sway. How completely callous to all the dictates of conscience and humanity, and how shamelessly sordid it has rendered this nation, let the history of the last two years testify. What have we seen? That which unless our eyes beheld, we could not have believed. We have seen the traffic in human beings pursued by one portion of our fellow citizens with an unfeeling and gloatingly avaricious eagerness, which would have made the early Spanish men-hunters of Cuba blush. Husbands and wives, and parents and children have been torn asunder with an utter recklessness of feeling, that equals, to say the least, anything of cruelty that the annals of savagedom can furnish, and all to make these victims toil and sweat un-thanked and unrewarded, in order to enrich their plunderers. But worse than this, ten-fold worse, and a thousand fold more alarming, we have seen Christians, not only engaging heart and soul in this horrid business, but Christian ministers also, nay, reverend divines, doctors of divinity, whole Presbyteries, Synods, and Conferences, solemnly and officially justifying it, appealing to the Bible - to the gospel of a compassionate Redeemer - to prove it all right, and that it had the sanction of Heaven. Shall a man believe this, even though it be told him? Posterity will not credit it, and yet it is nevertheless the truth, the sad reality. And scarcely less, if indeed not greater, has been the guilt, the criminal indifference, and often actual approval, with which these transactions have been witnessed in the free states. Men were either too busy in making money themselves, or too desirous to get a share of that earned by

the forced labor of the poor slave, to hear his groans. His tears, mingled with his blood drawn by the whip of the merciless taskmaster, fell unheeded to the ground; and what cared they if the soil he tilled were thus enriched, so that they were permitted to share in the profits of the crop? Nothing - absolutely nothing. Nay, they not only refused to express disapprobation themselves, but whoever did it, incurred their hot displeasure. And when the law could not punish those who dared to feel for the colored man, the power of the mob was resorted to. Elders of the church in Nashville scourged a brother for this crime, 'gentlemen of property and standing' in Boston, broke into an assemblage of females, and drove them from their knees because they were praying for the slave, Christian editors in New York, set on the mob to pull down, break up, and destroy the property and maltreat the persons of their fellow citizens, who had made themselves obnoxious by their efforts in behalf of bleeding humanity. These things are but specimens of what has been done in this Christian land for the last two or three years, and all to be traced to the *auri sacra fames* - the accursed love of gold, which has grown by what it fed on.

It could not be expected that such things could long endure; that the Lord would keep silence forever. He has spoken. He has come, in his Providence, and taken from us that for which we had sacrificed principle, humanity, duty, and now we find that we have 'filed our consciences' for nothing, and that our only reward is, what it deserved to be - remorse.

2. Another result of our worldly prosperity has been an alarming increase of luxury, licentiousness, and immorality of every kind. In our eagerness to grasp the bubble wealth, we have over-leaped all the restraints of religion and morality, and in our determination to enjoy its pleasures, we have disregarded the precepts of the gospel. The Sabbath, that blessed institution of heaven, given us purposely to be a barrier against the tide of corruption, flowing up from the bottomless pit, has been run over by our rail-road cars, and mail-stages, and steamboats, until it is pretty much entirely levelled in the dust, and the waves of vice and sin are accordingly sweeping over us with awful and almost resistless force, threatening to bear away, and indeed, in general having already done it, whatsoever thing is lovely and of good report among us. No hand but God's can roll back these bitter waters of perdition; and whether he will do it must depend upon the disposition he finds amongst us, to treat his hitherto despised ordinances with respect and reverence. 'Thou shalt reverence my Sabbaths.'

3. The only other evil to which we will now advert, is the disastrous influence that has been exerted upon the church. This has been in part adverted to, in the previous remarks. But it deserves a distinct mention by itself. It cannot be denied that the church in this country, has to an alarming degree, been carried away by the influences that have been at

work all around them. It is too true that many have left the work of the Lord, and have gone to work to get riches for themselves. Even ministers, in many instances, have forsaken the pulpit to enter lands, build rail-roads, erect steam-mills, make towns, etc. The less conscientious and pious Christians have done this openly, and without attempt at palliation, while the better sort have done it, under the specious pretext, with which they doubtless deceived themselves, that it was right to give one's self wholly up to the business of making money, provided we make it for the Lord. So that either one way or the other, pretty nearly the whole have yielded to the temptation.

So far as we know there is no ground for mutual recriminations among Christians, touching this thing; but there is ground for repentance and mutual confession of sin. We are all verily guilty in this matter.

The experience of the last two years has taught us, that the church is not yet sufficiently sanctified, to bear uninterrupted prosperity. A year or two more would have ruined us all. The present visitation of Providence, therefore, though a sharp, was yet a necessary remedy. It is the chastisement of a kind Father, who knows us a thousand times better than we know ourselves. If we humble ourselves under the mighty hand of God, he will have mercy; if we seek him in prayer and repentance, he will remove from our sky the clouds of his wrath, and again lift upon us 'the light of his reconciled countenance.' And may we all as Christians, and as citizens, remember that 'righteousness exalteth a nation, but sin is a reproach to any people.'"

TO THE REV. ASA CUMMINGS,
OF THE CHRISTIAN MIRROR

Alton, February 9th, 1837
Dear Brother,

I choose this personal mode of addressing you, because, while a sense of duty will impel me to speak with Christian frankness, I wish scrupulously to avoid all occasion of offence; and this has seemed to me the best method of effecting both. You will, I am sure, agree with me that the subject about which we differ is one of incalculable importance. Two millions and a half of our fellow-creatures are groaning in bondage, crushed to the earth, deprived of rights which their Maker gave them, and which are in themselves inalienable by any conceivable process except that of crime.

However men may theorize, and whatever men may wish, it is evident that this is a question of tremendous practical importance; and in the aspect which it presents to the Christian especially, he cannot fail to see enough to make him feel that here, at least, is no place for the indulgence of the pride of opinion or fondness for a beloved theory. Men may quibble about mere abstractions, and resort to all the arts of metaphysical attack and defense, in order to maintain a favorite position; but to do so when discussing a question like that of American Slavery, is little less than impious, and, in my opinion, argues a sad want of moral sensibility. The man who can deliberately do this, would find no difficulty in imitating Nero, who fiddled while Rome was burning. I have made these remarks, before proceeding to the more immediate subject of this communication, because a serious, candid, and honest state of mind, when we write or read on the subject of Slavery, cannot be too highly valued, nor too earnestly prayed for.

I come now to the question of "curtailing sermons." And how stands this matter? I suppose you will admit that no minister could, at the present time, in any of the slave states, preach what is called an "anti-slavery sermon," without being driven from his pulpit. Dr. Nelson attempted it in Missouri, and in consequence, had to flee for his life from the state, some leading church members being foremost in the persecution. I have lived about eight years in a slave state, and, except in one or two instances, I do not recollect ever to have heard slaveholders, whether in or out of the church, reproved for neglecting or abusing their slaves, although, at the same time, I have seen the slave sitting out on the carriage box, through all the service, while their masters and mistresses, whom they drove to church, were worshipping with great devoutness within. I have known church members sell all their slaves, at one time, into distant captivity, where they were to go beyond the reach of Christian instruction, yet never did I hear the pastor rebuke the deed. To preach against intemperance and Sabbath breaking, against covetousness and murder, and yet to pass over Slavery in silence, is, however you may regard it, in my opinion, "shunning to declare the whole counsel of God." I will give you a case in point.

Less than a year since, I heard in a city of a slaveholding state, the pastor of a Presbyterian church preach from the text, "It is the price of blood." The speaker first adduced several reasons for the command that man should not kill his fellow-man, such as that he had no right to take away what he could not restore, that it was insulting God to deface his image, etc. After briefly laying down these propositions, the main part of the discourse was occupied in showing what was and must be the moral character of those occupations, which were necessarily pursued at the expense of human life. The property acquired in this way, he told us, should legitimately be called "the price of blood." He dwelt upon this point with a variety and force of illustration and remark, that was painfully interesting, because painfully true. He spoke of the young men that were destroyed in the prime of life, of the families that were beggared, and the souls that were ruined, by the distillery and the dram shop; and he told those who made their property by this means, that the houses they dwelt in, and the fashionable dresses in which their wives and daughters appeared in the house of God, were "the price of BLOOD!" At this point of the discourse, a deep and thrilling interest pervaded the audience - men held their breath in expectation of what was coming - and it was evident what subject was uppermost in the minds of all; but the speaker closed by saying that other practices and other traffics might be mentioned, whose gains were the price of blood, but he should forbear, as he did not think it proper or prudent (I forget which was the word) to mention them. Now there was not, I presume, a single individual among his audience, that did not understand the preacher as referring to Slavery, - to the buying and selling human beings for the sake of gain. It was a topic of general conversation at the time, and some of the leading members of the church, were, as I learned, a good deal offended at even this distant allusion, by way of condemnation, to the source of their unholy gains.

Now the preacher might have acted wisely, or he might not, in thus forbearing to speak of the sin of Slavery. It is a question about which there will probably be a difference among good men; but in either alternative, my case is made good, that a minister cannot preach the whole truth to a slaveholding church and congregation. To dwell eloquently upon the sin of amassing money, by making and selling whisky and rum, and, at the same time, to pass over in silence the practice of amassing it by enslaving and selling human beings, when preaching to a congregation guilty of both, looks to me very much, comparatively speaking, like enforcing the "tithes of mint and cumin," while the " weightier matters of the law" are forgotten. I have said that there will doubtless be a difference of opinion, as to the propriety of the course pursued on this occasion; yet one thing is doubtless certain, had the preacher done otherwise, had he ventured to denounce Slavery as he had denounced intemperance, he never would have gone into that pulpit again. His church would not have endured such doctrine, and many of its leading members would have been among the first and the loudest to cry, "Crucify him, crucify him."

Yet I could not but feel at the time, that were I standing in his place, I should have done it, at whatever risk. As a minister of the gospel, *I* should not have dared to do otherwise. Nay, I felt that I would willingly have given one year of my life, to have stood on the vantage ground which the speaker then occupied, to have had the ear of that audience as he had, and then to have poured upon their startled consciences, the denunciations of God upon those who " oppress the poor and the needy, and the stranger within their gates." I would have done it, though, in so doing, I had expended my last breath.

This letter has already extended much farther than I at first intended, yet I cannot persuade myself to close it without a few additional remarks. It has been, and still is, to me a source of great grief, to witness the course which you, brother Cummings, together with the editors of the Vermont

Chronicle, the Boston Recorder, and the New York Observer, have pursued on the subject of Slavery. These are all brethren whom (though I have not the happiness to know them personally) I highly respect. Separately, and together, you wield an incalculable moral influence, and I need not say that your responsibilities are correspondingly great. These brethren, will, I am sure, pardon me, if I speak seriously, and in earnest, on this subject, for I speak in behalf of more than two millions of my fellow-beings, who are not permitted to open their mouths to plead their own cause. And I therefore tell you plainly, that you seem to me not at all to have understood your responsibilities, in relation to the subject of Slavery, or else to have trifled with them in a manner truly awful. I have seen the Mirror once and again, give the subject the go-by, with a dry joke or a half-concealed sarcasm, which none understand how to use better than he; I have seen the Recorder and the Chronicle, with column after column of their pages occupied by their acute and logical-minded editors, in reasoning coldly about sin and Slavery in the abstract, when the living and awful reality was before them and around them, disputing about words and terms, and the precise amount of guilt, even to the twentieth part of a scruple, to be attached to this or that slaveholder, as coolly, and with as much indifference, as if no manacled slave stood before them, with uplifted hands and streaming eyes, beseeching them to knock off their galling, soul-corroding chains. I have seen the New York Observer publish, week after week, and send it to its hundred thousand readers, the most partial and injurious representations of the characters and motives of those engaged in freeing the slave from bondage, while its columns have been hermetically sealed to all reply or confutation. And, as I have seen these things, I have asked myself, how long, oh! How long, shall these beloved, but mistaken brethren, continue to abuse their influence, pervert the truth, and retard the salvation of the slave?

Dear brother, lay aside your metaphysical spectacles, give up your undue attachment to well-worded theories, and look at the naked facts. If the wisdom of the schools cannot teach you the true character of Slavery, come with me, and let us interrogate yonder illiterate, untaught slave. He is just returning, faint and weary, from the toils of the day. He is an aged man, and has had for many years, a practical acquaintance with Slavery. Let us hear his reply to the question, "What is Slavery?" "It is to have my back subjected to the cowhide or the cart whip, at the will or caprice of my master, or any of his family. Every child has a right to curse, or kick, or cuff the old man. It is to toil all day beneath an almost vertical sun, with the bitter certainty always before me, that not one cent of what I earn, is, or can be my own. It is to depart from my hut every morning, with the sickening fear, that before I return at night, it will be visited by the slave-driving fiend. It is to return at night, and find my worst fears realized. My first-born son, denied even the poor privilege of bidding his father farewell, is on his way, a chained and manacled victim, to a distant market, there to be disposed of in shambles, where human flesh and sinews are bought and sold. It is to enter my cabin, and see my wife or daughter struggling in the lustful embraces of my master, or some of his white friends, without daring to attempt their rescue; for should I open my lips to remonstrate, a hundred lashes would be the consequence; and should I raise my hand to smite the brutal wretch, nothing but death could atone for the sacrilege. But above all, to be a slave, is to be denied the privilege of reading the gospel of the Son of God, to have no control over my own children, and, consequently to be deprived of the power and means of educating them in the principles of morality and religion. In one word, it is to be degraded from a man to a brute - to become, instead of a free moral agent, a thing, a piece of property, and to be used as such - to be deprived of all personal and all civil rights - to be shut out from all enjoyment in this world, and all hope in the next."

Such, brother Cummings, is Slavery, not that Slavery such as you may imagine or hope might exist, but Slavery as it actually now exists in eleven of these United States, nay, such as it exists in the church. And now, if you, and the brethren referred to, and others whom I might name, with these facts before you, resting not on my testimony only, but on that of hundreds of others, can deliberately make up your minds to continue to act the same parts which hitherto you have done, in relation to the present efforts to emancipate the slaves, why so be it. I cannot help it. Yet "my soul shall weep in secret places" over such an abuse of influence, such a perversion of talent, such a desertion from the cause of bleeding humanity, by those who ought to be foremost and most zealous in its defense. You can do, and you are doing, much to retard those efforts. But, in so doing, I declare to you my deliberate conviction, as I shall answer it at His bar, that you are fighting against God. The work I believe is his. He has owned it, he has set upon it the seal of his approbation, by raising up for it helpers when and where least expected. All good men, except, alas! a portion of the church in this country, are with it; the spirit of the age is with it; the precepts of the gospel are all on its side, and he were an infidel to doubt of its success. It will succeed, it will triumph, and that much sooner, I think, than even its friends, generally anticipate. You and I may yet live to have our ears gladdened and our hearts thrilled by the notes of that jubilee which shall sound from the Potomac to the Sabine, from the Ohio to the Gulf of Mexico, proclaiming "liberty to the captives, and the opening of the prison to them that are bound." Oh, who would forego the privilege of feeling that he had a right to join in that jubilee? - that it had been hastened in part by his exertions?

With much Christian affection, I remain,
Your brother in the Lord,
ELIJAH P. LOVEJOY

"The Abolitionists are beginning everywhere to throw off the mask, and boldly to advocate amalgamation; that is, the intermarriage of whites and blacks! - the union of persons that God by color, has put asunder, as much as he has separated midnight from noon- day!" - *Baptist Banner*

"Now, brother of the Banner, stop a moment, and do not go off at half charge, as you are somewhat apt to do. Let us reason together a moment - only for a moment.

In the first place, we ask you for the proof of the above statement. We deny its truth. We read most of the Abolition publications in the land, and we have never seen any such position taken by any one of them. Bring forward your proof, therefore, or acknowledge yourself mistaken, and that you have borne false witness against your neighbor.

But secondly, if God has put the black and white races so far asunder, how happens it that they come together so readily in the state where you live? Is not the Vice President of these United States, and one of your own citizens, an 'amalgamator,' as you phrase it? Are not his ' amalgamated' daughters among you, respectably married to men of pure Saxon blood - the sons of chivalrous Kentucky?

Moreover, go out into the streets of Louisville, the city of your residence, and where there are no Abolitionists, and tell me how many individuals among all the colored population that throng your streets, you can find whose faces shine with the pure gloss of an African complexion. Such persons are about as scarce in St. Louis as black swans are on the Mississippi, and we suspect the case is pretty similar in Louisville.

Now if this amalgamation must go on - certainly the taste of these individuals who practically favor it, is widely different from ours, but you know the old proverb, brother, *De gustibus*, etc. - if, then, it must go on, had it not better be so regulated as that it shall, in future, be in accordance with the Divine as well as human law, rather than, as now, in contravention to both?

If, for instance, an individual in Kentucky, like your illustrious citizen, the Vice President, should prefer the daughters of Ham rather than the daughters of Japhet, from whom to choose a wife, why should we who prefer the latter be restricted to one, while he is allowed a dozen, and indeed a whole harem if he please? And why, when we are bound to love, cherish, and maintain our wives till death, should he be allowed the privilege of making 'merchandise' of his and their children too, just as caprice or avarice may dictate?

Will the 'Banner' answer these questions satisfactorily, if he can, to his own conscience; and if he cannot, 'be ashamed and confounded, and never open his mouth more' about the ' amalgamation' of Abolitionists?"

"We have great respect for the acumen of brother Tracy, of the ' Boston Recorder,' but we do wish for his own sake, as well as truth's, that he were somewhat less given to the habit of deciding great questions of practical duty on metaphysical principles so subtle, that common folks need a magnifying glass to discover them. Brother T. has quoted Hudibras upon Mr. Phelps; will he excuse US if we also remind him that that same impartial and pious describer of the good men of his age, tells us of one

> 'who could divide
> A hair 'twixt north and north west side.'

And we may well suppose that after this was done, he could dispute in learned strain, as to which octagon section of the divided hair was the largest.

Does not a single glance serve to convince Mr. T. that the case he has supposed of the 'relation' commencing when the man is asleep is no case at all. For until the man awakes he can sustain no moral relation to anything or anybody, any more than the bedstead on which he lies. Go to him brother Tracy, and take Mr. Phelps along with you, wake the man up, tell him that his father has just left him a legacy of fifty human beings, and ask him what he intends to do in the case; if he say, 'I intend to hold them as my *property*' then Mr. Phelps will reply 'in so doing you sin against God;' and if we were there, most promptly would we add our own testimony to the same effect."

CHRISTIAN MIRROR

"We do not exactly understand what brother Cummings means in his paper of the 10th ult. when he talks about our compelling him to 'plume his wings,' and take his flight from this ' mundane sphere.' Be assured, brother, we have no wish to drive you out of the world, even if we had the ability. You have a work of repentance to perform, as it regards your course towards your colored brethren; and we love you too well to wish you to meet them at the bar of Him who is 'no respecter of persons,' until that work is performed. And then we want you to live long enough after that to evince your sincerity by 'bringing forth fruits meet for repentance;' and then we should be sorry to have you depart until you had witnessed the blessedness of immediate emancipation, and how groundless were all your fears respecting it. So that on the whole there seems to be no reason why you may not, so far as we are concerned, indulge the comfortable hope of attaining to your three score years and ten.

But now to business. You say in regard to the question whether the slaves are better treated at the South than in the West, 'Give us authentic testimony, and not random statements.' We find it very difficult, brother Cummings, to get any statements which you will consider 'authentic' if they make against your pre-conceived notions on the subject. We will make an effort, however. But first we must say and repeat, that it is a matter of unfeigned astonishment to us, that you should ask for evidence on this subject. We should not actually have been more surprised, had you seriously demanded of us, proof, that the Mississippi river was a larger and longer stream than the Santee, or Little Pedee. The ignorance here is almost great enough - perhaps quite - to be called absurd.

Your disposal of the 'strait-jacket,' is by no means satisfactory, nor is it candid. The phrase is surely proper enough, supposing it to be rightly applied. We certainly used the term 'strait-jacket,' that is the fact, but we did not apply them to an 'excellent aged minister,' as you said we did, and so said that which was not fact. Acknowledge your mistake, brother C.

Mr. Bailey has written a 'supplementary letter,' it seems, to explain away the testimony of his Synod, and you refer us to that. I tell you, brother C, that it is time to have done with these tergiversations. I call them tergiversations, and so they are, and they are a disgrace to anybody, much more to a Christian minister. I have read Mr. B.'s 'supplementary letter,' and I tell him, and I tell you, it is worthy only of a Jesuit. I will spend no time in refuting such special pleading, such vile sophistry. Pardon me if I speak plainly. The next thing I expect to be called on to prove, is, that negroes have not woolly heads in South Carolina. Mr. Bailey's supplementary letter has sunk him immeasurably in my estimation.

I am glad to hear you say that you think Slavery 'too desperate to be much longer tolerated by heaven or earth.' I never said there was 'not a chaste female in the church;' I said as a general truth there was not, and I repeat it."

THE RIGHT REMEDY

March 16th, 1837

"We frequently hear from many good brethren the remark, that whatever may be the evils of Slavery, the way to remedy them, is 'to preach the gospel.' In opposition to efforts made by anti-slavery societies, and anti-slavery presses, they say, 'If the gospel will not effect it (the abolition of Slavery) we despair of any instrumentality whatever.'

We would respectfully ask these brethren, what they mean by such remarks as these? We agree with them most cordially, that the gospel of the Son of God is the remedy for Slavery. But how? They certainly will not say, that it will prove this remedy as administered by those, their ministerial brethren, who maintain that the Bible sanctions Slavery; makes it right, and places it on the same footing in its code of morals, as the domestic relations of husband and wife, parent and child? Not in such hands will the gospel prove a remedy for the evils of Slavery.

But how much more good can it effect, when used by those who, notwithstanding they admit the remedy to be a good one, uniformly decline applying it for fear of irritating their patients? How long will it take the gospel to work a cure, if it is never applied to the diseased part? Will these brethren tell us? They seem to imagine there is some magic power about the preaching of the gospel, that is to do away with Slavery, while yet the authorized and accredited ministers of the gospel, never open their lips to declare that Slavery is condemned by it. If they do not mean this, we should be glad to know what it is they mean, by their constantly repeating ' the gospel is the remedy, the gospel is the remedy;' while yet they are as constantly condemning the conduct of those who seek to make it the remedy indeed, by proclaiming it to be, in all its principles and precepts, opposed to Slavery.

The Rev, James Douglass, whom we have known, and whom we highly respect as a devoted servant of 'Christ - in a communication to the Boston Recorder, which other eastern papers are copying, has much of this indefinite' ness of view about the gospel proving a remedy for Slavery. He would have anti-slavery men, instead of persisting in their present efforts to abolish Slavery, send ministers to the south, to 'preach the gospel,' to both masters and slaves. For, says he, 'where religion flourishes, slaves are well treated.' Aye, there's the very point. And this, then, is all the gospel as preached at the south, is able or expected to effect - the good treatment of the slave. Now we wish to aid in the preaching of no 'gospel whose ultimate aim, as it respects the slaves, goes no farther than this.' The 'gospel of the Son of God,' requires not the 'good treatment of the black man as a *slave*, but as a man, and a moral and accountable being; and the very first step in this good treatment is to set him free. Take an illustration of our meaning.

When the apostle Paul, went out into the Gentile world to 'preach the gospel,' he found his hearers all idolaters. He moreover found that in the practice of this idolatry, the most shameful rites abounded. The Heathen of both sexes were accustomed to spend their nights in the temples of their idols, in promiscuous, and most disgusting licentiousness. Now suppose he had commenced preaching the gospel to these polluted idolaters in this way: - 'I will not. Oh men of Athens and Corinth, require too much of you at once. I will say nothing of the divine honors you pay to Jupiter, and Mars, and Mercury, and Venus, and your other innumerable gods and goddesses; but I do require in the name of my Master, that, when you worship these deities, and especially the latter, you should do it in a little more respectable and decent manner. If you will cease these, your midnight orgies in the temples of your gods, and prosecute their worship no farther than to offer them daily libations, and to prostrate yourselves before their images, it is, I think, all the gospel requires of you at present. And for the rest, if indeed this be not sufficient, I leave you to learn it from my successor, Timothy.' And thus had the apostle Paul understood the 'preaching of the gospel,' as many of his modern successors seem to do, Christ would have died, not to abolish idolatry, but to 'remedy its evils,' and thus make it respectable! At least, this could have been the only result for two or three centuries after his departure from the world. If it be said that because we cannot abolish Slavery at once, that is no good reason why we should not rejoice to see, and as far as in us lies, endeavor to effect, the amelioration of the condition of slaves as slaves, we admit the correctness of the remark. When Paul was preaching the gospel to the Gentiles, he would undoubtedly be glad to see the Heathen quitting their licentious practices, even though they did not go so far as to abandon their idols. This was so much good effected; and so we are glad to see slaveholders treating their slaves with kindness, teaching them to read the Bible, (which however, they hardly ever do,) sending them to the Sabbath school and the church. But what we are protesting against, is the idea that the gospel is satisfied and its precepts fulfilled, when these things, and only these, are done. If you rob a man of ten dollars, it is better you should spend the money in disseminating copies of the Bible, than of Tom Paine's Age of Reason; but doing the former will no more justify the original theft than the latter. The gospel has no method of teaching the robber how to dispose of the avails of his violence, so that he may retain them without sin. It has, and can have, but one precept in the case - 'Restore what thou hast wickedly taken.' So if the gospel is to be preached to the masters of slaves, all it can say is, 'Restore the slave to himself; give him back those rights which belong to him, as he is man, and which cannot be taken away, without robbing both him and his God.'"

FAULT-FINDERS

August 17, 1837

"There is a large class of such men in this world. They are exceedingly sagacious in detecting errors in other men, but here all their sagacity ends. They never attempt anything themselves, but spend all their energies in thwarting the well-meant endeavors of others. You never find one of these men harnessed in to assist in pulling the ark of the Lord up the hill; no - they have as much as they can do to stand one side, and find fault with the way such an one takes hold to pull. He does not work to advantage - or else the traces are not made of the right material - they will be sure to break before you get half way up the hill; or yonder teamster speaks too loud, or uses too sharp a goad - or something else is wrong, no matter what. Sometimes you will find them hanging on to the wheels at the very steepest places of ascent, for no other reason than that they fear (considerate souls!) that the machine may possibly move too fast after you have got up the hill in going down on the other side! If you happen to ask any of these fault-finders, what they would have done, they never can tell you; all they can say is, 'Do differently from what you are now doing.' They can discern the wrong, but not the right. So there are certain animals whose instinct can direct them unerringly to putrid wells, while they can neither discern nor love the fountains of pure water that flow near their path.

There is nothing on which these fault-finders pride themselves more than on the superior equanimity of their tempers. They are never provoked to angry, harsh, or even inconsiderate expressions - not they; and hence they argue their own superiority in judgment, over those whom they are blaming. Now granting this assumption (of gentler speech) to be correct, (as to some extent it doubtless is,) yet what does it prove? Anything but what will be found creditable to these self-complacent gentlemen. Look at the relative condition of the parties. The one at their ease, walking backward and forward at gentle pace, doing nothing but finding fault; the other hard at work, with their heads bare, their 'shoulders peeled,' and every nerve excited to the utmost, in their efforts to 'accomplish as an hireling their day.' Is it wonderful, that under such circumstances, the working-men should occasionally manifest some impatience at the ill-timed (to say the least) reproofs and corrections of these idlers? We admit, that they ought to labor on, and always 'possess their souls in patience;' yet who that knows human nature can wonder that they sometimes rebuke these ill-omened idlers in no very courteous terms? And if haply they use a manifestly indiscreet term, or make an unwise movement, there is food enough for the fault-finders to chew upon for a long time, which they do with evident gust, and rather than it should fail them, not content with one masticating process, they ruminate its broken morsels.

There are two remarkable cases, which may be cited, illustrating the above remarks; and both have occurred within the memory of the present generation. The first is the Temperance Reformation. So soon as good men began to take hold of this work in earnest, just so soon the croakers began. Temperance societies were formed, sermons were preached, addresses delivered, books and tracts written, all for the purpose of arousing the nation to a sense of its danger and its guilt, in the matter of drunkenness. The fault-finders, many of them excellent men, and embracing in their number most of the dignitaries both of church and state, (for when was it known that men of this character commenced a work of self-denying reform?) immediately began to cry, 'innovation,' 'fanaticism,' 'ultraism,' etc., etc. They found fault (doubtless often with reason) with the temper, the spirit, the phraseology of the temperance reformers. They and all else who made any pretensions to decency were opposed to intemperance, but - and there they hung. Well, the friends of temperance, notwithstanding all their imperfections, (which were many and manifest,) triumphed. And now, no man of common understanding presumes to call himself the friend of total abstinence, who does not unite his name and influence with the Temperance Societies.

The other case to which we have referred, is that of Anti-Slavery. We are now in the midst of the developments of this great movement. It commenced, like the other, not with men in high places, so that in this, as in the temperance movement, when the glorious result aimed at shall be accomplished, it will then be seen that it was achieved 'not by might, nor by power, but by my Spirit, saith the Lord.' And as then, so now, we have the wise, the prudent, the cautious, in short, the conservatives of church and state, to contend with. They are at ease, and they do not like to be disturbed; or they have acquired a valuable reputation in former conflicts, and they do not like to put it to hazard in this. All such would gladly stand neuter in the present great conflict, and they cannot bear the idea of being disturbed, and compelled to take sides in the contest. Hence, their complacency towards slaveholders, and their anger towards those who are determined, God helping, that there shall be no neutrals in this moral warfare. And hence it is that when such men have been effectually roused, the first expression of their feeling is, not of hatred and abhorrence to Slavery, but of anger and resentment toward those who are opposed to this giant sin. This continues awhile, till conscience having been awakened and commenced doing its work, we soon begin to hear, 'I am opposed to Slavery as much as any man, but -.' But what? Why, but Garrison is opposed to the observance of the Sabbath, and Wright delivers lectures to children, and the Misses Grimke have no business to lecture in public, (we agree to this,) and Dr. Wardlaw hates the Americans, and George Thompson is employed by a society of ladies in Glasgow, and the American Anti-Slavery Society has seventy agents in the field, etc., etc. They have now got to a point where they must acknowledge their error, or continue to find fault. Hence it is just here that we often see the fault-finders redoubling their zeal and ingenuity, magnifying trifles, and converting mistakes into crimes.

The result, however, cannot be doubtful. All good men will come over - those who possess the greatest simplicity of Christian character will come first, and the rest will follow, as the truth reaches the heart. In the case of Anti-Slavery as of Temperance, the 'but' will be removed; and all will see that if the work of redeeming our beloved country from the sin and curse of Slavery, is not now well-managed, the greater the need why they should give their counsels, their prayers, and their aid, instead of holding themselves, as now, aloof for the purpose of fault-finding."

CHAPTER XII

During the winter and spring of 1836-7 no open hostility was manifested towards the "Observer" or its Editor. There were indeed some suppressed murmurings, which foreboded the coming storm. There were, too, a thousand false reports, calculated to injure his character and reputation, industriously circulated. But so accustomed was he, in common with others of like sentiments, to be abused, slandered, and reviled, that it was looked for as a matter of course. As a specimen of these reports, he was represented as declaring from the pulpit in Upper Alton, which he supplied during the summer - that if his wife should die that day, he would marry a black woman before Saturday night. And he was once asked by one, who could not be charged with extreme ignorance, if he had really made that declaration. And many such like things said they of him falsely.

In the "Observer" of June 29th appeared the subjoined editorial article.

DISTRICT OF COLUMBIA - PETITIONS

"We have received from the Secretary of the American Anti-Slavery Society, a communication requesting that we would endeavor to forward to them, as soon as possible, the names of *two individuals* in every county of the state, who will be disposed to receive and circulate petitions to Congress, for the Abolition of Slavery in the District of Columbia. We shall send on such names as we are able to designate by our own knowledge, immediately; but as there are many counties in the state where we have no acquaintance, we take this method of asking the attention of all the friends of humanity to the subject. We suggest the following,

1. Let all such individuals as are willing to undertake this work, forward their names to us, immediately, free of postage, stating particularly their county, and post office address.

2. Where the individual so writing is unknown to us, let him name some respectable individual in this place to whom we can refer, or if he cannot do this, in some other way forward to us satisfactory credentials. This is absolutely necessary to guard against imposition.

3. Let every individual who volunteers to engage in this work of circulating petitions, do it with the full understanding, that it will cost him some time, some trouble, and the good will of every advocate of Slavery. And if he is not willing to undertake the business at this expense, he had better not attempt it at all. And, moreover, let each one sending his name, send also the names of such other individuals in his own or adjoining counties, as he may think willing and qualified to circulate these petitions with zeal and success.

We need not add a word touching the vast importance of this subject. With Slavery in the several states we have nothing to do, except in the way of argument and persuasion; but let every freeman in this republic remember, that so long as Slavery exists in the District of Columbia, he is himself a slaveholder, and a licenser of the horrid traffic in slaves, carried on under the very shadow of the Capitol's walls. We have a right to interfere there, and that right brings with it a solemn duty, which we may not innocently neglect. John Quincy Adams presented the petitions of more than one hundred thousand freemen last year, he must have a million this. With proper effort we can furnish thirty thousand from this state."

To this, public attention was directed by its being copied into the Alton Spectator and Missouri Republican, and commented upon in a manner calculated to excite public indignation, July 6th, the "Observer" contained the following.

ILLINOIS STATE ANTI-SLAVERY SOCIETY

July 6th, 1837

"Is it not time that such a society should be formed? There are many, very many friends of the cause in this state, and their number is daily increasing. Ought not measures to be taken to embody their influence so as to make it tell with the greatest possible effect upon the holy cause of emancipation?

We would do nothing rashly, but it does seem to us that the time to form such a society has fully come. There are a number of local societies already existing in the state, and it would be every way better that their influence should be concentrated.

If it be decided that such a society ought to be formed, when and where shall the convention meet to form it? Shall it be in this place, or at Jacksonville, or Springfield, or elsewhere?

We take the liberty to throw out these questions for the consideration of our friends, and we suggest the propriety of their giving to them a speedy and candid consideration. Let as many as are in favor of the measure here proposed, send us their names for the purpose of having them attached to the call of the proposed convention, and let each one indicate the time and place of his preference for the meeting of the convention, with the express understanding that that place shall be selected which has the most votes in its favor.

We shall hope to have a response from the friends of the slave without delay. Every day do we feel more and more the necessity of action, decided and effective action, on this subject. With many we are already a 'fanatic' and an ' incendiary,' as it regards this matter, and we feel that we must become more and more vile in their eyes. We have never felt enough, nor prayed enough, nor done enough in behalf of the perishing slave.

This day (the 4th) reproaches our sloth and inactivity. It is the day of our nation's birth. Even as we write, crowds are hurrying past our window, in eager anticipation, to the appointed bower, to listen to the declaration that 'all men are born free and equal' - to hear the eloquent orator denounce, in strains of manly indignation, the attempt of England to lay a yoke upon the shoulders of our fathers, which neither they nor their children could bear. Alas! what bitter mockery is this. We assemble to thank God for our own freedom, and to eat and drink with joy and gladness of heart, while our feet are upon the necks of nearly three millions of our fellow men! Not all our shouts of self-congratulation can drown their groans - even that very flag of freedom that waves over our heads is formed from materials cultivated by slaves, on a soil moistened with their blood drawn from them by the whip of a republican task-master!

Brethren and friends, this must not be - it cannot be - for God will not endure it much longer. Come, then, to the rescue. The voice of three millions of slaves calls upon you to come and ' unloose the heavy burdens, and LET THE OPPRESSED GO FREE!' And on this day when every freeman's heart is glad, let us remember that -

> 'Wearily every bosom pineth,
> Wearily oh! wearily oh!
> Where the chain of Slavery twineth,
> Wearily oh! wearily oh!
> There the warrior's dart
>
> Hath no fleetness,
> There the maiden's heart
> Hath no sweetness.
> Every flower of life declineth,
>
> Wearily oh! wearily oh!
> Wearily - wearily - wearily -
> Wearily- wearily - wearily oh!
> Wearily oh! wearily oh!'"

As far as is known, these were the most obnoxious articles which appeared in the "Observer," and which by its enemies were thought worthy of special notice.

On Monday morning, the 8th of July, appeared an anonymous handbill, requesting those friends of the "Observer" dissatisfied with its course, together with the community generally, to meet at the Market House on the next Thursday. The doings of this meeting, as far as is necessary, are here given as reported by the secretary and published at the time. It was declared by the person stating the object of the meeting, that it was "to suppress Abolitionism in our town."

ANTI-ABOLITION MEETING

"Pursuant to public notice, a large and respectable concourse of the citizens of Alton, assembled at the Market House, early yesterday evening, in order to take into consideration the course pursued by the Rev. E. P. Lovejoy, in the publication and dissemination of the highly odious doctrines of modern Abolitionism, and the more to allay the spirit of an insulted people, which seemed brewing like a cloud, and darkening our social atmosphere. Although the combination of wealth, interest, and moral power were assiduously brought to bear upon the community in order to deter them from such a course; in boldly expressing their free and unbiased opinions on a subject of so delicate a nature, yet like men born to live and die, untrammeled by party, unseduced by mercenary motives, they met as freemen, determined to oppose, in a manly manner, and by a spirited resistance, the odious doctrine of modern misrule, which has stole on this community in direct violation of a *sacred pledge*.

The meeting was organized by calling to the chair, Dr. Halderman, and appointing J. P. Jordan, secretary.

The object of the meeting then being stated, on motion a committee of three was appointed to draw up resolutions -

Whereupon J. A. Townsend, Dr. H. Beall, and S. L. Miller, were appointed.

The committee, after retiring for a short time, returned and recommended to the meeting the following preamble, etc., which were unanimously adopted: -

Whereas, The citizens of Alton are called upon a second time to express their disapprobation of the course pursued by the Rev. E. P. Lovejoy, Editor of the 'Alton Observer,' in publishing and promulgating the doctrines of Abolitionism, and that, too, in violation of a solemn pledge, voluntarily given by him at a former meeting of the citizens of Alton, when an exile he sought their protection, that he would not interfere with the question of Abolitionism, in any way whatever, and that his intention alone was to publish a religious journal:

And whereas, On the strength of that pledge, and in full confidence that he would, as a clergyman of his profession, hold it sacred, we welcomed him as an acquisition to our place. But now finding, much to our mortification, that he has wantonly violated his pledge, and introduced into the columns of his paper, abolition doctrines of a most inflammatory character, and continued without regard to his solemn assertion to do so, which we as citizens of a state untrammeled with Slavery, deem it to be improper as well as impolitic, to agitate among us as we can have no benefit from it whatever, but on the contrary, much injury and damage, by eliciting from our sister states, a feeling towards us highly injurious to our community.

1. *Resolved*, That the Rev. E. P. Lovejoy has again taken up and advocated the principles of Abolitionism through his paper, the 'Observer,' contrary to the disposition and will of a majority of the citizens of Alton, and in direct violation of a sacred pledge and assurance, that this paper when established in Alton should not be devoted to Abolitionism.

2. *Resolved*, That we disapprove of the course of the 'Observer,' in publishing any articles favorable to Abolitionism, and that we censure Mr. Lovejoy in permitting such publications to appear in his paper, when a pledge or assurance has been given to this community, by him, that such doctrines should not be advocated.

3. *Resolved*, That a committee of five citizens be appointed by this meeting to wait upon and confer with Mr. Lovejoy, and ascertain from him, whether he intends in future to disseminate through the columns of the 'Observer,' the doctrines of Abolitionism, and report the result of their conference to the public.

After the committee had read the preparatory preamble and resolutions, they were submitted to the meeting, and warmly welcomed - upon which

It was moved that the President appoint the committee - when the following persons were designated:

B. K. Hart, L. J. Clawson, Col. N. Buckmaster, B. I. Gilman, Col. A. Olney, and Dr. J. A. Halderman, by request.

After which Col. A. Botkin arose, and making some pertinent preliminary remarks, offered the following resolution, which was cordially adopted:

Resolved, That we, as citizens of Alton, are aware that the Rev. E. P. Lovejoy still persists to publish an Abolition paper, to the injury of the community at large, and as we deprecate all violence of mobs, we now call on him, by our committee, and politely request a discontinuance of the publication of his incendiary doctrines, which alone have a tendency to disturb the quiet of our citizens and neighbors.

Dr. Halderman offering the four following resolutions, said briefly, he was glad to see such a spirit of independence in Alton - he was cheered to know he was not alone on this question - that the slaveholding states yet had friends even in a non-slaveholding state, to feel the wrongs and avenge the cause - he was moved to say, the liberty of our forefathers had given us the liberty of speech - and *continuing*, he added, it was our duty and our high privilege to act and speak on all questions touching this great commonwealth.

Whereupon, the resolutions being read, after some amendments by Messrs. Howard and Clifford, were unanimously adopted.

Resolved, That the recommendation in an editorial article of the 'Observer,' of a division in all the religious denominations on the *sole ground of Slavery*, is in our opinion destructive of the best interests of Christianity, and an unwarrantable assumption of arbitrary prerogative.

Resolved, That the immediate emancipation of the entire slave population, with their admittance to all the privileges, suffrages, offices, immunities, and preferments, civil, political, and religious, in common with ourselves, constitutes the doctrine of modern Abolitionism.

Resolved, That while we disapprove the doctrine of modern Abolitionism, we abhor and deprecate the evil of Slavery, and are ready and willing at any time, to give our influence and our money, to promote any system of emancipation, that will better the condition of that oppressed race of the human family, *that is agreeable to the slaveholding states.*

Resolved, That all the presses in the West and South, North and East, friendly to the cause' of colonization or gradual emancipation, in order to ameliorate the condition and freedom of the African race, are hereby requested to publish the foregoing protest and resolutions against the misrule of modern Abolitionism.

(Signed,)
J. A. HALDERMAN, Chairman
J. P. JORDON, Secretary"
July 11th, 1837

This meeting, though anything but respectable, either as it regards the number, or character of those who composed it, had an important influence in bringing about the bloody tragedy of the 7th of November. The Editor thought of denying ever having given a pledge; but being otherwise advised by his friends, did not do so. This was probably unwise, inasmuch as his silence, was, by many, construed into a tacit acknowledgment of the truth of the charge, and in consequence it was believed, to some extent both in Alton and abroad.

As to the facts about this pledge we would give the following document, merely premising that only four of the individuals whose names are attached to it are Abolitionists, several of them being opposed, and one decidedly hostile to the discussion of Slavery. And it is proper also to state that the paper was got up by one not an Abolitionist, and that it was signed, as far as is known, by all the individuals at the meeting, who were requested so to do.

"Whereas it has been frequently represented that the Rev. Elijah P. Lovejoy, late Editor of the 'Alton Observer,' solemnly pledged himself at a public meeting called for the purpose of taking measures to bring to justice, the persons engaged in the destruction of the first press, brought to Alton by said Lovejoy, not to discuss the subject of Slavery; We the undersigned declare the following to be his language in substance. 'My principal object in coming to this place, is to establish a religious paper. When I was in St. Louis I felt myself called upon to treat at large upon the subject of Slavery, as I was in a state where the evil existed, and as a citizen of that state I felt it my duty to devote a part of my columns to that subject; but gentlemen, I am not, and never was in full fellowship with the Abolitionists, but on the contrary, have had some spirited discussions with some of the leading Abolitionists of the East, and am not now considered by them as one of them. And now having come into a free state where the evil does not exist, I feel myself less called upon to discuss the subject than when I was in St. Louis.' The above, as we have stated, was his language in substance; the following we are willing to testify to be his words, in conclusion.

'But gentlemen, as long as I am an American citizen, and as long as American blood runs in these veins, I shall hold myself at liberty to speak, to write, and to publish whatever I please on any subject, being amenable to the laws of my country for the same.'

>GEO. H. WALWORTH,
>A. B. ROFF,
>SOLOMON E. MOORE,
>EFFINGHAM COCK,
>JOHN W. CHICKERING,
>JAMES MORSS, Jr.,
>F. W. GRAVES,
>W. L. CHAPPELL,
>A. ALEXANDER,
>CHAS. W. HUNTER."

In addition to the testimony of these gentlemen, we have the following editorial remarks in the first number of the "Alton Observer."

September 8th, 1837

"When the opposition to the 'Observer' commenced, nearly a year ago, in St. Louis, it was openly declared by the leader of that opposition, himself an infidel, that no religious paper should be permitted to be published in that city. During the absence of the Editor last spring, in attendance on the General Assembly, a leading grog-shop keeper in St. Louis was indicted for keeping open his shop on the Sabbath. Soon after his indictment a friend of ours happened into the house, and while there two of the grocery man's cronies came in, when all of them fell to cursing and swearing on the subject of the indictment. 'It was,' said they, 'all the work of the d----d Sunday School Union, and the Editor of this paper was at the bottom of the whole of it, and as soon as he returned they swore, with many oaths, that he should be mobbed.' *And they faithfully kept their word.* Of course we had nothing to do with the indictment, being at the time more than a thousand miles distant, and did not even know of it until after they had executed their threat.

When the Popish Cathedral in St. Louis was consecrated on the Sabbath day, amidst the pomp of military array, the roaring of artillery, the trampling of cavalry, and the sound of fife and drum, we published, from a correspondent, an account of this shameful desecration of the Lord's day. And scarcely had our paper containing the article, time to circulate through the city, before we heard from various quarters that our office was to be mobbed down for the offence we had given. Because we have declared- - an opinion which we conscientiously and solemnly believe, as we shall answer it at the bar of God - that the system of American negro Slavery is an awful evil and sin, that God has expressly forbidden us to separate husband and wife, parent and child, that no man has a right to traffic in his fellow-man, that it is the duty of every master to impart religious instruction to his slaves, and that it is the duty of us all to unite our hearty and zealous efforts, to effect the speedy and entire emancipation of that portion of our fellow-men in bondage amongst us; because we expressed our deep abhorrence of the act of a mob, by which a human being was sacrificed under circumstances of the most horrid cruelty, and because we would not submit to the imputation of Judge *Lawless*, that we had, with others, incited McIntosh to commit the crime for which he suffered - for these things, and for no other, has the mob been let loose upon us, and our printing office, together with considerable of our private property, been destroyed.

Now we ask every candid man, and especially every Christian, what sentiment of all those avowed above, ought to subject the individual advancing it, to the popular vengeance? There may be many who differ from us in some of the opinions here avowed - and they have a right to differ - but are there not enough who hold them, to make them, at least, respectable? And is it in this country, and this age of the world, that a man is to be persecuted, and crucified, for opinion's sake? And especially for such opinions? Is the Inquisition, banished even from Spain and Portugal, to be set up on the prairies of the West? Are the American people, with the Declaration of Independence in their hands, prepared to engage in a general crusade in favor of the perpetual Slavery of a portion of the human family?

'Can these things be,
And not o'ercome us like a summer cloud,

With special wonder?'

For one we distinctly avow it as our settled purpose, never, while life lasts, to yield to this new system of at- tempting to destroy, by means of mob violence, the rights of conscience, the freedom of opinion, and of the press. We intend not to deal in harsh denunciation, we wish to bring about or promote no disorder or disorganization in society, we would provoke no violence from any portion of the community; the only weapon we would use is the Truth, the only sentiment we would appeal to, the moral sense of the community. If we cannot be permitted to do this, except at the risk of property, reputation, and life, we must even take the risk. And the point now to be ascertained is, whether with these sentiments and this determination, we may rely upon being supported, in our present position, by the friends of morals and Christianity in the West. And it is precisely to ascertain this question, that the present article is written and sent forth to the public. With the friends of Truth, of Order, of the Rights of Conscience, and of God, we leave the decision."

We now return to the "Market House Meeting," as that held on the 11th of July is usually called. And here it is proper to remark, that although the invitation was principally given to the "friends of the 'Observer' who were dissatisfied with its course," yet not one of those appointed a committee to prepare resolutions for the action of the meeting, was a subscriber to the paper. To give their character does not consist with the design, nor comport with the dignity of this work.

It will be seen by the third resolution that a committee was appointed to "wait on Mr. Lovejoy and confer with him" as to his future course. And here it will be doing but justice to Mr. B. I. Oilman to say, that his name was used without his consent - he not being at the meeting - and that he refused to act, as will be seen by his name not being attached to the correspondence. No interview ever took place between this committee and the Editor of the "Observer." Their letter, together with the reply is given.

CORRESPONDENCE

"The correspondence below would have been laid before the public sooner, but for the difficulty of getting a meeting of the committee." - *Alton Telegraph.*

Alton, July 24th, 1837
To The Rev. E. P. Lovejoy:

Dear Sir - In the proceedings of a public meeting of the citizens of Alton, a copy of which is herewith transmitted to you, you will find the following resolution:

Resolved, That a committee of five citizens be appointed by this meeting, to wait upon and confer with Mr. Lovejoy, and ascertain whether he intends to disseminate through the columns of the 'Observer,' the doctrine of Abolitionism, and report the result of their conference to the public.

Whereupon, on motion, B. K. Hart, L. J. Clawson, Col. N. Buckmaster, B.I. Oilman, Col. A. Olney, and Dr. J. A. Halderman, were appointed said committee.

The committee have thought it most advisable, to address to you the proceedings themselves, instead of any written statement of their own. The views and feelings by which the citizens were actuated, and their wishes and expectations, are set forth with sufficient clearness in their reported proceedings, to which we respectfully invite your attention, with the utmost deference to your feelings as a man, and your rights as a citizen. We respectfully request that you will at your earliest convenience, answer the inquiries embodied in the above resolution, so that we may report the same to the public, in the discharge of our duty. Nothing but the importance of the question which the meeting was called to consider, and the dangers which its unwise agitation threatens, not only to the community, but to the whole country, could have induced us to take the step we have. With the wish that your answer may be dictated in wisdom, and prove such as will be satisfactory to the community, we subscribe ourselves with respect,

Your obedient servants,
B. K. HART,
L. J. CLAWSON,
N. BUCKMASTER,
A. OLNEY,
JOHN A. HALDERMAN."

Alton, July 26th, 1837
Messrs. B. K. Hart, L. J. Clawsox, N. Buckmaster, A. Olney, and John A. Halderman.

"Gentlemen - I have this day received through the Post Office, a communication signed by yourselves and addressed to me, enclosing a printed copy of the proceedings had at a public meeting held in this place on the 10th inst., to which proceedings you invite my attention.

Before replying more immediately to your communication, permit me to express my gratification at the kind and courteous terms in which it is made. In this respect it gives me pleasure to say, your letter is all I could desire. Be pleased, gentlemen, to accept my thanks. If therefore, my answer be not such, in some respects, as you might perhaps wish, I beg you will not attribute it to any want of respect to yourselves as individuals or to your opinions on the principal subject of your communication.

You will, therefore, permit me to say, that with the most respectful feelings towards you individually, I cannot consent, in this answer, to recognize you as the official organ of a public meeting convened to discuss the question, whether certain sentiments should, or should not be discussed in the public newspaper of which I am the Editor. By doing so, I should virtually admit that the liberty of the press and freedom of speech, were rightfully subject to other supervision and control, than those of the land. But this I cannot admit. On the contrary, in the language of one of the speakers at the meeting, I believe that 'the liberty of our forefathers has given us the liberty of speech,' and that it is 'our duty and our high privilege, to act and speak on all questions touching this great commonwealth.' I am happy, gentlemen, in being able heartily to concur in the above sentiments, which I perceive were uttered by one of your own members, and in which I cannot doubt, you all agree. I would only add, that I consider this 'liberty' was ascertained, but never originated by our forefathers. It comes to us, as I conceive, from our Maker, and is in its nature inalienable, belonging to man as man.

Believing, therefore, that everything having a tendency to bring this right into jeopardy, is eminently dangerous as a precedent, I cannot admit that it can be called in question by any man or body of men, or that they can with any propriety, question me as to my exercise of it. Gentlemen, I have confidence that you will, upon reflection, agree with me in this view of the case, and will consequently appreciate, with justice, my motives in declining to receive your communication, as from the official organ of the meeting to which you refer.

But as individuals whom I highly respect, permit me to say to you, that it is very far from my intention to do anything calculated to bring on an 'unwise agitation,' of the subject of Slavery, in this community. It is a subject that, as I apprehend, must be discussed, must be agitated. All virulence and intemperance of language, I should conceive to be 'unwise agitation.' It shall be my aim to resort and provoke to neither. I hope to discuss the overwhelmingly important subject of Slavery, with the freedom of a republican and the meekness of a Christian. If I fail in either respect, I beg that you will attribute it, gentlemen, to that imperfection which attends us all in the performance of our best purposes.

Permit me, respectfully, to refer you to an editorial article in the 'Alton Observer' of the 20th instant, headed, 'What are the sentiments of

Anti-Slavery men?' for the full expression of my views and principles on the subject of Slavery. If these views can be shown to be erroneous, I hold myself ready to reject them, and if you, or either of you, or any of my fellow citizens, deem them, and feel able to demonstrate them to be unsound, or of dangerous tendency, you and they are cordially invited to make use of the columns of the 'Observer' for that purpose.

With much respect,
Your friend and fellow citizen,
ELIJAH P. LOVEJOY"

From this time, threats of destroying the office of the "Observer" by violence, were openly and frequently heard. The Missouri Republican, a paper printed at St. Louis, did what it could, and that was not a little, to foster this spirit of lawlessness and outrage. Of this, however, the reader can judge from the following editorial extracts from that paper. The first was in the number containing the doings of the Market House meeting.

THE ALTON MEETING

"We give today all of the proceedings of the meeting held in Alton, on Thursday last, that our space will permit. We rejoice to see our neighbors taking this subject into hand. The proceedings of the meeting speak for themselves. They are not the intemperate ebullitions of excitement, or the temporary expression of a high wrought feeling; on the contrary, the proceedings throughout, manifest to us, the deep and settled purpose of men whose hospitalities have been slighted, and whose friendships have been abused, by one, who was bound by every moral and political obligation 'to have acted otherwise. The Editor of the 'Observer' has merited the full measure of the community's indignation; and if he will not learn from experience, they are very likely to teach him by practice, something of the light in which the honorable and respectable portion of the community view his conduct. He has, by his adhesion to the odious doctrines of Abolitionism, of which faction he now avows himself a member, and by his continued efforts to disseminate these odious doctrines, forfeited all claims to the protection of that or any other community."

The second was in the paper of the 17th of August, a few days, as will be seen, before the mob, and headed, Abolition.

"We perceive that an Anti-Slavery Society has been formed at Upper Alton, and many others, doubtless, will shortly spring up in different parts of the state. We had hoped, that our neighbors would have ejected from amongst them, that minister of mischief, the 'Observer,' or at least corrected its course. Something must be done in this matter, and that speedily! The good people of Illinois must either put a stop to the efforts of these fanatics, or expel them from their community. If this is not done, the travel of emigrants through their state, and the trade of the slaveholding states, and particularly Missouri, must stop. Everyone who desires the harmony of the country, and the peace and prosperity of all, should unite to put them down. They can do no positive good, and may do much irreparable harm. We would not desire to see this done at the expense of public order or legal restraint; but there is a moral indignation which the virtuous portion of a community may exert, which is sufficient to crush this faction and forever disgrace its fanatic instigators. It is to this we appeal, and hope that the appeal will not be unheeded."

On the 21st of August, he was taught by "experience the full measure of the community's indignation which he had merited," and began to learn by "practice" that he had not only "lost all claims to the protection of the community," but that, that protection was actually withdrawn. On this night, - two unsuccessful attempts having been made before - between the hours of ten and eleven, the office was entered by a band of fifteen or twenty citizens of that place, and press, type, and everything destroyed. Several of the hands were in the office at the time, together with a few other individuals. The mob commenced, as usual, with throwing stones into the building. One man was hit on the head and severely wounded; soon after which, the office was left, and the ruffians entered unopposed, and effected their work of destruction.

As it was early, a large concourse of citizens were collected, and witnessed the doings of the mob. Yet the strongest argument used to dissuade them from their felonious work, was, that if they would wait till morning he, the individual that addressed them, a wholesale merchant, would go in with them, help pack up the materials of the office, place them on some boat, put the Editor on top, and send them all down the river together! The civil authorities did nothing. The mayor did not even gain a "respectful" audience by words of persuasion. Had you on the next morning passed round from store to store, and from house to house, through the length and breadth of Alton, the expressions "good enough for him," "served him just right," "glad of it," would oftener have been heard, than any words of reprobation or regret, aye, ten to one.

The very narrow and providential escape of the Editor from the hands of the same ruthless miscreants that demolished his office, will best be given in his own words.

Alton, September 5th, 1837
Dearest Mother,

My press has again been mobbed down. I believe brother Owen has written to you about it. It was done the 21st of August, Monday night, about 11 o'clock, But I have thought perhaps you would like to hear from me, and I would have written sooner, but that I have been so hurried and worried, and so busy, that I could not snatch the time.

Do not think, mother, that I am disheartened or discouraged. Neither is true. I never was more convinced of the righteousness of the cause, and the certainty of its ultimate triumph. "As thy day is, so shall thy strength be." The truth of this promise, I have abundantly experienced. I have been enabled to bear things, easily to bear them, that I should once have thought would have crushed me to the earth. The Lord has indeed been to me a present, a very present help, in time of trouble. The Sabbath succeeding the mob, I preached from the text, " Thou wilt keep him in perfect peace, whose mind is stayed on thee, because he trusteth in thee." I understood that text as I never had before.

Perhaps you would like to have a brief description of the proceedings of the mob. About 9 o'clock I was returning from a friend's where I had been to marry a couple. I stepped into the apothecary's as I came through town, and got some medicine to bring home to my wife, she being very sick, as were also several other members of my family. We reside more than half a mile from town. And just as I was leaving the principal street I met the mob. They did not at first recognize me, and I parted their columns for some distance, and had just reached the rear, when some of them began to suspect who it was. They immediately wheeled their column and came after me; I did not hurry at all, believing it was not for such a man as I am to flee. They seemed a little loath to come on me, and I could hear their leaders swearing at them, and telling them to "push on," etc. By this time they began to throw clods of dirt at me, and several hit, without hurting me. And now a fellow pushed up to my side armed with a club, to ascertain certainly who it was. He then yelled out, "It's the d----d Abolitionist, give him hell;" whereat there was another rush upon me. But when they got close up, they seemed again to fall back. At length a number of them, linked arm in arm, pushed by me and wheeled in the road before me, thus stopping me completely. I then spoke to them, asking them why they stopped me. By this time the cry was all around me, "d--n him," "rail him," "rail him," "tar and feather him," "tar and feather him." I had no doubt that such was to be my fate. I then said to them, I have one request to make of you, and then you may do with me what you please, - I then asked them to send one of their number to take the medicine to my wife, which I begged they would do without alarming her. This they promised, and sent one of their number to do it, who did it according to their promise. I then said to them, "You had better let me go home, you have no right to detain me; I have never injured you." They began to curse and swear, when I added, "I am in your hands, and you must do with me whatever God permits you to do." They consulted a few moments, and then told me I might go home.

Thus you see how the Lord delivered me from those who rose up to do me hurt. Blessed be his name. During the whole of this trying scene my mind was as calm as it is now. I had time when I heard the mob coming, to lift up my heart to God, and he kept it in perfect peace.

Do write soon. My sheet is full. I am well, and so are we all but wife and child, and they are better. Love to all our brothers and sisters. May God bless them and you, my dearest mother.

ELIJAH P. LOVEJOY

That the world may know what were the principles, for believing which he "forfeited all claims to the protection of that or any other community," we give here his sentiments on the subject of Slavery, as contained in the "Alton Observer" of July 20th, 1837, alluded to in his answer to the Market House Committee.

WHAT ARE THE DOCTRINES OF ANTI-SLAVERY MEN?

"A young man had become exceedingly angry with an ancient philosopher, and had raised his cane to strike him. 'Strike,' said the philosopher - 'strike, but hear me.' He listened, and was convinced. There is not, probably, an individual, who reads this, that cannot recollect some instance in his life, in which his strong opposition to certain measures and principles, he now sees, was entirely owing lo groundless and unreasonable prejudices; and he is a fortunate man who can recollect but one such instance.

In respect to the subject now to be discussed, the writer frankly confesses no one of his readers can possibly be more prejudiced, or more hostile to anti-slavery measures or men, than he once was. And his, too, were honest, though, alas! how mistaken, prejudices. They arose partly from the fact that the 'new measures' came directly in contact with his former habits of thought and action, and partly, and chiefly, from the strange and astonishingly perverted representations given of leading men and their principles, in this new movement. We recollect no instance of parallel misrepresentation, except the charge brought against Christ of casting out devils by Beelzebub, the prince of devils. These misrepresentations were started by a few, and honestly believed by the many. They still prevail to a very great extent. Very probably some of our readers may be under their influence more or less. We ask them to be candid with themselves, and if they find this to be the case, to make an effort to throw them off, and come to the perusal of what follows, ready to embrace the truth wherever it is found. For truth is eternal, unchanging, though circumstances may, and do operate to give a different color to it, in our view, at different times. And truth will prevail, and those who do not yield to it must be destroyed by it. What then are the doctrines of Anti-Slavery men?

FIRST PRINCIPLES

1. Abolitionists hold that 'all men are born free and equal, endowed by their Creator with certain inalienable rights, among which are life, liberty, and. the pursuit of happiness.' They do not behave that these rights are abrogated, or at all modified by the color of the skin, but that they extend alike to every individual of the human family.

2. As the above-mentioned rights are in their nature inalienable, it is not possible that one man can convert another into a piece of property, thus at once annihilating all his personal rights, without the most flagrant injustice and usurpation. But American Slavery does this - it declares a slave to be a 'thing,' a 'chattel,' an article of personal 'property,' a piece of 'merchandise,' and now actually holds two and a half millions of our fellow-men in this precise condition.

3. Abolitionists, therefore, hold American Slavery to be a *wrong*, a legalized system of inconceivable injustice, and a sin. That it is a sin against God, whose prerogative as the rightful owner of all human beings is usurped, and against the slave himself, who is deprived of the power to dispose of his services as conscience may dictate, or his Maker require. And as whatever is morally wrong can never be politically right, and as the Bible teaches, and as Abolitionists believe, that 'righteousness exalteth a nation, while sin is a reproach to any people,' they also hold that Slavery is a political evil of unspeakable magnitude, and one which, if not removed, will speedily work the downfall of our free institutions, both civil and religious.

4. As the Bible inculcates upon man but one duty in respect to sin, and that is, immediate repentance; Abolitionists believe that all who hold slaves, or who approve the practice in others, should immediately cease to do so.

5. Lastly, Abolitionists believe, that as all men are born free, so all who are now held as slaves in this country were born free, and that they are slaves now is the sin, not of those who introduced the race into this country, but of those, and those alone, who now hold them, and have held them in Slavery from their birth. Let it be admitted, for argument's sake, that A or B has justly forfeited his title to freedom, and that he is now the rightful slave of C, bought with his money, how does this give C a claim to the posterity of A down to the latest generation? And does not the guilt of enslaving the successive generations of A's posterity belong to their respective masters, whoever they be? Nowhere are the true principles of freedom and personal rights better understood than at the South, though

their practice corresponds so wretchedly with their theory. Abolitionists adopt, as their own, the following sentiments, expressed by Mr. Calhoun in a speech on the tariff question, delivered in the Senate of the United States, in 1833: - 'He who *earns* the money - who digs it out of the earth with the sweat of his brow, has 3, just title to it against the Universe. *No one has a right to touch it, without his consent, except his government,* and it only to the extent of its legitimate wants: to take more is robbery." Now, this is precisely what slaveholders do, and Abolitionists do but echo back their own language, when they pronounce it 'robbery.'

EMANCIPATION - WHAT IS MEANT BY IT?

Simply, that the slaves shall cease to be held as property, and shall henceforth be held and treated as human beings. Simply, that we should take our feet from off their necks. Perhaps Ave cannot express ourselves better than to quote the language of another southerner. In reply to the question what is meant by emancipation, the answer is:

1. 'It is to reject with indignation the wild and guilty phantasy, that man can hold *property* in man. 2. To pay the laborer his hire, for he is worthy of it. 3. No longer to deny him the right of marriage, but to 'let every man have his own wife,' as saith the apostle. 4. To let parents have their own children, for they are the gift of the Lord to them, and no one else has any right to them. 5. No longer to withhold the advantages of education, and the privilege of reading the Bible. 6. To put the slave under the protection of law, instead of throwing him beyond its salutary influence.'

Now, who is there that is opposed to Slavery at all, and believes it to be wrong and a sin, but will agree to all this?

HOW AND BY WHOM IS EMANCIPATION TO BE EFFECTED?

To this question the answer is, by the masters themselves, and by no others. No others can effect it, nor is it desirable that they should, even if they could. Emancipation, to be of any value to the slave, must be the free, voluntary act of the master, performed from a conviction of its propriety. This avowal may sound very strange to those who have been in the habit of taking the principles of the Abolitionists from the misrepresentations of their opponents. Yet this is, and always has been, the cardinal principle of Abolitionists. If it be asked, then, why they intermeddle in a matter where they can confessedly do nothing themselves, in achieving the desired result? their reply is, that this is the very reason why they do and ought to intermeddle. It is because they cannot emancipate the slaves, that they call upon those who can to do it. Could they themselves do it, there would be no need of discussion - instead of discussing they would act, and with their present views, the work would soon be accomplished.

Who are they that hold Temperance meetings, form Temperance Societies, sustain and edit, and circulate Temperance ' Intelligencers' and 'Heralds'? Are they the men who own distilleries, or who sell or drink ardent spirits by the wholesale or retail? Directly the reverse. They are men who have been convinced of the evil and the sin of such practices, and having quit them, themselves, are now endeavoring to persuade their neighbors to do the same thing. For what purpose are the very efficient Executive Committee of the Illinois State Temperance Society now publishing their 'Herald,' and endeavoring to send it into every family of the state? Avowedly for the purpose of shutting up every distillery and dram shop in the state. The object is a noble one, and we bid them God speed; but how do they purpose to accomplish it? By doing violence, or exciting an angry community to do violence, to the persons or property of their fellow citizens? By no manner of means. They would not, if they could, shut up a single grog-shop belonging to their neighbors - and in this thing, all the inhabitants of the state, yea, of the world, are their neighbors - but they wish, and are determined, if light, and love, and argument, and fact, and demonstration can effect it, to persuade all to abandon a business so detrimental to all concerned in it, and to the community at large. Now this is precisely the ground occupied by Abolitionists in relation to Slavery. And let it be remembered that the objection of interfering in the business of others applies with equal force to the one as to the other. Should the friends of Temperance succeed, they will deprive many a man of what is now a very profitable business, and so will the Abolitionists. But in both cases the result will be achieved with the hearty and glad acquiescence of those more immediately concerned, and a great common good will be effected, infinitely over-balancing the partial evil, if evil it may be called, to deprive a man of the profits arising from rum selling or slave trading.

But, in the second place, as to the particular mode of effecting emancipation. This, too, belongs to the master to decide. When we tell a distiller or a vender of ardent spirits, that duty requires him to forsake his present business, we go no further. It belongs not to the preacher of Temperance to dictate to them, what particular use they shall make of those materials now so improperly employed. He may do anything, convert his buildings and appurtenances to any use, so that it be a lawful one. Yet advice might, perhaps, be kindly given and profitably listened to. We can tell the slaveholder what he may do with his slaves after emancipation, so as to do them justice, and at the same time, lose nothing himself. Employ them as free laborers, pay them their stipulated wages, and the results of the West India emancipation have afforded to us the means of assuring him that he will derive more clear profit from their labor as freemen than as slaves. Did the Abolitionists propose to remove the slave population from the country, the free inhabitants of the South might justly complain; for that would soon render their country a barren and uncultivated waste. But they aim at no such thing; nor yet would they encourage or allow the emancipated slaves to roam about the country as idle vagabonds; they would say to them, as to others, "They that will not work, neither shall they eat," and let the regulation be enforced with all proper sanctions. Only, when they work let them be paid for it.

AMALGAMATION EQUAL PRIVILEGES, ETC.

No charge has been more perseveringly made, or contributed more to render the cause of emancipation odious, than that its friends were also advocates of the amalgamation of the two races. Now, in answer to this, we reply:

1. The charge comes with an exceedingly bad grace from those who are loudest in making it; since they, that is many of them - (we speak within bounds when we say more than half of them) - do not only advocate, but actually practice amalgamation. The evidence of this is written in the bleached countenances of the slaves throughout all the slaveholding region. The law of slave descent is, that the children follow the condition of the mother; and the consequence is, that thousands hold as slaves their own sons and daughters, and brothers and sisters, and nephews and nieces. We know several cases of this sort. The Vice President of the United States has been, if he is not now, the father of slaves. And thousands have voted to elevate him to his present condition, who would crucify an Abolitionist on the bare suspicion of favoring, though only in theory, such an amalgamation. How shall we account for such inconsistency?

2. But, secondly, the charge is untrue - completely, and absolutely, and in every sense untrue. Abolitionists do NOT advocate the doctrine of amalgamation, but the reverse. And nothing can be more unjust than thus to charge them, without the least shadow of truth to sustain the charge. On the contrary, one reason why Abolitionists urge the Abolition of Slavery is, that they fully believe it will put a stop, in a great, and almost entire measure, to that wretched, and shameful, and polluted intercourse between the whites and blacks, now so common, it may be said so universal, in the slave states. As to equality of privileges, immunities, etc., the question of emancipation has nothing to do with these questions at all. Abolitionists are not so silly as to suppose' that merely setting the slaves free will at once make learned, virtuous, and influential individuals out of the degraded mass of slaves. They know better, though at the same time, they believe a process of purification and elevation would commence, which would gradually be productive of the most beneficial consequences. The question of civil rights is one entirely distinct from that of personal rights. Let the latter be restored and guar- anteed, and the whole object of

the Abolitionists, as such, is accomplished. Political rights are alienable, personal rights are not. Personal rights are often as secure under the government of a despot - Frederick the Great, of Prussia, for instance, as they possibly can be anywhere; while at the same time the subject has no political rights, give him these and you allow him to pursue his own happiness in his own way, provided he seeks it not at the expense of others. If in this pursuit he becomes the most virtuous, the most learned, the most eloquent, the most influential man in the United States, we see not how it is to be helped, nor who has a right to obstruct his course.

The above exposition of anti-slavery principles has been made at the request of a number of our respectable citizens. In preparing it, we have felt deeply our responsibility, and have trembled lest through any inadvertence of language we should make ourselves liable to be misunderstood, and thus repel the minds of those whom we wish to gain. In the correctness of these principles we have the most unshaken confidence, and that they finally will be properly understood and most universally adopted by our countrymen, we have no more doubt than we have, that Washington lived and Warren died to secure the blessings of civil and religious liberty. That they have met with such determined opposition, and brought upon their prominent supporters such extreme manifestations of popular hatred, is partly and chiefly owing to the fact that they have been strangely misapprehended, and partly that in their practical application in this country, they strike, or are supposed to strike, at self-interests of great magnitude.

Until the sentiments and principles set forth above shall prevail over the earth, the world can never be delivered from the bondage under which it has so long groaned. They are the sentiments which, though oftentimes dimly and feebly apprehended, have actuated the minds of the great and good of every age, who have mourned over the degradation of human nature, and have sought to elevate it, by ascertaining and securing those rights of man with which his Maker has endowed him. They are the principles which actuated a Thrasybulus, an Epaminondas, a Spartacus and a Brutus, of antiquity; a Doria, a Tell, a Hampden, a Sidney, a Russell, a Hancock, an Adams, a Washington, of later days. They brought our pilgrim fathers from the homes and fire-sides of old England to this country, then an unknown land, and a waste, howling wilderness. They sustained them to endure Toils, and hardships, and privations, until they made the 'wilderness to rejoice and blossom as the rose.' And now shall their children forsake these principles, and attempt to roll back the wheels of that reformation on whose banner is inscribed the liberty and equality of the human RACE, and which dispenses in its train, alike to all, the blessings of peace, of harmony, and the unmolested rights of conscience? No, they will not, they dare not.

We do not mean to be understood than in the oases referred to above, the manifestations of these principles were always proper. Enough, however, appeared to show that the minds of these patriots and sages were communing with their Maker, and were receiving from Him - though owing to the darkness of their minds, imperfectly understood and often misapprehended - revelations of the rights, duties, and privileges which he designed for the race.

> Did the form
> Of servile custom cramp their gen'rous powers?
> Would sordid policies, the barb'rous growth
> Of ignorance and rapine, bow them down
> To tame pursuits, to indolence and fear?
> Lo I they appeal to nature, to the winds
> And rolling waves, the sun's unwearied course,
> The elements and seasons; all declare
> For what the eternal Maker has ordain'd
> The powers of main, they felt within themselves
> His energy divine.

These principles, then, are eternal and immutable, for they are established by God himself, and whoever would destroy them, must first reach up to heaven and dethrone the Almighty. Sin had well-nigh banished them from the earth, when the Son of God came down to re-assert them, and died to sanction them. They are summed up, perfectly, in the language by which the angels announced the object of the Redeemer's mission - 'Glory to God in the highest, on earth peace, good will toward men.'"

CHAPTER XIII

Immediately after the destruction of the materials of the office, the friends in Alton had a meeting, at which there was but one voice, and that was, that the "Observer" must be reestablished and go on. A gentleman, one of the most wealthy in the place, said, that although he could not at that time advance the money to purchase new materials, yet rather than that the paper should not be again started he would mortgage every cent of his private property.

Thus encouraged, the Editor sent forth the following appeal on an extra sheet of the "Observer."

TO THE FRIENDS AND SUBSCRIBERS OF
THE ALTON OBSERVER

August 24th, 1837

After mentioning the demolition of his office, he continues:

I now appeal to you, and all the friends of law and order, to come up to the rescue. If you will sustain me, by the help of God, the press shall be again established at this place, and shall be sustained, come what will. Let the experiment be fairly tried, whether the liberty of speech and of the press is to be enjoyed in Illinois or not.

We need your help, and we must have it or sink. Let every man who ever means to do anything in the cause of civil and religious liberty, do it now. Let new subscribers send in their names, let former subscribers pay up their dues, and let everyone send in their contributions, as it will require not less than fifteen hundred dollars to re-establish the "Observer." Everything depends on you. If you take hold like men, like freemen, like Christians, all will be well; if you do not, mobism will triumph, but I shall be guiltless.

ELIJAH P. LOVEJOY

P. S. Let every man disposed to help, write me immediately, and let me know definitely, what he can do and what he will do.　　　　E. P. L.

The response to this appeal was full, prompt, decided and encouraging; and from almost all classes. Especially was this the case from his ministerial brethren. The letters before us, and there are many, from every part of the state, and not a few from other states, are uniformly expressive of sympathy and condolence towards the Editor, and approval of his course - assurance of assistance - and an earnest wish and confident expectation that his paper should go on. It is difficult to decide which is greatest, the surprise or indignation expressed in these letters. Surprise, because Alton had a name for morality and religion above every other place in the state; and indignation that any attempt should be made to destroy the freedom of the press, and that eight or ten thousand people should be deprived the opportunity of reading the paper of their choice.

Having, in Alton and Quincy, obtained by subscription a sufficient sum, he sent to Cincinnati to purchase the requisite materials for a new office.

Although his hands were thus made strong, and his heart encouraged, still the latter part of September, and the first of the next month, was perhaps the gloomiest season of the year: not from the deadly hatred of his enemies, though that was continually increasing, but from the waning ardor, and wavering resolution of many of his friends in Alton. There were some, however, who never swerved nor hesitated. And it must be acknowledged that there were many things to discourage them. The pecuniary burden had to a considerable extent fallen on them, and money matters were hard. But what contributed principally to this abatement of zeal, and partial desertion among his friends, was the pernicious influence of a certain pamphlet, full of gross perversions, gilded over with a smirking cant of Christian sincerity. This tract with a specious sophistry well calculated to deceive, endeavors to prove that the Holy Bible sanctions the system of American Slavery; and exhorts the conscientious slaveholder no longer to go with his head bowed down like a bulrush, oppressed with the feeling that God's "hot displeasure," is out against him for his oppression and injustice, but to go cheerily on in the good old time-honored path pressed by patriarchal feet, and guarded by apostolic injunctions!

Such was the influence of this pamphlet, seconded as it was by the efforts of a kindred spirit - the Rev. Joel Parker of New Orleans, that some were deceived and "went back," others disheartened; and all who were opposed, confirmed and strengthened in their hostility.

In consequence there was a want of union among those who had been supporters of the "Observer." Some wanted it to be a religious paper - which indeed it always had been - in other words that it should not meddle with the subject of Slavery. We speak now of those in Alton, with whom it was to decide whether the paper should start there again or not. Owing to this state of things, the following letter was written.

TO THE FRIENDS OF THE REDEEMER IN ALTON

Alton, September 11th, 1837
Dear Brethren,

It is at all times important that the friends of truth should be united. It is especially so at the present time, when iniquity is coming in like a flood. I should be false to my covenant vows, and false to every feeling of my heart, were I to refuse making any personal sacrifice to effect so desirable an object. Having learned that there is a division of sentiments among the brethren, as it regards the propriety of my continuing longer to fill the office of Editor of the "Alton Observer," I do not hesitate a moment to submit the question to your decision. Most cheerfully will I resign my post, if in your collective wisdom you think the cause we all profess to love will thereby be promoted. And in coming to a decision on this question, I beseech you as a favor - may I not enjoin it as a duty? - that you act without any regard to my personal feelings. I should be false to the Master I serve, and of whose gospel I am a minister, should I allow my own interests, (real or supposed,) to be placed in competition with his. Indeed, I have no interest, no wish, at least I think I have none; I know I ought to have none other than such as are subordinate to his will. Be it yours, brethren, to decide what is best for the cause of truth, most for the glory of God, and the salvation of souls, and rest assured - whatever my own private judgment may be - of my cordial acquiescence in your decision.

I had, at first, intended to make an unconditional surrender of the editorship into your hands. But as such a course might be liable to misconstructions, I have, by the advice of a beloved brother, determined to leave the whole matter with you. I am ready to go forward if you say so, and equally ready to yield to a successor, if such be your opinion. Yet let me say, promptly, that in looking back over my past labors as Editor of the "Observer," while I see many imperfections, and many errors and mistakes, I have, nevertheless, done the best I could. This I say in the fear of God; so that if I am to continue the Editor, you must not, on the whole, expect a much better paper than you have had.

Should you decide that I ought to give place to a successor, I shall expect the two following conditions to be fulfilled.

1. That you will assume in its behalf, all my obligations contracted in consequence of my connection with the "Observer." Some of them were contracted immediately on behalf of the "Observer," and some in supporting my family while its Editor.

2. As I have now spent four among the best years of my life in struggling to establish the "Observer," and place it on its present footing, I shall expect you will furnish me with a sum sufficient to enable me to remove myself and family to another field of labor. More I do not ask, and I trust this will not be thought unreasonable. I would not ask even this had I the means myself, but I have not.

3. On these conditions I surrender into your hands the "Observer's" subscription list, now amounting to more than two thousand one hundred names, and constantly increasing, together with all the dues coming to the establishment. A list both of the debts and credits accompanies this communication.

May the spirit of wisdom, dear brethren, guide you to a wise and *unanimous* decision - to a decision which God will approve and ratify, and which shall redound to the glory of his name.

Yours affectionately,

ELIJAH P. LOVEJOY

This paper we introduce for two reasons; first, as it is a part of his history; and secondly, that the reader may have the means of judging as it regards those charges of obstinacy and self-will which have so often been preferred against him.

At a meeting for the consideration of this resignation, the two following resolutions were introduced, for the sake of some definite action:

1. *Resolved*, That the "Alton Observer" ought to be established.
2. *Resolved*, That the Rev. Elijah P. Lovejoy ought to continue its Editor.

The first of these was passed, as far as is known, without debate, or a dissenting voice. The second, after being discussed through two or three successive meetings, was left without any definite action whatever. A gentleman playfully remarked one evening, on coming from one of these discussions, "we have been trying to kill your brother all the afternoon, but we cannot succeed." Thus the thing remained. Meanwhile, on the 21st of September, while the Editor was absent attending a meeting of the Presbytery, the press - the third which he had brought to Alton in little more than a year, arrived. It was landed about sunset, or a little after, and, surrounded by quite a number of friends, who had been apprised of its coming; was conveyed to the warehouse of Gerry and Weller. As it passed along the streets cries were heard, "there goes the Abolition press, stop it, stop it;" but no actual violence was offered. The mayor, apprised of its arrival, and also of the threats of its destruction, gave positive assurance that it should be protected; and expressed a wish that its friends should leave it in his hands. They did so. He posted a constable at the door, with orders to remain till a certain hour. As soon as he left, ten or twelve "respectable" ruffians, disguised with handkerchiefs over their faces, broke open the store, rolled the press across the street to the side of the river, broke it to pieces, and threw it in. While thus engaged, and before they had proceeded far in this work of robbery, the mayor arrived. He told them to disperse. They replied, that they would "as soon as they got through," and went on. This is literally true. The mayor returned, saying, that he never witnessed a more quiet and gentlemanly mob. The following letter will show that his enemies were not satisfied with merely destroying his press.

Alton, October 3d, 1837
My dear brother Leavitt,

I have just passed through a scene which I will try to describe to your readers.

On Sabbath, I preached for the Rev. Mr. Campbell, the Presbyterian minister of St. Charles, with whom I had formerly been acquainted, and who had lately arrived in this place from Wilmington Presbytery, Delaware. I preached in the morning, and at night. After the audience was dismissed at night, and when all had left the house but Mr. Campbell, his brother-in-law, Mr. Copes, and myself, a young man came in, and passing by me, slipped the following note into ray hand:

"Mr. Lovejoy,
 "Be watchful as you come from church tonight.
                                                              A Friend."

I showed the note to the two brethren present; and Mr. Campbell invited me to go home with him in consequence. I declined, however, and in company with him and Mr. Copes walked home, but a short distance, to my mother-in-law's. Brother Campbell went in with me, and Mr. C. passed on. This was about nine o'clock, and a very dark night. We received no molestation on our way, and the whole matter had passed my mind. Brother C. and I had sat conversing for nearly an hour; Mrs. L. had gone to another room and lain down; her mother was with her, having our sick child, while an unmarried sister of Mrs. L. was in the room with Mr. C. and myself. The rooms thus occupied were on the second floor, the first story of the house being tenanted as a store. The access to the rooms is by a flight of stairs leading up to a portico, on which the doors of the several rooms open.

About ten o'clock, as Mr. Campbell and myself were conversing, I heard a knocking at the foot of the stairs. I took a candle, and opening the door of the room in which I sat, to learn the cause, I found that the knocking had called up Mrs. Lovejoy and her mother, who had enquired what was wanted. The answer was, "We want to see Mr. Lovejoy, is he in." To this I answered myself, "Yes, I am here." They immediately rushed up to the portico, and two of them coming into the room laid hold of me. These two individuals, the name of one was Littler, formerly from Virginia, the other called himself a Mississippian, but his name I have not learned, though it is known in St. Charles. I asked them what they wanted of me. "We want you down stairs, d--n you," was the reply. They accordingly commenced attempting to pull me out of the house. And not succeeding immediately, one of them, Littler, began to beat me with his fists. By this time, Mrs. L. had come into the room. In doing so she had to make her way through the mob on the portico, who attempted to hinder her from coming, by rudely pushing her back, and one "chivalrous" southerner actually drew his dirk upon her. Her only reply was to strike him in the face with her hand, and then rushing past him, she flew to where I was, and throwing her arms around me, boldly faced the mobites, with a fortitude and self-devotion which none but a woman and a wife ever displayed. While they were attempting with oaths and curses to drag me from the room, she was smiting them in the face with her hands, or clinging to me to aid in resisting their efforts, and telling them that they must first take her before they should have her husband. Her energetic measures, seconded by those of her mother and sister, induced the assailants to let me go and leave the room.

As soon as they were gone, Mrs. L.'s powers of endurance failed her, and she fainted. I carried her into another room and laid her on the bed. So soon as she recovered from her fainting, she relapsed into hysterical fits, moaning and shrieking, and calling upon my name, alternately. Mrs. L.'s health is at all times extremely delicate, and at present peculiarly so, she being some months advanced in pregnancy. Her situation at this time was truly alarming and distressing. To add to the perplexities of the moment, I had our sick child in my arms, taken up from the floor where it had been left by its grandmother, in the hurry and alarm of the first onset of the mob. The poor little sufferer, as if conscious of danger from the cries of its mother, clung to me in silence. In this condition, and while I was endeavoring to calm Mrs. L.'s dreadfully excited mind, the mob returned to the charge, breaking into the room, and rushing up to the bed-side, again attempting to force me from the house. The brutal wretches were totally indifferent to her heart-rending cries and shrieks - she was too far exhausted to move; and I suppose they would have succeeded in forcing me out, had not my friend William M. Campbell, Esq. at this juncture come in, and with undaunted boldness, assisted me in freeing myself from their clutches. Mr. Campbell is a southerner, and a slaveholder; but he is a man, and he will please accept my grateful thanks for his aid so promptly and so opportunely rendered; others aided in forcing the mob from the room, so that the house was now clear a second time.

They did not, however, leave the yard of the house, which was full of drunken wretches, uttering the most awful and soul-chilling oaths and imprecations, and swearing they would have me at all hazards. I could hear the epithets, "The infernal scoundrel, the d----d amalgamating Abolitionist, we'll have his heart out yet," etc., etc. They were armed with pistols and dirks, and one pistol was discharged, whether at any person or not, I did not know. The fellow from Mississippi seemed the most bent on my destruction. He did not appear at all drunken, but both in words and actions manifested the most fiendish malignity of feeling and purpose. He was telling a story to the mobiles, which, whether true or false, (I know not,) was just calculated to madden them. His story was, that his wife had lately been violated by a negro. And this he said was all owing to me, who had instigated the negro to do the deed. He was a ruined man, he said, had just as lief die as not; but before he died he "would have my blood."

The mob now rushed up the stairs a third time, and one of them, a David Knott, of St. Charles, came in with a note signed "A citizen of St. Charles." I regret that I have mislaid it. It was short, however, requiring me to leave the town the next day at ten o'clock, in the morning. I told Mr. K. I presumed he expected no answer to such a note. He said he did not, and immediately left the room. As soon as he got out, they set up a yell, as if so many demons had just broken loose from hell. I had insulted them, it seems, by not returning an answer to their note. My friends now came round me, entreating me to send them a written answer. This I at first declined, but yielding to their urgent advice, I took my pencil and wrote as follows:

"I have already taken my passage in the stage, to leave tomorrow morning, at least by nine o'clock.
                                                Elijah P. Lovejoy."

This was carried out and read to them, and at first, after some pretty violent altercation among themselves, seemed to pacify them. They went away, as I supposed finally. But after having visited the grog-shop, they returned with augmented fury and violence. My friends in the house, of whom by the way, there were not many, now became thoroughly alarmed. They joined in advising me to leave the house, and make my escape, should an opportunity occur. This I at first absolutely declined doing. I did so on the principle I had adopted, of never either seeking or avoiding danger in the way of duty. "Should such a man as I flee," has been my sentiment, whether right or wrong. I was at length, however, compelled by the united entreaties of them all, and especially of my wife, to consent to do so, should opportunity offer. Accordingly, when the efforts of those below had diverted the attention of the mob for a few moments, I left the house and went away unperceived. I went up the street a few rods, and finding all still, I came back to reconnoiter, and after looking round awhile, and seeing or hearing no enemy, I went back into the house. Here, however, so far from being welcomed, I was greeted with reproaches in abundance for my temerity, as they called it, in venturing back.

And sure enough, scarcely had I seated myself before the mob returned again, as though they scented their prey. One man now went down to them, and by the promise of a dram, led them all away, and I was fain to escape, not so much from the mob, as from the reproaches of my wife and friends, by leaving the house a second time. It was now about midnight. Through the good hand of my God upon me, I got away unperceived. I walked about a mile to my friend, Maj. Sibley's residence. Having called him up and informed him of my condition, he kindly furnished me with a horse; and having rested myself on the sofa an hour or two, for I was much exhausted, I rode to Mr. Watson's, another friend, where I arrived about day-break, four miles from town. Here Mrs. L., though exhausted and utterly unfit to leave her bed, joined me in the morning, and we came home, reaching Alton about noon, meeting with no let or hindrance, though Mrs. L. was constantly alarmed with apprehensions of pursuit from St. Charles.

On our arrival in Alton, as we were going to our house, almost the first person we met in the street, was one of the very individuals who had first broken into the house at St. Charles. Mrs. L. instantly recognized him, and at once became greatly alarmed. There was the more reason for fear, inasmuch as the mob in St. Charles had repeatedly declared their determination to pursue me, and to have my life, and one of them, the fellow from Mississippi, boasted that he was chasing me about, and that he had assisted to destroy my press in Alton. This was the more readily believed, inasmuch as it was known that individuals from St. Louis, where this Mississippian now temporarily resides, were aiding in that work. The mobite from St. Charles also openly boasted here of their assault upon me in that place.

Upon these facts being made known to my friends, they deemed it advisable that our house should be guarded on Monday night. Indeed, this was necessary to quiet Mrs. L.'s fears. Though completely exhausted, as may well be supposed, from the scenes of the night before, she could not rest. The mob haunted her excited imagination, causing her continually to start from her moments of fitful slumber, with cries of alarm. This continued all the afternoon and evening of Monday, and I began to entertain serious apprehensions of the consequences. As soon, however, as our friends, to the number of ten arrived with arms in their hands, her fears subsided, and she sank into a comparatively silent sleep, which continued through most of the night. It is now Tuesday night. I am writing by the bedside of Mrs. L., whose excitement and fears have measurably returned with the darkness. She is constantly starting at every sound, while her mind is full of the horrible scenes through which she has so lately passed. What the final result will be for her I know not, but hope for the best. We have no one with us tonight, except the members of our own family. A loaded musket is standing at my bedside, while my two brothers, in an adjoining room, have three others, together with pistols, cartridges. Sic. And this is the way we live in the city of Alton! I have had inexpressible reluctance to resort to this method of defense. But dear-bought experience has taught me that there is at present no safety for me, and no defense in this place, either in the laws or the protecting ægis of public sentiment. I feel that I do not walk the streets in safety, and every night when I lie down, it is with the deep settled conviction, that there are those near me and around me, who seek my life. I have resisted this conviction as long as I could, but it has been forced upon me. Even were I safe from my enemies in Alton, my proximity to Missouri exposes me to attack from that state. And now that it is known that I am to receive no protection here, the way is open for them to do with me what they please. Accordingly a party of them from St. Louis came up and assisted in destroying' my press, the first time. This was well known. They came armed and stationed themselves behind a wall for the purpose of firing upon anyone who might attempt to defend the office. Yet who of this city has rebuked this daring outrage on the part of citizens of our state and city, upon the rights and person of the citizens of another state and city? No one. I mean there has been no public expression of opinion on the subject. Our two political papers have been silent, or if speaking at all, have thrown the blame on me rather than on any one else. And if you go through the streets of Alton, or into stores and shops, where you hear one condemning these outrages upon me, you will find five approving them. This is true, both of professor and non-professor. I have no doubts that four-fifths of the inhabitants of this city are glad that my press has been destroyed by a mob, both once and again. They hate mobs, it is true, but they hate Abolitionism a great deal more. Whether creditable to them or not, this is the state of public sentiment among our citizens. A leading member of the Presbyterian Church here, disclosed to me, in the presence of fifteen or twenty persons, that if the "Observer" were re-established here, he would do nothing to protect it from a mob again. A leading merchant here, and a Methodist minister, said the same thing, at the same time. Most of our leading men, whether in church or state, lay the blame all on me.

So far from calling the acts of the mob outrages, they go about the streets, saying in the hearing of everybody, "Mr. Lovejoy has no one to thank but himself." Of course the mob desire no better license than this.

The pulpit, with but one exception, is silent. Brother Graves was absent at the time of the first outrage. But since his return he has taken hold of the work with characteristic boldness and zeal. There is no cowardice in him, no shrinking from duty through fear of man. I wish I could say as much of our other pastors. Brother G. has told his people their duty faithfully and fearlessly. Whether they will hear him I know not, but he has cleared his skirts.

And now, my dear brother, if you ask what are my own feelings at a time like this, I answer, perfectly calm, perfectly resigned. Though in the midst of danger, I have a constant sense of security that keeps me alike from fear or anxiety. "Thou wilt keep him in perfect peace, whose mind is stayed on thee, because he trusteth in thee." This promise I feel has been literally fulfilled unto me. I read the promises of the Bible, and especially the Psalms, with a delight, a refreshing of soul I never knew before. Some persons here call me courageous, and others pronounce me stubborn; but I feel and know I am neither one nor the other. That I am enabled to continue firm in the midst of all my trials, is all of God. Let no one give me any credit for it. I disclaim it. I should feel that I were robbing Him, if even in thought, I should claim the least share to myself. He has said, "As thy day is, so shall thy strength be," and he has made his promise good. To him be all the praise. Pray for me.

We have a few excellent brethren here in Alton. They are sincerely desirous to know their duty in this crisis, and to do it. But as yet they cannot see that duty requires them to maintain their cause here at all hazards. Our Convention meets the last Thursday of this month. And of this be assured, the cause of truth still lives in Illinois, and will not want defenders. Whether our paper starts again will depend on our friends. East, West, North, and South. So far as depends on me it shall go. By the blessing of God, I will never abandon the enterprise so long as I live, and until success has crowned it. And there are those in Illinois who join me in this sentiment. And if I am to die it cannot be in a better cause.

Yours in the cause of truth and holiness,

ELIJAH P. LOVEJOY

CHAPTER XIV

Though cast down our brother was not destroyed. And notwithstanding the many discouragements which surrounded him, about the middle of October he sent for another press. Three, as will be recollected, had already been destroyed. One on his arrival, on the 21st of July, 1836, one on the 21st of August, 1837, and one on the 21st of September following. This last press he sent for on his own account, and at that time had not determined where it should be established. And here it will be proper to say a word in explanation of his "wish and determination" to leave Alton, as there has been some misapprehension on this point. His own judgment of the matter was always, that the press ought to remain at Alton, and be maintained there at all hazards. At the same time he thought it a sinful waste of property, to bring presses there to be thrown into the Mississippi, and consequently if friends remained idle and indifferent, and foes vigilant and active, it must of course be removed to some other place. His friends in Quincy were waiting to welcome and protect his press, and he felt disposed to go there, provided a sufficient number of friends could not be found in Alton to sustain it. We speak confidently on this subject, as one of us was with our brother at this time, and remember to have had a full and free conversation on this very point, viz., the unpleasant attitude of an individual placed in direct opposition to a large portion of his fellow citizens, and the duty of maintaining it. And the conclusion was, that a fair experiment had been made as to the protection to be expected from the civil authorities, and that unless volunteers appeared in the defense of the laws, it would be a hopeless contest. These conversations always ended by our brother's remarking, "Well we shall see when the Convention meets."

On the third week of this month, October, the Synod of Illinois held its annual session at Springfield. Here the Editor of the Observer had an opportunity of seeing his brethren from all parts of the state, and was greatly inspirited, and refreshed by the words of encouragement, and approbation which they spake unto him.

In mentioning the adverse influences which were at this time operating against the Anti-Slavery cause, and more or less directly against the Editor of the "Observer" as the organ or representative of that cause, it will be proper to mention a meeting of the Colonization Society of Upper Alton, on Tuesday before the Anti-Slavery Convention, which was to meet on the Thursday following at the same place. The history of this meeting is as follows: A few days previous, one of the most active members of this Society - which by the way had been dead for several years, accosted a very respectable lawyer of that town, and asked him if he would attend an anti-convention meeting and make a speech. The lawyer replied with some warmth and indignation, that if they would get up an anti-mob meeting, he would attend, and make a speech. In consequence of this answer, as it is supposed, they concluded to have a Colonization meeting. *Mutato nomine, idem manet.*

The Speakers were Hon. Cyrus Edwards, and J. M. Peck of Alton, and the Rev. Joel Parker of New Orleans. Mr. Parker represented the Abolitionists as bustling round with a great deal of ardor but with little discretion, and less wisdom, trying with all their might to get a lever under what they considered a great mass of corruption, in order to remove it at once. But like the Grecian philosopher they could find no stand point. Consequently their efforts were vain. He said, moreover, that owing to our associations, we could not respect the black man in this country. As an illustration he said, an Irish nobleman, might have a servant who should pay him almost as much reverence as a slave does his master. She might be amiable, affectionate, and faithful, and secure the love of her master, but he would not respect her. "Now," adds Mr. P. "by some unexpected turn of fortune, let this same servant become possessed of wealth, and let her marry a peer of the land, and be on terms of social intercourse and equality with her former master, and then he will begin to respect her." So, he continued, it is with the black man. Let him go to Africa, and let us think of him as associated with that country, and we shall begin to respect him. And he said he once actually knew a slave, who went to Africa with the name of Dick, - breathed the salubrious air of that climate, cast his slough, and came back Mr. Jones. "Now," says Mr. P., "this prejudice may be wrong, but so it is, and we must act on it." He was followed by Mr. Peck, who charged the Abolitionists as being of amalgamators, and of using abusive and unwarrantable epithets in regard to slaveholders, together with all those other charges so frequently preferred against them.

On Thursday the 26th of October the state Convention met. Attention to this subject had been invited in an editorial article in the "Observer" of the 29th of June, which has already been inserted.

The Editor of the "Observer" was not the first mover in this matter. He had received several letters from aged and judicious friends, suggesting the propriety of such a movement, and asking whether it was not time to make it. Some of these letters were received as early as the preceding spring. The first call, as has been seen, was definite and specific. Subsequently, in order to unite all good men, among whom there was some difference of opinion as to measures, a somewhat modified call was sent forth on an extra sheet of the "Observer." This call spoke of the importance of the subject of Slavery, the impossibility of remaining idle spectators in a moral contest which was agitating our country, and requesting those who "earnestly longed, and prayed for the immediate abolition of Slavery" to meet in Convention, for the benefit of mutual discussion and deliberation; not feeling themselves pledged thereby, to any definite mode of action. This was the substance of the call. It was signed by about two hundred and fifty persons from different parts of the state.

The delegates having convened in the Presbyterian Church in Upper Alton, were tailed to order, and the venerable Dr. Blackburn chosen Chairman. When the motion for Rev. Mr. Graves to be temporary clerk, was put, several voices cried out "no." These were from individuals who came in to disturb, and if possible to interrupt the doings of the Convention. Although the regular members of the Convention, at this time, outnumbered the others, the Chair not knowing the exact state of things, did not declare the vote in the affirmative. After this a desultory, and to some extent an angry and disorderly debate took place, which continued all the afternoon. At the commencement of the disturbance, the Editor of the "Observer" arose, stating the object for which they had met; that individuals from various parts of the state had come there, having been invited so to do, to discuss the subject of Slavery, and declaring that none, save those who entertained similar views to those embodied in the call, had any right to a seat in the Convention; asking them whether they could as gentlemen, come in and interrupt a meeting called for a specific purpose. Upon this, the reading of the call sent forth by himself, and also a subsequent one published by President Beecher, over his own name in one of the papers of that place, was called for.*

*(It will be proper to mention here, that Mr. B.'s name was attached to the first call, but that, as he stated in his note alluded to, it did not combine all the points which he expected it would, and especially as to the invitation, which he wished extended to all friends of the free discussion of the subject of Slavery; to this there was no objection, save that it was feared that the mob taking advantage of this invitation would come in and claim seats.)

When these calls had been read, the mob, through their chief speaker, declared that they responded to them, that they were friends of free discussion, nay courted it, - that they wished to meet the Abolitionists in fair and open field, argument with argument, fact with fact, reason with reason. All this seemed very fair: but mark the sequel. The afternoon of that day, Thursday, having been spent in this manner, they adjourned, without even organizing the meeting, to nine o'clock next morning. They met according to adjournment. The chairman then declared the doings of the meeting on the previous day as out of order, read the call to which two hundred and fifty names were attached, and declared that the test of membership, and that all who would subscribe to it should be considered as members of the Convention. Individuals present who wished, then signed their names, including not a few who were known to be opposed to immediate abolition. The Convention was then organized by the election of Dr. Blackburn for president, together with two secretaries. The forenoon was spent in organizing and adopting rules of debate, and appointing a committee of three to prepare resolutions for discussion. This committee consisted of Rev. Mr. Beecher, Rev. Mr. Turner, and Mr. Linder, who were to report in the afternoon.

It was agreed in the committee room that there should be but one report, although they were not agreed on all the resolutions; and that the chairman of the committee should state to the Convention, the resolutions on which they all agreed, and those which the majority and minority severally reported. This he did, and the report was accepted. The question was on its adoption. A motion was then made, which in reality divided the reports, namely, that the report of the minority, Mr. Linder, representing the Anti- Abolition part of the house, should be adopted. This vote was carried. A motion was then made that the report of the majority be also adopted. On this motion, the Rev. Mr. Hogan contended, that, by adopting the minority's report, they had virtually rejected that of the majority, and it was so decided. One of the resolutions was then discussed through the remainder of the day, and carried. It should be mentioned that throughout the whole day, runners had been on the alert to obtain signers to the call. A great many had thus become members of the Convention, who had no definite notion what they were about. In fact, as their conduct imported, they were "certain lewd fellows of the baser sort, men of Belial." With these the open space around the door, and a part of the aisles were crowded. So that after the adoption of the one resolution which had been discussed, a motion was made to adjourn without day, which was carried by acclamation! This was the free discussion which they desired!

Thus baffled, those who had come there in good faith, agreed to meet the next day at a private house, to form a State Anti-Slavery Society, no doubt now existing as to the propriety of such a measure. This they did. This meeting was composed of some of the most pious, and respected, and judicious men, ministers and laymen, in the state. And here the question whether the "Observer" should be re-established at Alton or not, was fully discussed. Dr. Miles, a gentleman from Cincinnati, said that it was all important that it should maintain its stand there; otherwise, he feared that the tide of violence and outrage, which had flowed from the East, would again flow back; and it was decided that it ought to remain at that place. This vote was unanimous, with the exception of one or two from Alton, who thought that it could not be maintained there. The Editor voted for its continuance; and it is proper to state that he was chosen Corresponding Secretary of the State Society.

The next week another colonization meeting was held, in the Lower Town, at which much the same doctrines were advanced as at the previous one, and by the same speakers. The Rev. Mr. Parker declared it an un-Christian thing to go into a community and promulgate doctrines which were calculated to excite that community, and that he should consider it his duty to refrain from speaking on any subject calculated to disturb, and agitate a people. This was on the last day of October. During this week several meetings of friends were held, at one of which President Beecher discussed, with much ability the propriety and duty of defending the press, which was now daily expected, by physical force. This is not the place for his arguments. He declared, however, that "he would enlist as a common soldier in defense of the law, and in protection of the press: and some who had been inclined toward the extreme "peace principles," as they are called, were convinced that there is, and of rigid ought to be, such a thing as civil government; and that the "powers that be are ordained of God," and consequently they became willing to maintain them.

On the 2d and 3d of November, meetings were held, which in their results and influence assume an importance and interest which otherwise would not belong to them. They may with propriety be considered the star chamber, where the death warrant of our brother was signed, and put into the hands of the mob for its execution. It was not a meeting of the rabble. Christians, and Christian ministers were there. Men who stand high in the estimation of their fellow citizens, and in many respects deservedly so. Had they planted themselves on the law and the right, the "damned spots" which now stain their hands, and will not "out" had not been there.

But we give the proceedings, merely premising that the meeting originated with the enemies of the "Observer," though some of its friends were invited to attend.

PUBLIC MEETING

"At a large and respectable meeting of the citizens of the city of Alton, held at the counting-room of Messrs. John Hogan & Co., on Thursday afternoon, Nov. 2d, 1837; Samuel G. Bailey, Esq. was called to the chair, and William F. D'Wolf appointed secretary.

Mr. Hogan then announced the object of the meeting to be, to take into consideration the present excited state of public sentiment in this city, growing out of the discussion of the Abolition question; and to endeavor to find some common ground, on which both parties might meet for the restoration of harmony and good fellowship by mutual concession - expressing a fervent wish that so desirable an object might be carried into effect.

He was followed by the Rev. Edward Beecher, of Jacksonville, who stated that the proposal of such a meeting had originated from Mr. Hogan, and that it had been deemed advisable by him and by Mr. Oilman, that the following resolutions, should be laid before the meeting for their consideration.

1. *Resolved*, That the free communication of thoughts and opinions, is one of the invaluable rights of man; and that every citizen may freely speak, write, and print on any subject, being responsible for the abuse of that liberty.

2. *Resolved*, That the abuse of this right is the only legal ground for restraining its use.

3. *Resolved*, That the question of abuse must be decided solely by a regular civil court, and in accordance with the law; and not by an irresponsible and unorganized portion of the community, be it great or small.

4. *Resolved*, For restraining what the law will not reach, we are to depend solely on argument and moral means, aided by the controlling influences of the spirit of God; and that these means, appropriately used, furnish an ample defense against all ultimate prevalence of false principles and unhealthy excitement.

5. *Resolved*, That where discussion is free and unrestrained, and proper means are used, the triumph of the truth is certain; and that with the triumph of truth the return of peace is sure; but that all attempts to check or prohibit discussion, will cause a daily increase of excitement, until such checks or prohibitions are removed.

6. *Resolved*, That our maintenance of these principles should be independent of all regard to persons or sentiments.

7. *Resolved*, That we are more especially called on to maintain them in case of unpopular sentiments or persons; as in no other cases will any effort to maintain them be needed.

8. *Resolved*, That these principles demand the protection of the Editor and of the press of the 'Alton Observer,' on grounds of principle solely, and altogether disconnected with approbation of his sentiments, personal character, or course, as Editor of the paper.

9. *Resolved*, That on these grounds alone, and irrespective of all political, moral, or religious differences, but solely as American citizens, from a sacred regard to the great principles of civil society, to the welfare of our country, to the reputation and honor of our city, to our own dearest rights and privileges, and those of our children, we will protect the press, the property, and the Editor of the 'Alton Observer,' and maintain him in the free exercise of his rights, to print and publish whatever he pleases, in obedience to the supreme laws of the land, and under the guidance and direction of the constituted civil authorities, he being responsible for the abuse of this liberty only to the laws of the land."

The meeting was then addressed at some length by Mr. Linder, in opposition to the resolutions; after which Mr. Hayden moved that the resolutions be laid on the table. At the suggestion of Mr. Hogan and Col. Botkin, this motion was subsequently withdrawn by the mover; when Mr. Hogan moved that the resolutions be referred to a committee, with instructions to report at an adjourned meeting. This motion was agreed to; and, it being ordered that said committee should consist of seven gentlemen, to be nominated by the chair, the Hon. Cyrus Edwards, and Messrs. John Hogan, Stephen Griggs, U. F. Linder, H. G. Van Wagenen, Thos. G. Hawley, and Winthrop S. Gilman, were appointed.

Mr. Linder then offered the following resolution, which was agreed to:

Resolved, unanimously, by this meeting, That in the interim between the adjournment and re-assembling hereof, if any infraction of the peace be attempted by any party or set of men in this community, we will aid to the utmost of our power in the maintenance of the laws."

The meeting then adjourned to meet at the court room, on Friday the 3d inst., at two o'clock, P. M.

Friday, Nov. 3d, 2 o'clock, P. M.

"The citizens met, pursuant to adjournment: and the meeting being called to order by the chairman, Mr. Linder offered the following resolution, which was unanimously agreed to without debate: -

Resolved, That this meeting shall be composed exclusively of the citizens of Madison County; and that it is requested that none others shall vote or take part in the discussion of any subject that may be offered for their consideration; but all persons in attendance, other than citizens, will consider themselves as welcome spectators.

The Hon. Cyrus Edwards, from the committee appointed at the previous meeting, then made the following report; which was read:

'The committee appointed to take under consideration certain resolutions submitted at our last meeting, beg leave to report: that they have given to those resolutions a deliberate and candid examination, and are constrained to say that, however they may approve their general spirit, they do not consider them, as a whole, suited to the exigency which has called together the citizens of Alton. It is notorious, that fearful excitements have grown out of collisions of sentiment between two great parties on the subject, and that these excitements have led to excesses on both sides deeply to be deplored. Too much of crimination and recrimination have been indulged. On the one hand, the Anti-Abolitionists have been charged with a heartless cruelty, a reckless disregard of the rights of man, and an insidious design, under deceptive pretexts, to perpetuate the foul stain of Slavery. They have been loaded with many and most opprobrious epithets, such as pirates, man-stealers, etc. etc. On the other hand, the Abolitionists have been too indiscriminately denounced as violent disturbers of the good order of society, willfully incendiary and disorganizing in their spirit, wickedly prompting servile insurrections, and traitorously encouraging infractions of the constitution, tending to disunion, violence and bloodshed. These uncharitable impeachments of motives have led to an appalling crisis, demanding of every good citizen the exertion of his utmost influence to arrest all acts of violence, and to restore harmony to our once peaceful and prosperous, but now distracted city. It is not to be disguised, that parties are now organizing and arming for a conflict, which may terminate in a train of mournful consequences. Under such circumstances, have we been convened. And your committee are satisfied that nothing short of a generous forbearance, a mild spirit of conciliation, and a yielding compromise of conflicting claims, can compose the elements of discord, and restore quiet to this agitated community. They are, therefore, forced to regard the resolutions under consideration as falling short of the great end in view; as demanding too much of concession on the one side, without equivalent concession on the other. Neither party can be expected to yield everything, and to acknowledge themselves exclusively in the wrong. In this there is no compromise. There must be a mutual sacrifice of prejudices, opinions, and interests, to accomplish the desired reconciliation - such a sacrifice as led to the adoption of the great charter of American freedom; which has secured to ourselves, and which promises a continuance to our posterity, of the blessed fruits of peace, prosperity and union. Whilst, therefore, we fully and freely recognize the justness of the principles engrafted upon our constitutions, that the free communication of thoughts and opinions is one of the invaluable rights of man, and that every citizen may freely speak, write, and print on any subject, being responsible for the abuse of that liberty; that the abuse of this right is the only legal ground for restraining its use; that the question of abuse must be decided solely by a regular civil court, and in accordance with the law, and not by an irresponsible and unorganized portion of the community, be it great or small - your committee would, with earnest importunity, urge as a means of allaying the acrimony of party strife, the unanimous adoption of the following preamble and resolutions:

Whereas, it is of the utmost importance that peace, harmony, order, and a due regard to law, should be restored to our distracted community; and whereas, in all cases of conflicting opinions about rights and privileges, each party should yield something in the spirit and form of compromise: Therefore,

1. *Resolved*, That a strong confidence is entertained that our citizens will abstain from all undue excitements, discountenance every act of violence to person or property, and cherish a sacred regard for the great principles contained in our Bill of Rights.

2. *Resolved*, That it is apparent to all good citizens, that the exigencies of the place require a course of moderation in relation to the discussion of principles in themselves deemed right, and of the highest importance; and

that it is no less a dictate of duty than expediency to adopt such a course in the present crisis.

3. *Resolved*, That so far as your committee have possessed the means of ascertaining the sense of the community, in relation to the establishment of a religious newspaper, such a course would, at a suitable time, and under the influence of judicious proprietors and editors, contribute to the cause of religion and good citizenship, and promote the prosperity of the city and country.

4. *Resolved*, That while there appears to be no disposition to prevent the liberty of free discussion, through the medium of the press or otherwise, as a general thing; it is deemed a matter indispensable to the peace and harmony of this community that the labors and influence of the late Editor of the 'Observer' be no longer identified with any newspaper establishment in this city.

5. *Resolved*, That whereas it has come to the knowledge of your committee that the late Editor of the 'Observer' has voluntarily proposed to the proprietors and stockholders of the 'Alton Observer,' to relinquish his interest and connection with that paper, if, in the opinion of his friends, that course were expedient; your committee consider that such a course would highly contribute to the peace and harmony of the place, and indicate on the part of the friends of the 'Observer,' a disposition to do all in their power to restore the city to its accustomed harmony and quiet.

6. *Resolved*, That we would not be understood as reflecting in the slightest degree upon the private character or motives of the late Editor of the 'Alton Observer,' by anything contained in the foregoing resolutions."

Mr. Linder then, took the floor, in support and explanation of the views taken by the committee, and urged the adoption of the resolutions reported by them with much earnestness. When he closed his remarks, Winthrop S. Oilman, Esq., one of the committee, handed the following protest against some of the sentiments expressed in the report; which he desired should be made a part of the record of the meeting.

W. S. Oilman, from the committee, protested against so much of the report as is contained in the resolutions; alleging it as his opinion, that the rigid enforcement of the law would prove the only sure protection of the rights of citizens, and the only safe remedy for similar excitements in future.

The Rev. E. P. Lovejoy, Editor of the 'Observer,' here addressed the meeting at some length, in a speech declaratory of his right, under the Constitution of this state, to print and publish his opinions, and of his determination to stand on this right, and abide the consequences, under a solemn sense of duty.

He was followed by Mr. Hogan, who took a wholly different view of the subject; and contended that it was the duty of Mr. Lovejoy, as a Christian and patriot, to abstain from the exercise of some of his abstract rights under existing circumstances. In the course of his remarks, the former referred to the pledge said to have been publicly given by the latter, when he first came to Alton; and observed, that at that time he most certainly did understand Mr. L. to say, that, inasmuch as he had left a slaveholding state, and had come to reside in a free State, he did not conceive it his duty to advocate the cause of emancipation, and did not intend doing so.

The Rev. F. W. Graves then rose in explanation; and asked Mr. Hogan whether Mr. Lovejoy did not, at the time referred to, distinctly state that he yielded none of his rights, to discuss any subject which he saw fit. Mr. Hogan replying in the affirmative, Mr. G. proceeded to remark, that when Mr. L. arrived in this city, he entertained the views attributed to him by the gentleman who had just taken his seat; that a change had subsequently taken place in his opinions; and that, at a certain meeting of the friends of the 'Observer,' he (Mr. L.) had made known this alteration in his sentiments, and asked advice whether it was best to come out in public on the subject. That, under the circumstances of the case, it was deemed most proper to let the paper go on - there then being no excitement in the public mind. Mr. G. next alluded to the present excited state of the popular feeling; and said that the friends of the 'Observer' had lately received communications from all parts of the country, and even from Kentucky, Missouri, and Mississippi, urging the necessity of re-establishing the press.

Mr. Linder followed in reply; and said he now understood the whole matter. It was a question, whether the interest and feelings of the citizens of Alton should be consulted; or whether we were to be dictated to by foreigners, who cared nothing but for the gratification of their own inclinations, and the establishment of certain abstract principles, which no one, as a general thing, ever thought of questioning. He concluded his remarks by offering the following resolution.

Resolved, That the discussion of the doctrines of immediate Abolitionism, as they have been discussed in the columns of the 'Alton Observer,' would be destructive of the peace and harmony of the citizens of Alton, and that, therefore, we cannot recommend the re-establishment of that paper, or any other of a similar character, and conducted with a like spirit.

The resolution having been read, Mr. Edwards rose, and expressed the hope that its adoption would not be pressed at this moment. He dwelt with great earnestness and effect on the importance of calmness in our deliberations; and trusted that the present meeting would be productive of good to the community. The resolution was then laid on the table.

Judge Hawley then made a few very eloquent and appropriate remarks, on the subject for which this meeting had been called: and concluded by offering the following preamble and resolution; which were read, and laid on the table for the present.

Whereas, great and general excitement has for some time past prevailed with the people of the city of Alton, in relation to the publication of the doctrines of Abolition, as promulgated by Mr. E. P. Lovejoy, in a paper called the 'Alton Observer;' and whereas, as a consequence of that excitement, personal violence has been resorted to in the destruction of said press: Therefore,

Resolved, That whilst we decidedly disapprove of the doctrines, as put forth by the said Lovejoy, as subversive of the great principles of our union, and of the prosperity of our young and growing city, we at the same time as decidedly disapprove of all unlawful violence.

The question on agreeing to the report of the committee was then called for; and, on motion of Mr. Hogan, the resolutions being taken up separately, were severally disposed of as follows: resolutions 1, 2, and 4, were agreed to unanimously; and resolutions 3, 5, and 6, were Stricken out. The report, as amended, was then agreed to.

The resolution offered by Mr. Linder, and laid on the table, was then taken up, and agreed to; as was also that subsequently introduced by Judge Hawley, after striking out the preamble from the latter.

Mr. Krum then offered the following resolution; which was also agreed to.

Resolved, That as citizens of Alton, and the friends of order, peace, and constitutional law, we regret that persons and editors from abroad have seen proper to interest themselves so conspicuously in the discussion and agitation of a question, in which our city is made the principal theatre."

The meeting then adjourned, *sine die.*

SAM'L G. BAILEY, *Chairman,*

W. F. D'WoLF, Secretary.

These proceedings speak for themselves. Some of the speeches were of a most violent kind, attacking not only Abolition, but religion and its ministers. It will be seen that by rejecting the third resolution, they virtually declared that no religious paper would be tolerated, although under the management of "judicious proprietors and editors," and started at a "proper time."

The remarks of our brother referred to in the doings of the meeting, were as follows.

Having obtained the floor, he went to the desk in front of the assembly, and said:

"Mr. Chairman - it is not true, as has been charged upon me, that I hold in contempt the feelings and sentiments of this community, in reference to the question which is now agitating it. I respect and appreciate the feelings and opinions of my fellow citizens, and it is one of the most painful and unpleasant duties of my life, that I am called upon to act in opposition to them. If you suppose, sir, that I have published sentiments contrary to those generally held in this community, because I delighted in differing from them, or in occasioning a disturbance, you have entirely misapprehended me. But, sir, while I value the good opinion of my fellow citizens, as highly as any one, I may be permitted to say, that I am governed by higher considerations than either the favor or the fear of man. I am impelled to the course I have taken, because I fear God. As I shall answer it to my God in the great day, I dare not abandon my sentiments, or cease in all proper ways to propagate them.

"I, Mr. Chairman, have not desired, or asked any compromise. I have asked for nothing but to be protected in my rights as a citizen - rights which God has given me, and which are guaranteed to me by the constitution of my country. Have I, sir, been guilty of any infraction of the laws? Whose good name have I injured? When and where have I published anything injurious to the reputation of Alton? Have I not, on the other hand, labored, in common, with the rest of my fellow citizens, to promote the reputation and interests of this city? What, sir, I ask, has been my offence? Put your finger upon it - define it - and I stand ready to answer for it. If I have committed any crime, you can easily convict me. You have public sentiment in your favor. You have your juries, and you have your attorney, (looking at the Attorney-General,) and I have no doubt you can convict me. But if I have been guilty of no violation of law, why am I hunted up and down continually like a partridge upon the mountains? Why am I threatened with the tar-barrel? Why am I waylaid every day, and from night to night, and my life in jeopardy every hour?

"You have, sir, made up, as the lawyers say, a false issue; there are not two parties between whom there can be a compromise. I plant myself, sir, down on my unquestionable rights, and the question to be decided is, whether I shall be protected in the exercise, and enjoyment of those rights - that is the question, sir; - whether my property shall be protected, whether I shall be suffered to go home to my family at night without being assailed, and threatened with tar and feathers, and assassination; whether my afflicted wife, whose life has been in jeopardy, from continued alarm and excitement, shall night after night be driven from a sick bed into the garret to save her life from the brickbats and violence of the mobs; *that sir, is the question.*" Here, much affected and overcome by his feelings, he burst into tears. Many, not excepting even his enemies, wept - several sobbed aloud, and the sympathies of the whole meeting were deeply excited. He continued. "Forgive me, sir, that I have thus betrayed my weakness. It was the allusion to my family that overcame my feelings. Not, sir, I assure you, from any fears on my part. I have no personal fears. Not that I feel able to contest the matter with the whole community, I know perfectly well I am not. I know, sir, that you can tar and feather me, hang me up, or put me into the Mississippi, without the least difficulty. But what then? Where shall I go? I have been made to feel that if I am not safe at

Alton, I shall not be safe anywhere. I recently visited St. Charles to bring home my family, and was torn from their frantic embrace by a mob. I have been beset night and day at Alton. And now if I leave here and go elsewhere, violence may overtake me in my retreat, and I have no more claim upon the protection of any other community than I have upon this; and I have concluded, after consultation with my friends, and earnestly seeking counsel of God, to remain at Alton, and here to insist on protection in the exercise of my rights. If the civil authorities refuse to protect me, I must look to God; and if I die, I have determined to make my grave in Alton."

A writer who was present, after giving the substance of these remarks, observes:

"His manner - but I cannot attempt to describe it. He was calm and serious, but firm and decided. Not an epithet or unkind allusion escaped his lips, notwithstanding he knew he was in the midst of those who were seeking his blood, and notwithstanding he was well aware of the influence that that meeting, if it should not take the right turn, would have in infuriating the mob to do their work. He and his friends had prayed earnestly that God would overrule the deliberations of that meeting for good. He had been all day communing with God. His countenance, the subdued tones of his voice, and whole appearance indicated a mind in a peculiarly heavenly frame, and ready to acquiesce in the will of God, whatever that might be. I confess to you, sir, that I regarded him at the time, in view of all the circumstances, as presenting a spectacle of moral sublimity, such as I had never before witnessed, and such as the world seldom affords. It reminded me of Paul before Festus, and of Luther at Worms."

The press was now daily expected. Consequently there was no little excitement and anxiety. As soon as the puff of a boat was heard, the friends started for the landing-place to receive and protect it. The mob were no less vigilant, and had declared that it should be destroyed at the landing. One of their number was stationed at St. Louis - where all the boats touch on their way up the river, to ascertain when it arrived. A friend also remained there for about a week waiting its arrival, and prepared to act in concert with those at Alton. An arrangement was at one time made, to have it landed at a place called Chippewa, about five miles down the river, and conveyed secretly to Upper Alton. But not coming the day that it was expected, and the roads becoming bad in consequence of heavy rains, that plan was abandoned. At length it came into St. Louis on Sunday night the 5th, and by expresses, an arrangement was made with the Captain to land it at three o'clock Monday night, or rather Tuesday morning. The exact time of its arrival was known to a few only, though that a press was expected, was known throughout the city. On Monday Mr. W. S. Gilman and our brother went to the Mayor, told him of the expected arrival of the press, and of the threats made of destroying it, which indeed were notorious; and requested that special constables might be appointed to keep the peace. This request the Mayor communicated to the Common Council, stating at the same time, that from the confidence placed in the persons making these representations, as well as from what he himself knew, he had good reason to believe that there would be some infraction of the laws, and submitted to them whether some action would not be necessary. After a few moments silence, Mr. King, one of the aldermen, moved "that a note be addressed to Mr. Lovejoy and his friends, requesting them not to persist in establishing an Abolition press in Alton, and setting forth the reasons for the same." We have a paper signed by the Clerk of the Common Council containing the above, as an extract from the records of the said Council. The phrase "setting forth the reasons for the same," is obscure. Probably it means setting forth the reasons to "Mr. Lovejoy and his friends why they should not establish an Abolition press." The Mayor told them that that vote was not answering the proposition which he made to them, and that consequently he should not sign it if passed. It was laid on the table, and the Council adjourned, and nothing more was done about it. On Monday evening between forty and fifty citizens met in the warehouse of Godfrey, Oilman & Co., where the press was to be stored, in order to form themselves into a volunteer company, to act under the direction of the Mayor, in defense of the law. About ten o'clock several left; not far from thirty remaining in the building, with one of the city constables to command them. They were armed with rifles and muskets, mostly the former, loaded with buckshot or small balls. The Editor of the "Observer" was not there. His dwelling had been attacked but a few nights before, and himself and sister narrowly escaped being hit with a heavy brickbat, sufficient to take life. In consequence of the nightly expectation of an assault, he made arrangements with a brother then with him, to watch alternately every other night, at home and at the store. At three o'clock the boat arrived containing the long looked for press. It was a light night, and the sentinel of the mob had been seen, at intervals all night on the shore, who immediately gave the alarm, and horns were blown throughout the city. As soon as the boat was heard, the Mayor was called, and came into the building. He requested those within to remain there, and keep quiet, till called upon. He said he should go out and attend the storing of the press, and if any mob collected should command them to disperse - if they refused, and offered any violence, he should command those in the building to fire.

Owing, however, to the lateness of the hour, the mob were unable to muster their forces, to any considerable number, and the press was stored without molestation, except the firing of a few stones. The press thus safely-deposited in the garret of a firm stone warehouse, was thought to be secure. The great contest was expected at the landing, as it would be more difficult to protect it there, and of course additional advantages would be afforded the mob for its destruction.

No very unusual excitement prevailed on Tuesday, though it was noised through the city that "the Abolition press" had arrived. On Tuesday night the volunteers already spoken of again met at the same place. At nine, all but twelve (one or two dropped in afterwards) went away. Our brother remained, who with one or two others, was the only Abolitionist there. They were there not as Abolitionists but as citizens.

And here it will be proper to describe the building, so that the reader may have a clear conception of the scene. The Mississippi River, whose general course, as is known, is southerly, at this point runs nearly east. The building is composed of two stores, with two separate roofs, communicating with each other within. The gable ends are north and south - one of them of course, next the river. All the windows, and also all the doors, with the exception of one which opens into the basement story on the east side, are in the two gable ends. It is three stories high on the north end, and four on the south, the one next the river. It stands alone; a street being on the north end, the river on the south, and several rods open space on the two sides, so that it is accessible on all points.

About ten o'clock, the drunkeries and coffee-houses began to belch forth their inmates, and a mob of about thirty individuals, armed, some with stones, and some with guns and pistols,* formed themselves into a line on the south end of the store next the river, knocked and hailed the store. Those within were stationed in different parts of the building. Mr. Oilman, one of the owners of the store, asked them from the garret door, what they wanted. Their leader, William Carr, replied, "the press." Mr. Gilman then told them that it would not be given up, and added, "we have no ill feelings towards any of you, and should much regret to do you any injury; but we are authorized by the Mayor to defend our property, and shall do so with our lives." Carr again replied that they had determined to have it even at the sacrifice of their lives, and presented a pistol towards Mr. G., who then retired into the building. The mob then went round to the opposite end of the warehouse, and commenced throwing stones, which soon demolished several windows. Those in the building had agreed not to fire unless their lives were endangered. After throwing stones for some time, the mob fired two or three guns into the building, without however wounding any one. The fire was then returned from within, two or three guns discharged upon the rioters, several of their number wounded, and one by the name of Bishop, mortally. This checked the efforts of the mob and they departed, carrying away those that were wounded. The number is not known as they were concealed by their friends. After a visit to the rum-shops, they returned with ladders and other materials to set fire to the roof of the warehouse, shouting with fearful imprecations and curses, "Burn them out, burn them out!" They now kept themselves on the side of the building where there were no windows, so that they could not be annoyed or driven away by those within the building, unless they came out. This of course would be extremely dangerous, as the night was perfectly clear, and the moon at its full. The Mayor and Justice Robbins were then deputed by the mob to bear a flag of truce to those within, proposing as terms of capitulation, that the press should be given up, and on that condition, they might be permitted to depart unmolested, and that no other property should be destroyed. The Mayor made known the terms of surrender to the little band, at the same time informing them that the mob had determined to fire the building. They promptly replied, that they came there to defend their property, and should do it. Mr. Oilman then requested him to call upon certain citizens to prevent the burning of the store. The Mayor replied, that so numerous were the mob, and so desperate withal, that he could do nothing but command and persuade, which he had already tried without effect. He was then asked if they should defend their property with arms, he replied as he had repeatedly before, that they had a perfect right so to do, and that the law justified that course. On returning and reporting the result of his embassy, the mob set up a shout, and rushed on with cries of "Fire the building, fire the building," "Burn 'em out, burn 'em out," "shoot every d----d Abolitionist as he leaves."

It was now near midnight. The bells had been rung and a large concourse of citizens assembled, who stood inactive spectators of these deeds of arson and murder. The mob now raised their ladders and placed them on the north-east corner of the store, and kindled a fire on the roof, which although of wood, did not burn very readily. About five individuals now volunteered to go out and drive them away. They left the building on the south end, came round to the south-east corner of the building, turned the angle, and two or three fired upon the man on the ladder, drove him away and dispersed the mob. They then returned into the store and re-loaded. Our brother and *Mr. Weller, with one or two others again stepped to the door, and, seeing no one, stood looking round just without the threshold, our brother being a little before the others and more exposed. Several of the mob had in the meantime, concealed themselves behind a pile of lumber that lay at a short distance. One of them had a two-barreled gun and fired. Our brother received five balls, three in his breast, two on the left and one on the right side, one in the abdomen, and one in his left arm. He turned quickly round into the store, ran hastily up a flight of stairs, with his arms across his breast, came into the counting-room, and fell, exclaiming, "Oh God, I am shot," "I am shot," and expired in a few moments. Mr. Weller received a ball in the calf of his leg, but has since recovered. Some in the building were for continuing the conflict, but they finally resolved to yield. One of their number the Rev. Mr. Harned, then went up to the scuttle, and informed the mob that Mr.

Lovejoy was dead and that they would give up the press, provided they might be allowed to escape unmolested. When this announcement was made the mob set up a yell of exultation which rent the very heavens, and swore that they should all find a grave where they were. Mr. Roff then determined to go out at all hazards and to make some terms if possible. As soon as he had opened the door, and placed one foot without, he was fired upon and wounded in the ankle. He too has nearly recovered. A Mr. West then came to the door on the north end of the store, and cried to those within, "For God's sake leave the building and let them in or all the property will be destroyed," stating also that the roof was already on fire, and that it was useless to remain. All except two or three then laid down their arms, left the building at the southern door, and fled down the river. As they escaped, they were fired upon by the mob, and one individual had a ball pass through his coat near his shoulder. The mob then rushed into the building, - the fire being extinguished - threw the press out of the window upon the shore, broke it to pieces, and threw it into the river. They destroyed no other property except a few guns. They offered no indignity to their murdered victim, who lay on a cot in the counting-room. Dr. S. M. Hope, one of their number, insisted on taking the ball from Mr. Weller's leg, but he refused, saying that he would rather die than receive assistance from one of the mob.

About two o'clock the mob dispersed. On the door of the building where some of those who had escaped had taken refuge, figures of coffins were drawn, under which was written, "Ready-made coffins for sale, inquire of etc.," referring to individuals who had been in the store that night.

The next morning the bloody remains of our brother, were removed by a few friends from the warehouse to his dwelling; and as the hearse moved slowly along through the street, it was saluted with jeers and scoffs, which showed that the hatred of his enemies still raged in their breasts, unsatisfied even with his blood. One who had been a principal actor in the horrid tragedy of the previous night, said, "If he had a fife he would play the dead march for him." He was buried on Thursday the ninth of November, just thirty-five years from the day of his birth. There was not a large number who attended his funeral. He looked perfectly natural, but little paler than usual, and a smile still resting upon his lips. He sleeps in a grave-yard a short distance from his dwelling, between two large oak trees, one standing at his head and one at his feet.

His wife was not at home at the time of his death, having gone to Upper Alton, that same day in order to avoid that state of continual alarm and apprehension, which attended her while at Alton. When told that her husband was killed, she sank down senseless, "trembling," says one present, "as though an arrow had pierced her heart." She remained in this state for several days, so that she was not able to attend the burial of her husband. After her partial recovery she stopped for a few days at her house. On the day she left Alton for her mother's at St. Charles, where she now is, she rode to the grave of her husband. She wept freely but was not very much agitated. She said on her return, that she hoped she might live to train up her little son to imitate the example of his father.

She has but one little boy, Edward Payson, who was born in March, 1836. If she lives she will probably give birth to another child. Her health is now, February, 1838, comparatively good.

That our brother, for we knew him well, has gone to a world where hatred cannot disturb, nor violence injure, we cannot doubt. We cannot doubt that those ties which twined so closely around his heart, and which were so rudely and wickedly sundered, have been healed in that place of peace and blessedness dimly shadowed forth in the following lines from his own pen.

From the Alton Telegraph, January 21st, 1838

*RIOT TRIALS

Contrary to general expectation, the persons recently indicted for having participated in the fatal riot of the 7th of November, were brought to trial on Wednesday and Friday of last week, and severally acquitted - the assailants and defendants being tried on different days. Our business engagements having put it out of our power to attend in either case, we are indebted for the following brief notes of both trials to the politeness of two gentlemen present, who have kindly furnished them at our request.

"On Wednesday last, our City Court was occupied from half-past nine in the morning until ten at night, in the trial of the cause of the People vs. Enoch Long, T. B. Hurlbut, Wm. Harned, Geo. A. Walworth, A. B, Roff, Winthrop S. Gilman, James Morss, Jr., George H. Whitney, John S. Noble, Henry Tanner, Royal Weller, and Reuben Gerry, upon an indictment fora riot on the memorable night of the 7th November last, in defending a printing press then in the possession of Godfrey, Oilman & Co. The indictment contained two counts; one of which charged the defendants with resisting an attack made by certain persons unknown, to destroy a printing press, the property of Godfrey and Gilman, and then being in their possession; the other count charged the defendants with unlawfully defending a certain warehouse - being the property of Godfrey and Gilman, - against an attempt by certain persons to force open and enter the same. Mr. Davis, one of the counsel for Mr. Gilman, moved for a separate trial as to Mr. Gilman; which, after much argument, was granted, upon the condition that the other eleven defendants should stipulate to be tried jointly. At this stage of the cause, a petition signed by some sixty citizens was presented to the court, praying that the Hon. U. F. Linder, Attorney General of the State, might be permitted to assist the City Attorney in the prosecution of the indictment. The court, in answer to the petition, remarked, that it was wholly without its province to interfere with the subject matter of the petition; inasmuch as the City Attorney alone, could say who should and who should not assist him; and consequently, the court, in discharge of its duty, and with all respect for the petitioners, would be compelled to deny the request; but that the Attorney General could appear in the cause, if the counsel for the people and the defendant should so consent. Mr. Davis then arose, and stated to the court, that neither Mr. Gilman nor his counsel had any objection whatever to the Attorney General's appearing on behalf of the People. The City Attorney consenting, Mr. Linder appeared in aid of the prosecution.

A jury was without much difficulty impaneled; and the prosecution proceeded in the examination of the testimony, which developed most clearly this whole transaction from its origin down to its lamentable termination. One of the witnesses on the part of the prosecution, H. H. West, Esq. stated, that early in the evening, about dark, a person called upon him, and informed him that a mob was to be gotten up that nighty with a view of destroying the press then in the warehouse of Godfrey, Gilman & Co., and that the assailants had determined to obtain the press, and destroy it, either by burning the warehouse, or blowing it up; that the person giving him the information urged him to go and see Mr. Gilman, and inform him of the fact; that he, in company with E. Keating, Esq. did repair to the warehouse of Mr. Gilman, where he found a number of individuals assembled, all of whom were armed with muskets; and that he there stated to Mr. Gilman what he had been told, and the rumor that was current through the town; that Mr. Gilman expressed great astonishment at the information, and could not credit it; and said he did not expect any attack would be made that evening. Mr. West also stated that the attack commenced on the outside, by throwing a volley of stones at the windows and doors, and that two guns were fired from the outside previous to any guns being fired from within. Mr. Keating corroborated in every respect the testimony of Mr. West, and also testified that the firing of guns commenced on the outside, and at the time the first attack was made upon the building. All the witnesses agreed in this particular; and the Mayor of the city, in his testimony stated that he saw the assailants, when they first went to the warehouse, many of whom were picking up stones as they proceeded towards it, and that one man had a gun. There was one other witness, besides the Mayor, called on behalf of the defendant, who corroborated the statement of the witnesses on the part of the prosecution, as to the attack first being made on the outside with stones and firearms, and who stated further, that he was one of the individuals in the building, who had repaired there with a view of defending it; that it was well understood and agreed among them, that they were in no case to act except upon the defensive; and that a resort to fire-arms was not to be had unless driven to it in the preservation of their lives. He further stated that they all supposed they were acting under the authority of the Mayor. The above is the substance of the testimony, both on the part of the prosecution and the defense, and which will serve to give the public some idea of the facts developed in the cause, until they shall be enabled to see a minute statement of the whole trial, which, we are informed, is now preparing - a gentlemen having taken full notes for that purpose- and which will be published in pamphlet form as soon as the circumstances will admit of it. The counsel for the defendant then proposed to submit the case without argument to the jury; which being objected to on the part of the prosecution, it was summed up by F. B. Murdoch, City Attorney, Samuel G. Bailey, and U. F. Linder, Attorney General, Esq'rs., on the part of the prosecution, and Geo. T. M. Davis and Alfred Cowles, Esq'rs. on the part of the defendant. No instructions being asked for by either side, the cause was submitted after the argument of counsel without any instructions from his honor the Judge to the jury; who, after an absence of ten minutes, returned into court the verdict of Not Guilty. The next morning the City Attorney entered a *nolle prosequi* as to the other eleven defendants.

On Friday, the 19th of January, there came on for trial in the Municipal Court of this city, the case of the People against Frederick Bruchey, William Carr, James M. Rock, David Butler, Horace Beall, Levi Palmer, Nutter, Jennings, and others. Two of the defendants had left the city: the others came in voluntarily, and entered the plea of Not Guilty. The indictment was for riot, and charged that the defendants, on the 7th of November, with force and arms, riotously and routously entered the warehouse of Benjamin Godfrey and Winthrop S. Gilman, and forcibly broke and destroyed a printing press, then and there being, the proper goods and chattels of the said Godfrey and Gilman, contrary to the statute in such case made and provided. An indictment had been found against Winthrop S. Gilman and others, who had entered the said warehouse to defend the press from threatened destruction by the mob without. That indictment was tried on Wednesday, the 17th day of January, which trial resulted in the acquittance of Mr. Gilman, who was tried separately; after which the City Attorney dismissed the prosecution as to the other defendants, jointly indicted with him. This trial having led to an examination of the whole case, as well of those assaulting the warehouse, as of those defending it, the members of the jury of the regular panel had formed opinions in relation to the matter, so as to disqualify themselves. It therefore became necessary to select a new jury from the by-standers, for the purpose of trying the last case.

On the part of the People, it was proved, that the press had arrived by steamboat a day or two previous to the 7th of November, consigned to Mr. A. B. Roff; but was landed at Messrs. Godfrey and Gilman's warehouse, where it was stored; that said warehouse was built by those gentlemen in 1832, and has been since that time owned and occupied by them, as forwarding and commission merchants; that on the afternoon of November 7th, one of the defendants had told the witness, (H. H. West, Esq.) that the boys were going to attack the warehouse, and that it would be either blown up or burned, unless the press was given up; and that some of the defendants were in a company of about twenty-five, that formed a line from a certain grocery, swearing that they would have the press at all hazards. It was also proved that two guns or pistols were fired from the outside of the warehouse at those within; that showers of stones were discharged against the front of the building, by which the windows were demolished; that during the attack a man named Bishop was shot from the inside of the warehouse; that some of the defendants were seen carrying away his body observing that one of their men had been wounded; that Mr. Gilman addressed the crowd from the third story of the building, requesting them to desist, and stating that he was defending his property, which he felt it his duty to do at the risk of his life; that he was replied to by one of the defendants, as spokesman for the rest, who observed that they were determined to destroy the press, if it cost them their lives.

It was also proved by the Mayor, and S. W. Robbins, a Justice of the Peace, that they identified several of the defendants, with arms in their hands, declaring that they would have the press; that a man was seen going towards the warehouse, with fire in his hands, swearing that he would burn down the building; that a ladder was set up against the side, and the fire actually communicated to thereof; that at this time, Mr. West went in with the Mayor, to propose a capitulation, by which it was stipulated that if those inside would leave the warehouse, and give up the press, they should not be injured, and no other property, except the press, molested; that the building was accordingly abandoned by Mr. Gilman, and its other defenders, as the only means left them to prevent its destruction, and that of their own lives; that they were fired upon by some of the crowd as they retreated; that upon their leaving the warehouse, it was immediately entered by some of the defendants and others; that the press was thrown out, and demolished with a sledge hammer, etc.

This constitutes the sum of the evidence on the part of the prosecution. On the part of the defendants, it was proved by Mr. Gilman that he was not the owner of the press, and had no further interest in it, than the liability of himself and partner for its safe-keeping. After argument by counsel, the case was submitted to the jury, who returned a verdict of Not Guilty. Counsel for the people, F. B. Murdoch, City Attorney, and Alfred Cowles, Esq'rs; for the defense, U. F. Linder, Esq., Attorney General. [See the Mayor's evidence at the end.]

THERE IS AN ISLE

"There is an isle, a lovely isle,
    Which ocean depth's embrace,
Nor man's deceit, nor woman's wile,
    Hath ever found the place.
How sweet 'twould be, if I could find
This isle, and leave the world behind.

See from the heaven-born Pleiades,
    Comes the young-, blooming spring;
Her light car yoked unto a breeze,
    With aromatic wing;
Gaily she drives around its shores.
And scatters all her purple stores.

Ten thousand Naiads sport along,
    Her ever joyous train;
And life and love are poured in song,
    And bliss in every strain;
So soft, so sweet, so bland the while,
That even despair itself would smile.

Eternal calm hangs o'er its plains,
    Its skies are ever fair;
In nectar'd dew descend its rains;
    No fire-charged clouds are there,
To speak in thunder from the path
Of God come down to earth in wrath.

Its silvery streams o'er crystals flow,
    Where sparkling diamonds be,

And, sweetly murmuring, gently go.
    To meet a stormless sea;
And in their clear, reflective tide.
In golden scales the fishes glide.

Melodious songsters fill its groves.
    To harmony attuned;
Where saints and seraphs tell their loves,
    Their golden harps around.
In strains as soft as charmed the hours.
When man was blest in Eden's bowers.

No birds of blood, nor beasts of prey.
    Can in its woodlands breathe;
Peace spreads her wing o'er ev'ry spray,
    And beauty sleeps beneath;
Or wakes to joy her varying note,
From ev'ry golden-feather'd throat.

No gloomy morning ever gleams
    Upon this isle so fair;
No tainted breeze from guilty climes
    Infects the evening air;
For in the light of ev'ry star
Are angels watching from afar.

Oh! I would leave this wretched world,
    Where hope can hardly smile;
And go on wings by faith unfurled,
    To reach this happy isle;
But that some ties still bind me here,
Which while they fetter, still endear.

And I would not that these should part,
    Till He, and He alone.
Who wound them finely round my heart.
    Has cut them one by one:
And when the last is severed, then
Upon this isle 'twill heal again."

                      E. P. L.

Hallowell Gazette, Nov. 7th, 1827

CHAPTER X

We now approach the end of our painful task. A constant attention, for several weeks, to the scenes at Alton, has drawn largely upon the sympathies of the heart. By night and by day the image of a murdered brother has been present to the mind. It has indeed been both soothing and refreshing to trace the abundant evidences, in his public and private writings, that he was "ready to be offered." We have simply narrated the facts in regard to his life, and presented some portion of his writings, according to the best of our judgment and ability. We offer no remark, draw no inferences, make no appeal, seek no coloring. Of the whole painful tragedy, it has been justly said, "no language can exaggerate the naked atrocity of the facts - no oratory can deepen the dark colors - the simple statement is the strongest - the plainest narrative the most condemning."

We had hoped to obtain an engraving which would give an accurate conception of his person. This however was found wholly impracticable as no portrait of him had ever been taken.

He was of middling stature, thick set, his height being about five feet nine inches. His complexion was dark, with black piercing eyes and full countenance. His feelings were naturally ardent. As a man, he was courageous, firm, and independent. As a companion, cheerful and social. As a Christian, meek and prayerful. As a minister, dignified and solemn. As a writer, clear and forcible, drawing at pleasure, for the illustration of his subject, from the stores of a well-furnished memory. In the social relations, as husband, son, and brother, he was kind and sympathizing - greatly beloved.

After his return to the West, in 1833, he acquired and retained a large share of the confidence and esteem of his brethren, in the ministry and in the churches. He was ordained as an evangelist in .Tune, 1834. He was frequently called to attend protracted meetings, and visit the destitute churches in the vicinity of St. Louis and Alton. He felt a lively interest in the various benevolent societies of the West, and was secretary of four or five of them for several years. At the time he left St. Louis, he was moderator of the Presbytery there, and also of the Presbytery at Alton when he died. There is no evidence that the Christian community were at all withdrawing their confidence from him. On the other hand, there is abundant testimony that he had a place in the warm affections of a great majority of the wise and good throughout Illinois, and in many other states. The difficulties which he had to encounter were local - they all arose from his course upon two subjects. Popery and Slavery. The only valid accusation that even his enemies have preferred against him is; that he too much he revered the command, "Thou shalt love thy neighbor as thy thyself." We here insert a letter from the Rev. Dr. Chaplin, who was President of

Waterville College, while our brother was a member of that institution. Also an extract from the sermon of Mr. McKeen.

Willington, Conn., January 30th, 1838
Rev. Jos. C. Lovejoy,

Dear Sir: - In compliance with the wish expressed in your letter of the 15th inst. and repeated in that of the 23cl, I set down to record some things in relation to the late Rev. E. P. Lovejoy, your unfortunate and justly lamented brother.

From the commencement of his collegiate course to the time of his graduation, I was intimately acquainted with him. During this period, he made no pretensions to experimental religion. As far, however, as my acquaintance with him enabled me to judge, he was never chargeable with making light of sacred things, or with favoring the cause of infidelity. According to the best of my recollection, his attendance on the services of the chapel was regular and respectful. I have besides the satisfaction of being able to say, that he sustained a fair moral character, and was exact in his obedience to the laws of the college. He uniformly treated its officers in a gentlemanly manner, and seemed desirous of exerting all the influence he possessed over his fellow-students in favor of order and good morals. I think his natural disposition was kind and amiable. His temperament was, indeed, uncommonly sanguine, as everyone must have perceived who was at all acquainted with him. And this, we should naturally suppose, must frequently have led him to the adoption of measures, or at least to the use of expressions at variance with the dictates of sound reason. There are, some excellent men who, in consequence of possessing too much warmth, are frequently betrayed into indiscretions which greatly diminish both their comfort and usefulness. But this was not the case with Mr. Lovejoy, at least during his residence at Waterville. He had such a fund of good sense and good nature that, although exceedingly ardent, he seldom gave offence, or had cause to be sorry on account of the measures which he adopted. A hundred young men like him might, it seems to me, be more easily governed than half a dozen of those (falsely called) choice spirits, who frequently reside in the walls of a college.

In regard to the intellectual powers of your deceased brother, I do not hesitate to say, that they were of a superior order. He seems to me to have approached very near to the rank of those distinguished men who have been honored with the title of universal geniuses. Du- ring his collegiate course he appeared to have an almost equal adaptation of mind to the various branches of science and literature, usually studied at our seminaries of learning; and, what is more, he took hold of each with giant strength. It was my lot to hear his class in Greek and in metaphysics, and I well remember that in both of these departments of knowledge, he appeared to great advantage at the daily recitations, and also at the examination of his class before the board of visitors. I think he was rather more fond of languages and polite literature, than of intellectual philosophy and the exact sciences. In the latter, however, he acquitted himself in a highly creditable manner.

After what I have said respecting his attainments, it seems almost superfluous to add that he was a close applicant. I mention this as one of his distinguishing excellencies. In the course of my life I have been acquainted with some individuals of fine talents, who, in consequence of their disrelish of intellectual labor, never attained to a very high rank as literary men. And this would, unquestionably, have been the case with your brother, had he not been willing to toil in the pursuit of knowledge. But he was willing to toil by night and by day. And this enabled him, not only to make rapid progress in science and literature himself, but to exert a highly beneficial influence on the progress of his fellow-students.

In closing this communication, I cannot refrain from expressing my sympathy with you, my dear sir, and with your widowed mother and other relations, in view of the heavy afflictions which you have all experienced in the untimely death of one so deservedly dear to your hearts, and my hope that you will not only be supported under it, but find it yield in you the peaceable fruit of righteousness.

With great respect, I am
Your friend and servant,
JER. CHAPLIN

Extracts from a sermon preached at Oldtown, Maine, December 31st, 1837, on the occasion of the massacre of the Rev, Mr. Lovejoy, by request of the mother and other relatives of the deceased in that place, by the Rev. Silas McKeen, of Belfast, from Psalm lxxvi. 10, - "*Surely the wrath of man shall praise Thee.*"

Let us now consider briefly some of the principal objections which have been made to the course which Mr. Lovejoy thought it his duty to pursue.

It has been insisted that no one ought to so go before or run counter to public opinion, as to make himself odious or create disturbance in the community, and that as Mr. Lovejoy did this, he acted imprudently, and virtually forfeited his claim to legal protection. If so, Galileo deserved to be condemned and punished as he was, for daring to invade the Romish darkness by teaching that the earth is a sphere, turning on its axis, and revolving round the sun. William Tindall deserved to be strangled and burned for offering such an insult to public sentiment, as to prepare and publish a translation of the New Testament in English, that his countrymen might have an opportunity of reading for themselves those holy books. And the apostles merited their fate by attempting to bring into contempt the established doctrines and usages of Heathenism, in order to introduce and establish Christianity. The sentiment is base and abominable and ought to be repudiated with scorn.

It has again been said that when Mr. Lovejoy saw that he had excited public indignation, prudence required that he should have gone to some other place. That this in many, perhaps in most cases of persecution, is proper, when practicable, seems evident from our Lord's direction to his apostles, "When they persecute you in this city, flee ye into another." But suppose one to be thrown into such circumstances that no security will be gained, or that important principles will be abandoned, and a dangerous precedent set in, can he flee; is this general rule binding then?

Take the case of Shadrach and his companions who firmly refused to worship the image which their king had set up, and yet attempted not to flee from his wrath; of Daniel, who in view of the peril of being cast into the den of lions, continued to make his prayer publicly unto his God, as he had done aforetime; and of Nehemiah, who, on being informed of the murderous designs of his enemies, and advised to conceal himself in the temple, boldly replied, "Should such a man as I flee? who is there that, being as I am, would go into the Temple to save his life? I will not go in." Our missionaries, Worcester and Butler, remained at their station in opposition to the unconstitutional and unrighteous laws of Georgia, until they were cast into the penitentiary; and were justified by the highest legal tribunal in this nation, in so doing. What shall we say of the conduct of all these men? We cannot but admire it. Our Savior fled several times from his enemies; but when he knew that the time was at hand for him to suffer, he made no further attempt to escape. The primitive martyrs very generally might have saved their lives, by what those who comprehended not their views, considered a very reasonable and easy compliance with public law and sentiment; but they could not yield, because they believed they ought not. So now, a man may be thrown into such a critical and responsible situation, that it would be wrong for him to flee even to save his life. Our lamented friend believed that such was his case, and I see not how it can be proved that his belief in regard to this point was not well founded. If he ought to have quietly yielded to popular prejudice or violence, every editor, every minister, every magistrate, ought, in similar circumstances, to do so; and law and justice are but empty names.

Let those who call him imprudent, provided they are men of principle, be thrown into such circumstances that they must relinquish sacred rights and set dangerous examples by yielding to the dictation of mobs, and they will themselves do what some others who have no sympathy with their objects, will call imprudent. No doubt some considered the Rev. Mr. Parker, of New Orleans, exceedingly imprudent a few years ago, to return to that city, when he knew there was high indignation against him, and to inform the men of influence, who had resolved to drive him away, that he should stay, be the consequences what they might. But he thought he acted, and undoubtedly did act, in a manner worthy of his truly excellent character. Happy is he who condemneth not his brother in the thing that he alloweth.

Again, it has been said that Mr. Lovejoy and his friends had no right to resort to the use of deadly weapons in their defense; that they had no more right to fire on the mob, than the mob had to fire on them; that they were in fact, two mobs conflicting with each other; and that his fall was an evidence of the divine disapprobation of his conduct.

We pretend not that our friend was infallible; we feel under no obligation to justify, indiscriminately, everything which in the midst of his manifold difficulties, and perils and cruel persecutions he may have said and done. But let us look at this matter candidly, and with due discrimination.

If failure and death by violence be evidence of the divine displeasure in regard either to the object or measures pursued, the converse of the proposition must be admitted to be equally true; and then every robber and murderer who has been successful, and escaped with impunity, must be considered as having thereby received indubitable evidence of Heaven's approbation. Even the bloody assassin who shot our brother to the heart, may continue to lift up his blood-stained visage with triumph, inasmuch as he took the sword and has not perished by it. The position cannot be maintained for a moment.

That the men assailed were in any sense a mob, standing in that respect on a level with, the assailants, is a false and base insinuation. As well might you say, that the crew of a merchant vessel, who resist the pirates who attack them, are themselves pirates in so doing; or that those who resist robbers, violators, and murderers, are no better than they. The parties stood on ground altogether different. The one stood in defense of sacred rights; the other came to wrest them away. The one stood on ground environed and secured to them by the constitution and laws of their country; while the other came of their own unauthorized will to break through that enclosure, and to put those who had fled to it for shelter, under the ban of mobocracy.

Again, Mr. Lovejoy and his friends acted with the countenance, and virtually under the authority of the chief officer of that city, whereas their assailants acted in direct contempt of his authority.

Civil governments are ordained of God, and magistrates are appointed by such governments expressly for the purpose of protecting those who do well, and for restraining, punishing, and, if need be, cutting off by death those who violate the order of the community, and the rights of their fellow-men. It is God's will that they should not bear the sword in vain; but act as his ministers, in the character of avengers, to execute wrath upon those who do evil. They ought in all instances to suppress riots, to put down mobs, even by force and arms, when it cannot be otherwise effected. With this view they applied to the Mayor of Alton. He acknowledged the justice of their claim; but owing to the state of public sentiment and feeling there, was not able, or at least did not venture, to furnish them with requisite protection. He told them, however, that they had a right to arm and defend themselves, and in two instances he had acted with them while thus armed, before the night of the fatal encounter; once while President Beecher was delivering an address on Slavery; and again, the night the press was landed. He did not, indeed, require them to arm, but confessed their right, and gave them countenance. On the fatal night he commanded the mob to disperse; but he did not command them to disperse, or to lay down their arms. Single handed he could do nothing, and they were the only men who stood firmly by him in support of the laws. If then you would not condemn a military company who should come forth by the call of authority to put down riot, why will you, so far as the legality of the proceedings is concerned, condemn these persecuted men for acting as they did?

But should it still be insisted on by any, that they were in no sense authorized by the Mayor to defend their property and persons, which we do not admit, yet had they not, according to the constitutions, laws, and usages of all countries, especially of their own, a natural and civil right to defend themselves when their unalienable rights were assailed, and no protection from government could be obtained? Has not the solitary traveler a right to break the robber's grasp from his throat; and to turn away his dirk from his breast, though he should perchance break that robber's arm or head in the attempt? Has not the master of a family, when roused from his couch at the midnight hour, a right to repel with such weapons as he can lay his hand upon, the wretches who are attempting to plunder, violate, and murder his family, and to burn him and them together to hide their iniquity? For my part T have not the shadow of a doubt respecting the right of defense in such cases as these. Neither have I any doubt of the legal right of Mr. Lovejoy to defend himself as he did. All the blood which was shed there on both sides, is, and must forever be on the heads of the rioters; until they apply to such a fountain of purification as -earth cannot afford, to wash it away, and the civil authorities of the place are bound if possible to bring the murderers to justice.

But was not the defense which he attempted contrary to the command of the Savior, which required him to do unto others as he would have them do to him, and therefore morally, religiously, if not legally, wrong? I know not what right we have even on this ground to condemn him. Obedience to this law is not inconsistent with the exercise of civil justice, or the maintenance of unalienable rights. It requires us to cherish benevolence to all, and to do towards others as in reversed circumstances it would be right and best that they should do towards us. Everyone with such light as he can obtain, must decide and act, and answer to God for himself. In regard to the case before us a very worthy minister in Vermont (Rev. Chester Wright of Hardwick) has published this declaration. "I hereby declare that if I ever assault a family with murderous intent, I would that the head of that family resist me unto blood, if he cannot control me otherwise - I would that if I join a mob to destroy a printing press to stifle free discussion, if I assault the defenders of that press, and attempt to lire the building in which they have entrenched themselves, that some lover of his country, some bold defender of its sacred liberties, some generous friend of the oppressed and trodden down slave, under the influence and by the authority of the great law of love, would shoot me dead." Mr. Lovejoy no doubt took the same views of the matter, and fell in the exercise of philanthropy, and with a good conscience towards God.

But if he had a right to attempt defense, was it wise and prudent for him, situated as he was, to use that right? I have been inclined to think it was not. I do think that in pertinaciously defending his rights as he did, when compassed about by an opposition so powerful, he acted injudiciously; in this respect, that he had not sufficient reason to believe that it was possible for him to secure his object. Should a strong band of robbers break into your habitation at night, and having shown you that they had you completely in their power, declare they would spare your life only on condition you would make no resistance, no outcry, let them do what they pleased with your property and family, perhaps prudence, abstractedly considered, might require you to acquiesce in the condition, however cruel. But yet you would find the actual submission a very different thing from mere speculation about its expediency. Charging Mr. Lovejoy with imprudence in seeking to defend his press and life, is one of the severest reflections which can be cast on the authorities and people of Alton. The more evident it is that he acted injudiciously in this attempt, the more manifest it is that a most disgraceful disregard of law, of justice, and even of humanity, prevailed in that city. What would you think of a community where it would be imprudent for you to use your own property and faculties in a lawful manner, and according to your own convictions of duty? But Mr. Lovejoy's imprudence is palliated by two circumstances. One is that friends in whom he placed confidence hoped that he might succeed, and encouraged him to go on. He and they trusted that a stoic of determined resistance would be sufficient, and that no blood would be shed on either side. If the affair had so turned out, his decision would no doubt have been generally commended. The other is that he appears to have believed that even if he failed in securing his immediate object, still the ultimate benefits which would accrue from his effort, would be sufficient to justify any lawful sacrifices by which they might be obtained. And who can disprove it? On this principle the patriotic men who fell in the war of the revolution, were willing to expose their lives in contending for liberty, even unto death. And in the spirit of martyrs our missionary brethren in China are, as we suppose, persisting in their pious efforts under the sword of civil authority uplifted to smite them. They are encouraged by the church in so doing. If tidings should hereafter come that they have been sacrificed, it will undoubtedly be said by many that they acted imprudently in remaining; but still their example of firmness and perseverance, in the midst of perils, will not have been presented in vain, nor their blood have been shed in vain; but like that of the primitive martyrs will multiply converts to righteousness. So if any choose, or feel constrained, to say that our lamented Lovejoy was imprudent, that he acted injudiciously in abiding at his post, and warring for Liberty at such fearful disadvantage with its enemies, still it must be allowed that he acted nobly, and died heroically, and has left an example of invincible firmness in the maintenance of what he believed to be true and right, which is likely to be remembered long, and to have great influence. His work is done, his warfare accomplished, and his spirit gone, we confidently trust, to that blessed world where the remembrance of the scenes of conflict and suffering, through which he and his fellow- worshippers passed while here, will occasion no sorrow; but serve to inspire them all with profound and everlasting admiration of the wisdom and power of their God, who causes the wrath of man to praise him, and restrains the remainder.

Let us now advert, briefly, to a few of the beneficial consequences which under the government of the Almighty, have resulted, and may yet be expected to result from this terrible out-breaking of wrath.

In the first place, it shows to all men, what many have been slow to believe, that the spirit of American slave-holding is deadly hostile to human liberty. What has this spirit done? It has subjected millions of our countrymen to a state of abject bondage, has deprived them of all their inalienable rights, even of the privilege of calling their bodies or souls their own, and debarred them from all means tending to raise them to a more elevated condition. It cannot endure that a word should be uttered, that a sentence should be published, in favor of their elevation to freedom. To prevent this in some of the slave states, the most strict and sanguinary laws have been enacted, subjecting the man to death who shall open his lips in favor of the dumb; and in the absence of such laws in others, men on the slightest suspicion of sympathy for the down trodden, have been seized by infuriated mobs, and under mock forms of justice, treated with barbarous cruelty. Not satisfied with absolute domination in the dark land of the slaves, this spirit of despotism is struggling to grasp and strangle Liberty in the free states, and to subdue all things to itself. The public mail has been broken open and rifled of its contents, that everything tending to enlighten the public mind on the subject of Slavery might be destroyed. Printing presses have been again and again demolished, and their editors, humane and noble-minded men, hunted from place to place by blood-thirsty assassins. Peaceable assemblies have been violently assailed, and even females treated with abuse, because they wished to hear anything on this subject. Officers of colleges have been driven from the seats of learning, and ministers-of the gospel dragged from the altars of God, because they testified against this oppression. The Legislatures of the North and East have been loudly called on by those of the South to silence effectually all discussion of this subject. In the absence of such laws, large premiums have been publicly offered by slaveholders, for the heads of such men in the free states as they considered most forward and able in advocating the duty of emancipation. And now when the Editor of the "Alton Observer" could in no other way be silenced, he has been shot down, beside his press, which slaveholders and their abettors greatly feared, and his murderers are suffered to go unpunished; because the officers of justice either sympathize with, or fear their vengeance. Those balls which pierced his heart were aimed at the heart of Liberty! Your liberty and mine; and intended to strike every one dumb who had dared to advocate the rights and liberty of mankind. This spirit of slaveholding is intolerant of all opposition, however mild, and breathes out threatenings and slaughter against all who would by manly expostulation, induce it to relinquish its grasp upon the throats of its victims. What it has done to Lovejoy it threatens to do to others, who advocate the same cause. Is it not then violently intolerant of all freedom, which interferes in the least with its own acts of unjust and cruel oppression?

Secondly, The Alton tragedy has proved that by the power of truth the encroachments of the slaveholding spirit upon our liberties, may be effectually resisted and its reign everywhere in due season terminated. Why are slaveholders, and those who sympathize with them, so engaged against all who, by speech or the press, publish and animadvert on their laws and usages in regard to the colored people? Why do they stone public lecturers, demolish printing presses, and offer rewards for the heads of Abolitionists? Why have they imbued their hands in the blood of our brother? Why are they so highly exasperated when petitions are sent in to Congress, praying for the termination of Slavery in the District of Columbia, and threaten the dissolution of the Union if those petitions are even read? Why do they attempt to strike down any and every torch which throws its light upon them, as would a company of evil-doers, when at midnight suddenly detected in the midst of their nefarious deeds by the officers of justice? It is my friends, because there is a power in truth which the slaveholding spirit cannot bear. It is conscious that its principles are unsound, that its doings are unjustifiable; and therefore will not come unto the light; will not suffer the light to come into its dark and hateful dominions, lest it should be exposed and reproved. False statements it could easily refute; but truth is endued with fearful energy. Before the power of speech and the press unrestrained, it cannot stand. It is sensible that it cannot, and is therefore making desperate efforts to prostrate and trample down that power. If it fails in this attempt it knows that all its strongholds must be battered down; that its deeds of oppression and violence must be abandoned. Let the light of truth, then, be poured upon this oppressive spirit and its doings, in stronger effulgence than ever. We have no need of carnal weapons in this aggressive warfare; let the light of truth shine as it ought and the spirit of slaveholding will die of itself; nauseated, convulsed, and overwhelmed, with an insupportable conviction of its own loathsomeness.

Thirdly, this terrible out-breaking of human wrath is furnishing slaveholders and those who favor their cause with evidence which must convince them, if not infatuated, that the freedom of speech and of the press cannot be suppressed by violence. True, printing presses have been and may again be destroyed, an editor of distinguished worth has been shot down, because he insisted on the rights which the laws of his country had guaranteed to him. Other editors may be assassinated. But the spirit of freemen has been aroused, and an abundance of other presses are ready for the service; and other editors, talented, high-souled, and self-sacrificing men are ready to succeed to the place which the hand of violence has vacated. When men contend for principle, for what they deem their sacred and inalienable rights, threats and deeds of violence, and gag-laws cannot effectually restrain them; but on the contrary, they call forth the mighty, the indomitable, deathless energies of the soul to make more determined and persevering efforts. So it has been in all times past; is now, and ever will be.

Therefore, finally, we trust that God will make the wrath of man exhibited at Alton, eminently instrumental of accomplishing the downfall of Slavery, The whole subject is undergoing a new examination, and the true nature of it is being better understood. Those who were previously enlisted in the cause of human rights are fired with new zeal, and grasp their principles with stronger determination to defend and propagate them. New friends are coming forth to enlist in the cause, and more will now, probably, be effected in one year for the benefit of the down trodden, than would have been done in several, if this costly sacrifice of our brother's blood had not been poured out upon the altar of liberty - had not been shed in defense of his and our sacred rights. And on you, free men, free women, and free children, the voice of that blood, the groan of millions of your fellow-countrymen deprived of all their inalienable rights, the menaces and outrages of slaveholders, and the authority of your God, are all, in different ways, but with concentrated power, calling loudly, that you see that no man deprive you of your proper liberty, or be suffered to encroach upon it at all; that in the use of this liberty you never encroach on that of others or give countenance to those who do; but boldly plead the cause of the oppressed; and never cease from an enlightened, benevolent, most determined and vigorous opposition to Slavery, until you shall be released by death, or Slavery shall be exterminated from the world. Truth, benevolence, and equity, must, and will prevail.

I would speak a word to this bereaved mother, and these other mourners, on whom this cruel out-breaking of wrath has burst with such desolating fury. But what can I say? My dear friends enter into the secret chambers of divine love and protection, and there meditate on the character and government of God; commit yourselves wholly unto him, to do and suffer all his pleasure; and you will be sustained. Forget, as much as possible, your private griefs, and think of the excellent character of your and our beloved Elijah; of his firmness unto death in maintaining truth and rectitude, of the glory to which his spirit, so devoted to God, has now attained; of the honor which is paid to his memory by multitudes who never personally, knew either you or him; which will be paid by true patriots and philanthropists in coming ages; of the immense benefits which will result from his martyrdom; think of the emotions of gratitude and praise to God, with which emancipated millions will hereafter speak of his sufferings for their sake; of the happiness which will be enjoyed by all mankind, when Slavery shall everywhere have ceased, and paternal love shall prevail among all the races of the great family of man; think of the swiftly approaching day when you, if true Christians, will meet all the martyrs, indeed the whole company of the redeemed before the throne of God, and lift up your voices with them in everlasting songs of praise, even for the sufferings through which you are now destined to pass; and you must, you will be comforted. Trust my friends in the Lord, for in the Lord Jehovah is everlasting strength. He will cause the wrath of man to praise him, and the remainder of wrath he will effectually restrain. To him be glory and dominion now and forever. Amen."

The remainder of this, and the following chapter will be made up of expressions of public sentiment, variously uttered, in relation to his death and the circumstances connected with it. We can however only give a mere fraction of the numerous expressions of the press and of public meetings. The admirable address to the "Citizens of Alton" is from an unknown hand. It was sent to New York with the name and place of the author carefully concealed. The gentlemen whose speeches are inserted, will accept our sincere thanks, for their "sincere tribute of a swelling heart."

RESOLUTIONS OF PUBLIC MEETINGS

BANGOR, MAINE

At a special meeting of the Bangor City Anti-Slavery Society, November 27th, 1837. Whereas the late Rev. Elijah P. Lovejoy, of Alton, Illinois, was a native of this state, his aged and excellent mother and other members of the family being still resident in our vicinity, and well known to at least many of us -

Resolved, That in our judgment, he was an intelligent, talented, upright, noble-hearted man; a sincere and consistent Christian; an able, independent, and faithful minister of the Gospel; a bold, uncompromising enemy of oppression in all its forms; a self-sacrificing friend and defender of civil and religious liberty, of truth and righteousness, whose name and whose virtues deserve to be embalmed in the memory of every friend of God and man.

BELFAST, MAINE

In pursuance of a notice previously given, a public meeting was held at the North Church, on the evening of the 30th of November, 1837, for the discussion of resolutions expressive of the sentiments of our citizens, relative to the assassination of the Rev. E. P. Lovejoy. The Hon. Alfred Johnson being chosen chairman, and B. P. Field, Jr., secretary. The following resolutions were reported by a committee, discussed and unanimously adopted.

Resolved, That in pursuance of the public notice which called this meeting, we have assembled, not as men of any party, civil or religious, but on the broad ground of American citizenship, to pass resolutions in regard to the topics specified, as truth and the good of our country may in our estimation demand.

That the Rev. E. P. Lovejoy, a highly respected citizen, recently of this state, who was on the 7th inst. assassinated by a mob at Alton, in Illinois, in consequence of an attempt on his part to protect his property, liberty, and life, when no legal protection could be obtained - has fallen a martyr in defense of rights which are guaranteed to every freeman by the constitutions of the general and state governments; rights of which our country has made her highest boast, and which are dear to every American citizen.

PLYMOUTH, NEW HAMPSHIRE

Meeting of Abolitionists, December 13th, 1837

Resolved, That this meeting and the people throughout this land, have a vital and solemn interest in the death of the Rev. E. P. Lovejoy, late Editor of the "Alton Observer," who has fallen by the hands of our countrymen, in defense of the liberty of the press, in one of the non-slaveholding states of this republic.

That on the citizens of influence and office in Alton - on "the property and standing" of that bloody little city, and not on the poor, infuriated and drunken mob who were their instruments, rests immediately before God and impartial human judgment, the guilt of this riot and murder.

That the only preventive of these mobs which now outrage the whole land, and threaten to prostrate all law and security at their ruffian feet, is in the prevalence and triumph of anti-slavery principles - in other words - the Abolition of Slavery.

DORCHESTER, NEW HAMPSHIRE, ANTI-SLAVERY SOCIETY

Resolved, That we consider the conduct of the Attorney-General, of the state of Illinois, at a meeting a few days previous to the murder, in stating publicly that Mr. Lovejoy, would be killed within two weeks, worthy of the frowns of an injured community.

That, as application was made by Mr. Lovejoy to the Common Council of Alton, to defend his person and property from violence, the Council by refusing to comply with his request, well knowing the imminent danger to which he was exposed, are guilty of his blood.

CHICHESTER, NEW HAMPSHIRE

At a public meeting of citizens in the Congregational meeting-house, December 14th, 1837

Resolved, That we commend the decision, firmness, and courage of the Rev. E. P. Lovejoy in his endeavors to establish and sustain a free religious press at Alton, Illinois; - who, though deserted by the civil powers, which, by the constitution and laws of the state, and by solemn oaths, were pledged for his protection, yet, not acting for himself merely, but in behalf of insulted humanity, and the liberty of speech and of the press, and in behalf of posterity, - nobly withstood unrighteous and murderous violence, and died a martyr to the holy cause of right, and truth, and freedom.

CONCORD, NEW HAMPSHIRE

That in the destruction of the "Alton Observer," the freedom of conscience and of religious opinion was assailed, and that it specially behooves the pulpit and the PRESS to lift up their voices in vindication and defense of that freedom, and against any attempt to infringe its full exercise.

That in the opinion of this meeting, the blood of E. P. Lovejoy is no less an offering in behalf of the constitutional rights of American freemen, than it is in behalf of the enslaved.

NEW HAMPSHIRE A. S. SOCIETY

Resolved, That our beloved brother, the late E. P, Lovejoy, in laying down his life in vindication of his just rights, has become a martyr not only to the doctrines of Abolition, but to the principles of law and order; and that the blow aimed at him in the destruction of his life and property, has struck at the liberties and rights of every American citizen, and of every human being.

That the persevering determination of Mr. Lovejoy to publish his paper at Alton, his exposure of property and life, and firm resistance even unto death, of the outrageous and murderous attempts to destroy his press, so far from a spirit of obstinacy and reckless defiance, was the result of a duty which he owed to the principles of liberty, the rights of conscience, and the freedom of the press, and should be honored and revered by every Christian and freeman.

MARLBORO, MASSACHUSETTS

That we view the Rev. Mr. Lovejoy, who lately fell at Alton, Illinois, without reference to the particular cause in which he was engaged, as a martyr to the great and inestimable rights of the freedom of the press, and freedom of discussion.

PLYMOUTH, MASSACHUSETTS, ANTI-SLAVERY SOCIETY

Resolved, That we have every reason to believe that had the citizens of Alton been faithful in sustaining the laws of the land, and in frowning upon the conduct of those who destroyed the press of Mr. Lovejoy, the blood of that good man would not, as it now does, cry to Heaven for vengeance, on those who have been accessary to his death.

That the much lamented Lovejoy, in asserting his undoubted and constitutional right, the right of enjoying and protecting life, liberty, and property, in refusing to yield to the threatening dictation of a blood-thirsty mob, thereby sacrificing his life as a martyr in the holy cause of Abolition, deserves a name to be held in everlasting remembrance.

WASHINGTON COUNTY, NEW YORK

That the martyrdom of the Rev. Mr. Lovejoy, had no other provocation than his untiring zeal in attempting to continue a religious newspaper, whose columns were open to the free discussion of the great principles of freedom embodied in the declaration of independence.

That all those citizens, whether in the editorial chair or elsewhere, who persist in representing his death as the consequence of the rash attempt on his part, to establish an Abolition paper on the frontier of Slavery, are either willfully ignorant, or wickedly perverse.

COLORED CITIZENS OF NEW YORK

Public meeting, November 23d, at the Rev. Theodore S. Wright's Church

Resolved, That we most cordially respond to the feelings and views embodied in the proceedings of the Executive Committee of Am. A. S. Society, touching the deliberate and brutal murder of the Rev. Elijah P. Lovejoy, who gave up his life on the 7th of November, in sustaining the liberty of the press and the holy principles of Abolition, to which he was honored of God to become the first Martyr in this nation.

That in common with the friends of law, order, and oppressed humanity of our nation, we solemnly deplore and mourn the loss of this holy and able advocate of the rights of man, and express our deep and heartfelt sympathy for his heroic wife, who has been thus painfully bereaved of a kind and faithful husband; and implore the blessings of the God of the oppressed, to descend upon her, and her dear fatherless children.

PHILADELPHIA

At a large public meeting of the citizens of the Northern Liberties, held on the evening of the 27th instant, at the Temperance Hall, in pursuance of a call of the committee of arrangement of a former meeting, held for the purpose of expressing and making known their sentiments in relation to the late murder of the Rev. E. P. Lovejoy, at Alton, Illinois, for the great crime of maintaining his rights as an American citizen, and also for the purpose of expressing their opinions in relation to the right oi free discussion, and the liberty of the press.

After an address by Judge Price, it was unanimously *Resolved*, That the right of free discussion, though guaranteed, was not conferred by our constitution and laws of our country, but that it is the gift of God, and inherent in our moral nature, and therefore a right which human government cannot take away.

That the exercise of the right of free discussion is essential to the maintenance and security of our other rights; and that without this, other rights would be of little value.

That, should the public apathy continue to give toleration and immunity to mobs, while their fury is directed against the advocates of human rights, we must not be surprised when artful demagogues shall mount the whirlwind and direct the storm, against the property, the peace, and the lives of other portions of the community.

SUSQUEHANNAH, PENNSYLVANIA COUNTY

That so long as the right of a citizen to defend his property, himself, and his country, shall be acknowledged, so long ought the noble daring of E. P. Lovejoy, and the "sublimity of his heroism,*' to awaken universal admiration, and elicit universal applause.

That duty to his country, duty to the cause of liberty, required that Mr. Lovejoy should stand thus firmly upon his inalienable rights, and in yielding up his life in obedience to that duty, is and ought of right to be, honored as a martyr in the cause of the human race.

PORTAGE COUNTY ANTI-SLAVERY SOCIETY

Resolved, That it is the imperious duty of all who would cherish our free institutions to discountenance in a becoming manner the high handed act of violence and outrage.

That Mr. Lovejoy laid down his life in a cause worthy of so noble a sacrifice, the cause of free discussion, of human rights, and the freedom of the press.

That his name should ever be held in remembrance as the heroic friend and devoted advocate of those free institutions, which the patriots of the Revolution, like him, freely laid down their lives to establish and maintain.

SALEM, OHIO

This meeting, convened without distinction of sect or party, having had a statement of the late riot at Alton, Illinois, laid before it, deems it advisable that an expression of abhorrence should be set forth, and that its humble voice should constitute one item in the strong effort now being made to arouse the sleepers, (if it be not too late.)

Resolved, That to withhold a decided expression of disapprobation regarding the Alton tragedy, is virtually giving it our sanction.

That we pledge ourselves to each other and to the community, to spare no exertions, to protect men in their rights when pursuing lawful vocations, and to vindicate the supremacy of the laws.

That when an individual or a community announces the expectation of a mob, it virtually invites one; and that there has rarely been a riot in our country in which the instigators and actors were the same persons. "The people will be excited." "We shall be unable to prevent violence," with similar expressions, are significant, and seldom fail to produce that excitement and its concomitants, which they cunningly and hypocritically deprecate.

That the "compromise" meeting at Alton, together with the course of the Mayor and other civil authorities, had the direct tendency adverted to in the last resolution.

That before we will tamely submit to have our lips sealed at the bidding of mobocratic despotism, we will suffer our bodies to be immolated on the spot upon which we may perish contending for our rights, and our name to be enrolled with that of E. P. Lovejoy, as martyrs to the cause of law, of liberty, and of free discussion.

VOICE OF THE PRESS

The blood of Mr. Lovejoy, we believe, lies at the door of civil authority. They have slept for weeks and months over the heating volcano, and they knew they were doing this; and they, we believe, were rather willing it should be so. We believe Mr. Lovejoy has fallen a sacrifice to liberty, and that the voice of his blood will only be appeased by the triumph of this principle. And we can cheerfully add, in the language of a contemporary, "Thus died the first martyr in the cause of Abolitionism. Long will his name be used as a talisman in that cause, and the mention of it will infuse new vigor into its swelling ranks, and incite its votaries to renewed action and fresh energies, until every fetter is sundered, and every chain broken. May God hasten the day,"
- *Maine Wesleyan Journal*

The hand so often raised to bless, lies powerless; the lips which moved in prayer, will move no more - his spirit, so gentle, yet so firm, is happy with its God. His affectionate wife, who so lately periled her life in defending his, was by the last accounts still insensible - his children are fatherless, and their mother a widow. Who would say the work of the murderer is incomplete? They desired to silence him, and he is dead - and the press they feared is destroyed. And yet, though Lovejoy has earned the crown of martyrdom, and been taken from among us, he speaketh, and in a voice of thunder that shall penetrate where his living voice would never have been heard - and move thousands of hearts which his arguments never could have moved.
- *Maine, Portland Transcript*

Mr. Lovejoy was educated in this vicinity, and was regarded as a young man of great promise. This idea of mobbing and killing people to stop the freedom of speech and of the press, will never do in this age and country.
- *Gospel Banner*

The curse of God be on the heads of the infernal mob. This will do more for the Abolition cause, than could a score of presses and a hundred

missionaries. Lovejoy was a native of Albion, Maine. He has died a martyr in the cause of liberty of speech and the press.
- *Belfast Journal*

A martyred Lovejoy has unloosed the tongues of thousands, and compelled them to speak out for God and their country. That oppressed portion of our fellow-men, however degraded by the awful curse of Slavery, for whom he labored, have, by his martyrdom and death, gained a phalanx of firm and decided friends. Instead, then, of being .disheartened, let the friends of freedom and the press arise from their lethargy; let them urge with ten-fold more earnestness the cause of their countrymen in chains - let the pulpit lift up its voice - let the fervent orisons of all the professed followers of Him who "went about doing good," ascend on high - let everyone who fears God and loves man, be filled with a new, a reanimating impulse to press forward in the cause of freedom, until every chain is broken; and soon shall we see the oppressed delivered out of the hand of the spoiler, and our country saved from a fearful destiny.
- *Maine Eastern Baptist*

The civil authorities, to their deep disgrace, did not attempt to shield this freeman, battling to protect the freedom of speech, of the press, and of all the sacred rights secured to the citizens by the constitution of these United States. Lovejoy was a man of talents, piety, and worth, whose untimely fate v/ill not only be mourned by all who knew and honored him, but it will long be mourned by all who cleave to the freedom of speech, and of the press, as the sheet anchor of our liberties.
- *New Hampshire Courier*

It is not merely for the murder of E. P. Lovejoy as a man, the image of God smitten down by the hand of fierce wrath, that we should mourn and cry aloud - but for the deadly blow struck at liberty, as impersonated in that man, for the violence done to democratic and Christian principle, for the outrage committed against rights, inalienable and immutable, the birth-right and possession of every human being. Not only has a minister of the gospel been martyred for attempting, in meekness and firmness, to obey the departing command of the Savior - "Go ye into all the world and preach the gospel to every creature" - but the dearest and holiest right which all ministers possess - freedom of speech - has been assailed. Not only has an editor been murdered for publishing his opinions, but the press throughout the country has had an outrage committed on it, and the rights which every editor possesses have been rudely and ruthlessly violated.
- *New Hampshire, Herald of Freeman*

The refusal of the civil authorities to extend efficient protection to Mr. Lovejoy, while it was well known by those authorities that his life was sought, and in imminent danger, day after day, and week after week; the Attorney-General of the state having himself declared, a short time previous to the actual accomplishment of the tragical event, that Mr. Lovejoy would be destroyed in less than a fortnight - the neglect, as far as we have heard, in the same authorities, since the commission of the bloody deed, to take any measures for bringing the murderers to justice - the wicked hardihood of some public journals in excusing the murderous mob from blame, and casting the responsibility and guilt altogether upon the innocent, butchered victim - the slight manner in which many others pass over the subject, some being quite dumb in relation thereto - the extensive insensibility of our citizens, and even of some, if not many professed Christians, even ministers - all these circumstances, and more circumstances than these, indicate a danger that this nation will not, by thorough repentance, and by executing justice upon the guilty, put away that BLOOD GUILTINESS with which, in the sight of the just Judge of all the earth, it is now so deeply stained.
- *New Hampshire Morning Star*

He died in defense of what should ever be dear to American citizens, the right of free discussion, subject to the law - but in a portion of our land, the law has no restraint. We hope the murderers will yet be identified and punished. It should be remembered, that Bishop was killed previously by a random shot from the castle - every man's house is his own castle - and that no resistance with fire-arms was made, until the mob had broken the windows of the building, fired into it, and attempted to set it on fire. Had half a dozen been killed, and the mob so dispersed, it would have been perfectly justifiable, and far better than that one man should have lost his life in defense of his property, and constitutional rights.
- *New Hampshire Keene Sentinel*

In the main, the tone of the press betokens a sound and healthy state of public feeling. In some few instances the comments of editors have been little short of cold blooded apology for the murderers. If we mistake not, this offering of blood upon the altar of free discussion, will arouse the nation to a just sense of its hitherto criminal indifference and apathy on this subject, and lead to an assertion of the right, thus smitten down by mob violence, that shall forever place it beyond question.
- *Vermont Argus*

Thus has fallen - in the very place to which he was invited - unprotected by "the friends of free discussion" - in a free state, the first martyr to the cause of humanity. The theatre of murders, of bloody and

outrageous deeds of infamy, has been transferred from Vicksburg to Alton. Let this place be forever remembered - let its name be written in the catalogue of all that is execrable - let the emigrant avoid it as he values his liberty - let him pass by on the other side of this Sodom of the West, lest, if he should tarry in it, the wrath of insulted heaven in fire and water, should descend and destroy the place, with its wicked, pusillanimous, and shameless inhabitants, who, like base cowards, permitted the murder of one of their fellow citizens. There can be no excuse offered on their part. Their duty was plain - they should have armed themselves, rallied in support of the Mayor, and shot down, without ceremony, the first and every invader of the rights of citizenship.
- *Vermont Caledonian*

The murdered Lovejoy died, a Martyr to the freedom OF THE PRESS. It was a noble cause. Looking upon him as a freeman, bravely laboring for the right; as a patriot, taking his own life in his hands, as of less consequence than the establishment of one of the dearest and most precious blessings of our free constitution, we would embalm his memory, and plant the emblem of immortality to grow above his grave.

As a patriot, a lover of the constitution and laws of his country, and the rights of freemen, his name should be written beside those venerable compeers who have battled with the minions of corrupt power, and the doctrines of man's inferiority.

Why was it that Lovejoy was left to struggle alone for a common right? Where were the executors of the law? Where the Common Council of Alton, and especially the Mayor, its chief executive officer? The official station of the Mayor, made it his duty to exert himself to the utmost in calling out the moral and physical force of the city, to suppress every outbreak. He should have aroused the Common Council, and when hints of slaughter were openly proclaimed, and deeply muttered, he should have prepared himself for a vigorous defense - more - he should have carried the war into Africa, and seized the cold-blooded villains, who were daily threatening to trample, rough shod, upon the rights of property and life. A noble-hearted freeman should have been protected in the assertion and exercise of his rights. But where do we find the Mayor, with the robes of his official station? and how employed? Doing the bidding of an unlawful mob - the obedient messenger, the pliant servant, the supple attorney for the destroyers, to demand of a free citizen a surrender of property, of liberty and principle, or be murdered on the spot! How his craven heart and his degraded station, and violated oath of office, must have blanched his cheek with the mantle of shame and disgrace, when, in return to such a demand, he received the spirit stirring and noble reply, that they had assembled to protect their property against lawless violence, and were determined to do so. A Mayor, with a little of the good old blood of our revolutionary fathers, would sooner have breasted the storm by a rally among the police, and his chosen friends, and laid his body upon the threshold of the store, and died like a patriot in defense of law and liberty.

Let him occupy the niche to which fame now points!
- *Vermont, Brattleborough Phoenix*

We have to record this week one of the most atrocious and cold-blooded murders ever committed. Rev. E. P. Lovejoy, late Editor of the "Alton (Illinois) Observer" - a man alike distinguished for his piety, and for his devotion to the sacred cause of liberty - has been murdered by a brutal mob. No crime is charged against him - no palliation for this monstrous outrage is to be given - unless firmly and fearlessly to advocate the sacred cause of the oppressed, is a crime worthy of death, or an excuse for the shedding of human blood! He has fallen a martyr in the cause of freedom - a victim of the accursed system of Slavery. To shed his blood, slave- holders, or their emissaries, invaded the limits, disturbed the peace, and violated the laws of a free state; and we fear these assassins have also succeeded in making their escape, and found a sanctuary in the slave state of Missouri. It would only be carrying out the spirit of this atrocious act, should the government of Missouri refuse any aid in arresting the perpetrators. But we shall see.
- *Vermont Watchman*

Incarnate fiends and assassins have robbed a wife of a husband, children of a father, and society of a pure minded man; for what? Because he stood under a shield of the constitution, and defended the liberty of the press. A glorious cause to die in! Let his memory be embalmed. The blood of that innocent man will not sink into the ground. It will be required at the hands of all those who have raised this infernal spirit of mobism against free discussion and a free press. The blood of a murdered Lovejoy is on the heads of those men, who, on the 17th of August, 1836, assembled in Faneuil Hall, to vote down free discussion, and whose hands afterwards were' barely stayed from being reeked in the blood of Garrison. Free discussion has now her martyr, and it will rouse men who have souls, to the defense of that dearest right, as did the murder of Morgan, to the defense of the rights of free citizens against a secret despotism.
- *Boston Daily Advocate*

Vicksburgh has for some time enjoyed a pre-eminence of murderous notoriety; but Alton, Illinois, has lately stepped forward to dispute this unenviable station, and has far outrun Vicksburgh in the career of blood and infamy. The people of Vicksburgh acted under a sudden impulse; the people of Alton are responsible for a deliberate and long plotted murder. They have not only violated the law, they have trampled also upon the

rights of hospitality - in every honorable mind, more sacred, if possible, even than the laws themselves.
- *Boston Atlas*

The Moloch of America, (Slavery,) demands the sacrifice of a citizen, a Christian, a philanthropist, a minister of the gospel, a noble defender of the rights of man, and straightway it is given by his devotees, to gratify his ire, which burns against the philanthropists of the age. This is only the commencement. The spirit of Slavery demands the sacrifice, not only of the rights and dearest privileges of American citizens, but their lives and their blood also. Silence or death is the mandate of the evil genius of Slavery. Lovejoy is dead! May his mantle fall upon a kindred spirit, who shall accomplish the work which he began. We trust that the Abolitionists of America will never cease their efforts till a free press is established at Alton, which shall pour forth a flood of light, that will scatter the midnight darkness now hovering over that devoted city. From thence, may a light shine out and blaze upon the naked conscience of every oppressor and mobocrat in the land. There may the spirit of Lovejoy live, and still, by his example, his sufferings, and blood, continue to speak in tones of thunder to this nation, till every heart is made to quail before the omnipotent truth in the defense of which he died.
- *Boston Christian*

Do you ask why these men hated Mr. Lovejoy so? It was not so much because they hated him, as because they wished to please the slaveholders, that they killed him. He believed it was wicked to hold slaves, and he tried to convince all the readers of the "Observer" that the slaves had a right to their liberty. This was the truth; but those who love Slavery were not willing to have the truth told. They therefore destroyed the presses, and murdered the man who dared to use them, to publish such truths.

We see by this that the spirit of slave-holding is the spirit of murder. The tyrants of Europe and Asia are not willing to have men print what they please, for fear their subjects should become wise enough to know that they have a right to be free. But in this case, the people in a state called free, unite in killing a man for publishing facts about Slavery in another state.
- *Boston Cabinet*

Another noble heart is added to the angel choir above, who lean eagerly from their high sphere to watch our course and cheer us onward, in the deliverance of the slave. We have been too tame and too slow. Oh! shall the blood of this first martyr sink into the earth for naught? No. Let the anti-slavery presses thunder anew, and louder than ever! Let all those

who have hung back from prudential motives now come up to the help of the Lord and show what, side they are on - let them boldly assert their principles, in the pulpit, in the domestic circle, and in the public streets, until the whole country is agitated from Maine to New Orleans, until the bloody south reels and trembles beneath the shock as if an earthquake rent her unhallowed borders. Let us insist strenuously and more strenuously than ever that our captive brethren shall be free. The manacled hands of those dusky millions are raised to Heaven in earnest prayer for one breath of that sweet liberty about which our native orators are howling in the public halls, as if in mockery of their fettered countrymen. Let not the widow's tears be dry before those chains are riven - let not the moans of the fatherless be hushed before this high-handed and damning enormity is swept from our land. The disenthralled spirit of Lovejoy is hovering around us as we write, and a voice from his tomb cries, Onward! the time is come!
- *Boston Wanderer*

What freeman - who but a savage, or cold-hearted murderer would now go to Alton? Meanness, infamy, and guilt are attached to the very name. Hereafter, when a criminal is considered too base for any known punishment, it will be said of him - "he ought to be banished to Alton;" or, "he ought to be banished to a place as vile and infamous as Alton - a place where freedom is disowned - where the defenders of freedom are murdered by the consent of the inhabitants - where the inhabitants themselves are land pirates - where the Attorney-General, the representative of the state, instead of bringing criminals to judgment, encourages - spurs them on, to the perpetration of the foulest crimes, the basest murder; and the Mayor of the city sits as a judge advocate for the mob.
- *Massachusetts Lynn Record*

The press throughout the country, ought to raise its voice against the conduct of the Mayor of Alton, during the late riot at that place. Taking his own account of the transaction, he is an accessary before the fact, as well as at the very time of its perpetration to the horrid crimes of arson and murder. Not only did he neglect to exert his authority, and the authority of the law to quell the riot - but he identified himself with the mob, by becoming their messenger, to ask of Lovejoy and his associates the surrendering of their property and their rights, and to threaten them with the consequences which ensued, if they failed to comply. Is he not, then, as guilty as the worst incendiary present on that fearful occasion.
- *Worcester Republican*

Mr. Lovejoy was a clear and vigorous writer; open, manly, and fearless in the declaration of his sentiments, active and industrious in editorial labors. He was guilty of few errors, except such as arose from the too great haste of a benevolent heart, intent on doing good, and ready to sacrifice self for its accomplishment. The St. Louis Observer, which he established and conducted to its close, was a paper of more than usual interest. He engaged warmly in the controversy with the Roman Catholics. He stated that the true cause of the hostility against him was, his opposition to Popery; and that the charge of Abolitionism was fabricated as an excuse for the attack, and as a means of exciting odium against him.
- *New York Observer*

Where were the civil energies of Alton? Where was their regard for American character? Where their regard for the cause of the slave, the liberty of the north, the rights of man, and the laws of God? Where was the Mayor in this hour of peril? According to his own self-condemning evidence, waiting with imbecility or connivance to behold the sacrifice, siding with the assailants, and meanly asking the property to be given up as the only price of peace. But where was the victim - where the devoted Lovejoy? In his place, ready to be offered. He stood forth an American citizen, and in the assertion and exercise of all the great rights of man, he fell a martyr to the liberty of the press, and to the cause of the slave, in the land of the free! Was it for this that Washington, Hancock, Franklin, Jefferson, Adams, Henry, and Lafayette (peace to the ashes of the Frenchman! he died in season) toiled and bled? Was it for this that the Declaration of Independence was signed, and a government organized which guarantees to every citizen the inalienable rights of life, liberty, AND THE PURSUIT OF HAPPINESS?
- *New York Evangelist*

It now remains to be seen, whether the perpetrators of this atrocious crime will be made to pay the penalty of life, or whether they will be suffered to go unpunished. If the latter, then we may truly say that the rights of American citizens are but a name; that our laws are inadequate to the protection of life and property, or even to the vindication of their own majesty against transgressors.

Mr. Lovejoy we understand, was a man of excellent character and moral worth; and the only fault, it is presumed, which his murderers could allege against him, was, that he was an Abolitionist, and was determined to publish an Abolition paper at Alton. It ought to be recollected, however, that he had once changed his place of publication in consequence of popular excitement, having established his paper originally at St. Louis.

The enemies of Abolition must be very stupid indeed, if they expect to put it down, in this free country, by mob violence, and especially by

assassination and murder. The old maxim, that "the blood of the martyrs is the seed of the church," is just as true in the case of Abolition, and for similar reasons.
- *New York Journal of Commerce*

For our own part, we approve, we applaud, we would consecrate, if we could, to universal honor, the conduct of those who bled in this gallant defense of the freedom of the press. Whether they erred or not in their opinion, they did not err in the conviction of their rights as citizens of a democratic government, to express them; nor did they err in defending this right with an obstinacy which yielded only to death and the utmost violence.
- *Evening Post*

We loathe and abhor the miserable cant of those that talk of Mr. Lovejoy as guilty of "resisting public opinion." Public opinion, forsooth! What right have five hundred or five thousand to interfere with the lawful expression of a free man's sentiments because they happen to number more than those who think with him? We spurn the base tyranny - this utter denial of all rights, save as the tender mercies of a mob shall vouchsafe them. If Mr. Lovejoy's views were erroneous, let them be refuted; if his motives were corrupt, (but this is not pretended,) let them be exposed and contemned; if his actions were unlawful, let them be lawfully punished. But, right or wrong, none of these were better or worse for the fact that they were unacceptable to the majority. He had as perfect and absolute a right to proclaim and defend his sentiments in Illinois, where nine-tenths may be opposed to them, as though all were enthusiastic in their favor; and he who would deny or in the least degree abridge this right, is an enemy to freedom, and a hypocrite if he dare pretend to republicanism.
- *New Yorker*

The blow by which Mr. Lovejoy fell, was aimed not at "him only. His body was cut down merely because it stood between the press and the weapon raised for its destruction. But that blow has fallen upon every press in this nation. And the death of that man calls WITH a thousand TONGUES, IN TRUMPET TONES UPON THE PRESS for redress. Surely no one can doubt for a moment, but a corrupted, time-serving press, has created that state of feeling which has resulted in this tragical event, especially when it is seen how such papers as the Courier and Enquirer, the New York Gazette, and some others, speak of this horrid outrage, calling it an Abolition mob, and throwing the whole blame upon the murdered Lovejoy.
- *New York Zionist Watchman*

A Great Man has fallen. - The martyrdom of the Rev. E. P. Lovejoy has excited among our brethren a spirit of holy ambition and action, calculated to emancipate a world. The combined powers of all the embodied and disembodied tyrants in the universe, cannot withstand it. The enlightened abhorrence of our people, to oppression of every kind, will be a powerful engine in expelling Slavery and caste, from our otherwise favored land.

Colored men cannot be enslaved nor oppressed much longer in America. Slavery and oppression are exotics, which can never become indigenous in an American climate, nor soil. They may be forced for a while, but the time must of necessity be short.
- *New York Colored American*

The issue is now fairly made up, whether the laws or the mob is to prevail - whether the press, so long the boasted palladium of our liberties, is to be the sport of popular passion, or whether it shall be protected and secured by the laws.

Mr. Lovejoy is said to have been a man of high character and worth. As an Abolitionist he had the same right to print and publish, as the advocates of Slavery. We trust this horrid transaction will not be allowed to sleep without some more general and formidable expressions of public feeling than mere newspaper notices, important as they certainly are. The innocent blood shed at Alton, unavenged, must remain an indelible national stain.

The whole country will be held responsible for it abroad, and who that has the spirit of a man, but must hang his head and blush, when he reflects that in this vaunted land a ferocious mob may violate with impunity all the private and personal rights of a peaceable citizen-shoot him down as they would a wild beast - fire his house, and save his family and friends from indiscriminate slaughter only on condition of private obedience to its demands! Shame be to us, if we let this thing pass!
- *Newark Daily Advertiser*

Alton Massacre. - The thrill of sensibility which seems to have been produced by the murder of Rev. E. P. Lovejoy, at Alton, has called forth from every part of the land, a burst of indignation which has not had its parallel in this country since the battle of Lexington, 1775. One thing which appears from looking over our exchange papers, has struck us with amazement, and that is, that the most decided expressions of disapprobation and abhorrence of the dead are from the slaveholding states. With a large list of southern papers before us, we find not one attempt at an apology for the murderous outrage. The only apologists for it are found in our northern cities, and among editors who have a circulation at the south, and some others who have a pecuniary interest in retaining the favor of southern customers. The question, whether law or mobs shall rule, must be decided. And if the blood of Warren flowed not guiltily forth on Bunker's Hill, in resisting the despotism of England, the very angels of freedom must have hovered around Lovejoy as the warm current of his heart ebbed away, in resistance to the infinitely worse despotism of lawlessness and mobs. The right of discussing the subject of Slavery is now the very Thermopylae of American freedom. Let this right be surrendered, and what comes next? Why, the Whig or the Tory press must be silenced by the voice of the ruling party, or torn down by riotous mobs; and the politician must count the people before he can dare to attack or defend the bank; and then Unitarian churches must blaze before orthodox mobs, or evangelical piety flee away before the successful riots of infidelity. Our liberties hinge upon the decision of this question. We ought to be ready to sacrifice everything that is dear in life, rather than in such an hour as this to shrink from duty. Life without liberty is of little worth; and if we cannot enjoy the privilege of speaking freely and of writing freely, we ought like Lovejoy, freely to die.

- Boston Recorder

CHAPTER XVI

TO THE CITIZENS OF ALTON

Years have elapsed since I enjoyed the hospitality of your then infant settlement. Since then I have never ceased to feel a lively interest in your prosperity. Most gratifying have been the reports of your growing wealth and commerce, and, especially, of your liberality, correct morals, and enlightened public sentiment. Should the domestic institutions of bordering states ever enfeeble in them the spirit of freedom, among you, it was hoped, she would still be found vigorous and hardy as your own giant youth. Against the invasion of servile sentiment, here, it was presumed, would be an impregnable barrier - here, the rights of man were to find a sanctuary, the persecuted of any name, or of however delusive a creed, were to obtain constitutional protection. Should the lights of American liberty elsewhere grow dim, amid your wild cliffs her torch was still to burn, as brightly as on Bunker's heights, or the Plymouth Rock. These anticipations, in sorrow, not in anger I say it, are no more. They have been most cruelly swept away. The associations connected with you, in the public mind, I need not tell you, are sadly, fearfully changed; the bright colors have faded, and dark, and dismal, and bloody hues are on them. A tumultuary, lawless, fanatic power, overmastering or overawing the civil authority, enslaving public sentiment - paralyzing the public conscience - freezing with fear the sympathies of even the generous, the intelligent, and the good, and, with a few noble exceptions, making the mind of your whole city hold its breath, and crouch in silence before it - ferocity victorious over right, brute force over free opinion - a gang of ruffians claiming to be regulators of speech and the press, usurping the name of the people, and grasping in the same polluted clutch, the functions of accuser, judge, and executioner - "making night hideous" with their loathsome triumph - in the presence of unresisting multitudes, demolishing buildings, firing your city, publicly murdering an American citizen for the crime of exercising rights, most sacredly guaranteed to him by the Constitution of the United States, and the state of Illinois - and finally, with fiendish malignity, and a meanness more than fiendish, in" violation of their express stipulations, firing upon the unarmed and unresisting. Such are the images that now start at the name of ALTO>r. Are they mere horrid phantoms? Would to God they were SO. Oh, no! they have left enduring memorials in broken hearts, bereaved infancy, and untimely graves - they have left a community disgraced, freedom of speech awed into silence, and the majesty of law trampled underfoot. In the dishonor of the American name, in the wound given to the cause of universal liberty, and the outraged feeling of mankind, they have left abiding monuments. The muse of history turns aside her head, and weeps, as she chronicles in crimson the record.

I doubt not, you generally regret, as sincerely as I do, the guilty acts that have been perpetrated among you, and it is far from my wish, in thus addressing you, by exaggerated statement, or high-wrought coloring, to swell that tide of reprobation and abhorrence, that is setting in upon you from the wise and good in all parts of our land, and which, I doubt not, will be increased by the indignant sentiment of all liberal Europe. Such an attempt would be most idle. No language can exaggerate the naked atrocity of the facts - no oratory can deepen the dark colors of the truth. Amplification would enfeeble - the simple statement is the strongest - the plainest narrative the most condemning. But to inflame public odium is as far from my wish, as from my power. For you as a people, I have ever cherished sentiments of kindness and well wishing. And vindictive, indeed, must be the temper that would add to the griefs or disgrace of your position. Other towns can often look back with pride to their early history, and relumine, in the associations of the past, the waning love of liberty and truth. Boston has her Faneuil Hall, Charleston her Fort Moultrie; but Alton must wear it upon her escutcheon, in characters imperishable as the rocky bluffs around her - that in her early youth she crouched, before not one, but an hundred masters, that in her, freedom of speech found its first American martyr - that she did all, than in her immaturity and feebleness she could do, to bury freedom of the press, and with it, the American Constitution, in a bloody grave. The sacrifices of life may have been small - that of principle was mighty - the infamy of it, not the tide of all coming years, nor the flow of your ever-rolling Mississippi can wash away. Upon the internal and domestic situation, to which you seem to have sealed yourselves by this act, I can reflect only with pity and horror. Deep and cruel as may have been the injury done to your country and your kind - the first and bitterest fruits you must reap in your own bosom. Living in a community without law, with a blood-baited and fanatical populace for your masters, with the fatal evidence before you, that that populace can be restrained in the course of its impulses by no right, human or divine, but are ready upon provocation to waste your city with arson and murder - the condition you exhibit is most deplorable. But add to this the fact, that that populace have, many of them, brought upon themselves the guilt and frenzy of murder, and have placed themselves in a situation which requires the perpetual prostration of law, and the permanent ascendancy of the mob, in order to their personal safety - and the frightfulness of the picture is consummate.

Nor do I address you, because I think that with you the principles of liberty and morality are peculiarly unsound, or that popular depravity with you is without parallel. Alas, it finds guilty fellowship in but too many places in our land. But the outrage perpetrated among you was one of aggravated enormity - both as it regards the individual, and principles sacrificed. It was no gambler, no ruffian, no malefactor defying or evading justice, whose blood is upon your hands. It was not a case where an indignant populace, in the impulse of an evil hour, inflicted a vengeance, due to its object, though rendering the avengers more guilty than the victim. It had not even the miserable justification of those instances, where, in a zeal for justice, all justice is trampled underfoot, and in punishing one crime, are committed a thou- sand. It was a man, in the eye of human law, without reproach, a man of undoubted piety, and giving evidence of a devotion sincere, however misguided you may have deemed it, to the great cause of human rights - a man wrong, if wrong at all, only in his views of a great moral question, and in the fearless expression of those views - a man who, however imprudent or misjudging "you may have thought him, you must at least acknowledge could not be deterred by self-sacrifice, or intimidated by the fury of the multitude, or seduced by popular opinion from supposed duty, but who dared in the assertion of the right even to die - it is for shedding the blood of such a man, that mankind hold you responsible. There was too at stake, not individual rights only, but vast principles. Whether our General and State Constitutions, with their solemn guarantees, should be of sovereign authority, or a mere splendid delusion and a snare, was in controversy. Moreover, he who strikes at the freedom of speech, is guilty of treason, not only to his country, but to his kind; he strikes at the great means to the ultimate triumph of truth, and the anticipated improvement of the human race. It is these considerations - that the atrocity committed among you was provoked by no crime - that you made, as far as you could, a solemn oblation of the principles of universal liberty and of the future hopes of the race, upon the same ensanguined altar, that sink your hitherto fair fame far below the infamous murders of Vicksburg and St. Louis.

Before entering upon the question of responsibility for the past events, permit me to remark, what should perhaps have been premised before, that in addressing the people of Alton in general, I do not mean to embrace, in any censure implied, that noble few, that to the utmost of their ability, defended the rights of the citizen, and the majesty of the law. To them, I would accord my humble tribute of respect and gratitude. From my heart I thank them, that they succumbed not to the fanaticism of the populace, and the despotic ferocity of force.

There are two means of preventing popular outrages, moral influence, and, in the last resort, physical force. The former is the more humane, and generally the safer and more efficient expedient, but where it fails, we must have recourse to the latter, or permit society to be broken up. Let me then ask of the people of Alton, are you satisfied, that in the use of both these means yon have fully discharged your duty? The approach of the evil was deliberate and gradual, and gave full opportunity for the use of moral preventives. Public meetings had been held, parties had been organized, and press after press destroyed. What means of counteraction or prevention had you employed? Had you expressed your unqualified detestation of such outrages? Had you endeavored to rectify public sentiment and to arouse the community to consciousness of its guilt and its peril? Had you fearlessly indicated your uncompromising hostility to the adoption of lawless means under any pretext or against any evil? or did you palliate, or at least divert public indignation from acts you could not justify, by condemning the obstinacy and fanaticism of a man, who would not consent to silence his press at the will of a mob? Of the influence you exerted in private and domestic intercourse, I have no knowledge except from results; the inference they would warrant I will not draw. Of your endeavors to correct the popular mind by your public acts, your public resolves, and solemn expressions of opinion, we have, unhappily for your fame, your own record. It is difficult for an American to read that record without a burning blush. You had been expressly called together to consult for the tranquility and order of your city. Repeated instances of lawless violence had taken place, indications of an anarchical spirit were thick around you. You had full reason to be aware of your danger, and of the responsibilities under which you were acting. And what was the question which was convulsing your community? It was whether an American citizen should be permitted to exercise a most sacred constitutional right, or forego it at the pleasure of the mob. The vast importance of the principle' at stake was most obvious. The case was too plain to admit of argument. Did you then, the independent and enlightened men, meet the exigencies of the crisis by the decided nature of your resolves? By strong remonstrance, and unqualified rebuke, did you attempt to stay the popular infatuation and iniquity? Especially did you determine to sustain the law in all cases, and at all hazards? Resolutions to this very effect were brought before you. How could you have done otherwise than adopt them? Yet these, you rejected; and on what grounds? Because it was said they *put one party entirely in the wrong*: they would have done so. The parties were the American people and a gang of ruffians. And so because resolutions for sustaining the law and the constitution would have "put one party entirely in the wrong," they were to be rejected! What spirit of delusion, what smooth-lipped Belial could have induced you to swallow down such logic? One would have thought your understandings, if not your consciences would have retched at it. And what did you adopt in their stead? A resolution to enforce the laws *until the report of your committee was received*. And what was the report of that committee? A set of resolutions which in their popular impression at least, justified the mob by condemning the object of their hate - which recommended to him a removal from your city, and a sacrifice of his constitutional rights to a rabble of ruffians, and called it compromise. History, I apprehend, will pronounce it compromise, on your part, of duty and right, of honor and safety. These you adopted. Did you, then, the report of your committee having been received, renew your resolution to enforce the law, and that without limitation? No. Why did you not? Was it that you dared not, or that you wished not to do so? And what was the concluding resolution of this peculiar assemblage, introduced by one, who, 'most of all must have felt the responsibilities of his position - your Mayor? An expression of regret at interference from abroad in the matters of your city and community; as if, forsooth, wresting away the rights of any American citizen, and introducing into your state the pernicious precedent of mob violence triumphing over the freedom of the press, and infecting the body politic with this foul leprosy, were simply a domestic concern. As well might you consider firing one's house in the midst of a vast city, or importing into it garments infected with the plague, as merely affecting an individual interest. What must the introducer of the resolution have thought of it on that shameful night, when at last he found that there was no salvation for itself in Alton, and that his staff of office was but a polluted and paltry gewgaw? When he was compelled to become envoy truly "extraordinary" for the mob, he must have felt little disposed to deprecate aid from any quarter. He would, I imagine, have felt relieved at the sight of an army of intermeddlers, and that with the sword and the bayonet. Thus, having irritated the ferocity of the populace against their destined victim - having set your seal upon prejudices you ought to have enlightened - having sanctioned ulterior violence by a resolution of limited resistance, and by neglecting to renew that resolution - having given the mob a triumph by failing to take a fearless and unflinching stand in favor of civil rights, with a few faint salvos for the honor and majesty of law, your assembly, which happily has few parallels in modern times, broke up, losing an opportunity which was never to return. I firmly believe, if even at that late hour, you had taken the high and determined position you ought to have taken long before, if with your disapprobation of the course of Mr. Lovejoy, did you deem it necessary to express it, you had united a declaration of your fixed and unqualified purpose to sustain the law at all hazards, all yet might have been well. This you would not, or you dared not do. The occasion was lost; and blood and tears were to follow, of which what has already flowed may be no more than the first faint shower-drops. Such, as far as I have been able to learn, is the nature and amount of the moral prevention you used!

Let us next inquire what was your conduct in the use of the second means of prevention specified, coercion. And first: after the destruction of former presses, what measures had been taken by the civil authorities, and by your citizens to guard against, or to punish these out-rages? If any were made, that they were feeble, inefficient, and heartless, seems inferable from the results. And finally, upon the day of the arrival of the last press, when indications of premeditated violence were rife all around you, what precautionary measures were employed? Your Mayor consulted the City Council on the subject, and - they refused to act! - Their reasons remain in their own bosoms. The public demand to know them - they have a right to know them. Who were that City Council? The infamy of such a seemingly flagrant betrayal of trust, requires a definite resting-place. And at the last dark catastrophe, when the alarm bells had summoned you from your beds, and you saw a band of infuriated and drunken wretches besetting a warehouse, containing a number of your most respectable citizens, with deadly weapons - when you heard the discharge of fire-arms, and the blasphemies of rage, and the vows of murder, and saw them setting fire to the building, and hemming in the besieged with the avowed determination of burning the edifice and its occupants together - when you beheld a mob of about one hundred and fifty, about fifty of whom only are supposed to have been armed, engaged in these atrocities, what was your conduct? Undoubtedly your sympathies, if not your patriotism, were at length aroused- you eagerly offered your services to your Mayor- you could not be restrained - you rushed to the rescue. No, alas! no, not such were the facts. You looked quietly on, and saw the work of destruction and murder consummated!

For the above facts I am chiefly indebted, not to hearsay, or rumor, but to the published reports of your own meeting, and the statement of your Mayor. Whether, in view of the above facts, your consciences will acquit you of dereliction of duty, in the use of moral and coercive means - whether the public sentiment of your country, and the solemn tribunal of the human race, and the high Chancery of Heaven will hold you guiltless, is to you an inquiry of fearful interest. The decision, which all these might perhaps authenticate, it is not my wish to pronounce. My aim is not to upbraid, but to awaken to a serious and impartial review. Not, certainly, without the amplest evidence, should I feel warranted in bringing in a verdict of conviction of a guilt so opprobrious and so tremendous. Whatever justification the case admits, will be carefully and gratefully listened to. That there are some among you, who deserve no share in the infamy of the above transaction, we know - that there are more we should be glad to hope. That the individuals, whose well-known and hitherto respected names are made to appear as endorsers for the transactions of that strange meeting, were blinded by fear and overawed by the mob, and were not guilty of deliberate wickedness, charity leads us to presume. Perhaps it would be hazardous for common virtue to be thrown in their situation.

We can hardly give assurances how even ourselves will act, until circumstances have tried us.

But it is vain to attempt to shift the blame by impugning the motives and previous conduct of the Sufferer. To degrade him, were it in your power, would not exalt you- it would only add to the "deep damnation of his taking off" the coward malice that seeks shelter behind the carcass of its victim. To term him "rash," "headstrong," and "imprudent," is the strongest sentence of self-condemnation you can utter. Why was it "rash" or "imprudent" to exercise the most sacred of American of human rights - freedom of speech - in Alton? Was it because he ought to have known that there was not law, nor conscience, nor patriotism, nor intelligence, among you, to protect him? And if these elements were not found among you; you, and not he, were responsible for their absence. Nor do the results, melancholy as they are, though they argue your delinquency, necessarily convict him of rashness. There are in moral, as in political conflicts, Thermopylæs, where we must make a stand or perish - where yielding would be treason to our principles, our country, and our race - where it becomes a most solemn duty - to die! Perhaps nothing less than the shedding of blood could awaken the conscience and salutary fears of this nation, and open its eyes to that dreadful Tarpeian, on whose verge it is tottering. Whether such was the fact in this case, it concerns not my present purpose to inquire. Nor is it of importance to examine the vulgar charge that he died with the blood of a fellow-being on his hands. The charge, according to the testimony of those who were with him in the building, and who alone could know, is false. After the doors and windows had been broken in, and guns had been fired into the building, the fatal shot was discharged from within, but not by Mr. Lovejoy. But were the charge true, he had a right to shoot down that, or any other individual among the assailants, as he would so many beasts of prey. They were no more than midnight robbers. Pardon me - they *were* more, they were *traitors*. Had his hands been stained with the blood of a hundred of them, the decision of any court, human or divine, would have washed it all away. He had the right of self-defense, which is given to all - and he had in this case more, the direct warrant of the civil authority. The last act of Mr. Lovejoy does not imply the existence of any other emotions in his breast, than those which, with reference to other men, and other countries, and times, we are wont to ascribe to the highest heroic virtue. As it regards the charge of an unavailing waste of human life, nothing but the result proved it unavailing. It was the opinion of judicious men, that resistance to lawless violence, and the enforcement of law, were feasible; and had the guard from the Upper Town been present, there is little doubt they would have been effected. If we feel inclined to regret, that a minister of the gospel attempted to defend the rights of the citizen, and the laws of his country by force, this act should be viewed at least with indulgence, by those who are wont to regard with admiration, examples in their own Revolutionary history, where the pulpit was exchanged for the battlefield. Never was there a cause more sacred than that in which he fell. Nor will it avail you to charge him with having violated a pledge never to agitate the Slavery question in Alton. Such a pledge he never gave, nor had he a right to give. Such a pledge you had no right to receive, much less to enforce. All that he did, or ought to have done, was to express an existing intention, subject however to his future views of duty. And his right to print when, and where, and what he pleased, we must remember was not gained, nor could it be forfeited by the will of those to whom that intention was expressed.

But it is not relevant to my present purpose to be his apologist or condemner. It is enough for me to know that Mr. Lovejoy was an American citizen, in the exercise of his undoubted right, and that for this, he was in the face of your city openly murdered. How obnoxious soever his sentiments may have been, he had unquestionably the right to publish them, and for the abuse of this right he was amenable, not to a tumultuary, anarchical power, but to the legal tribunals, and those only. This you knew, and you knew it was your most solemn duty to maintain the law at all hazards. Call him imprudent, infatuated, fanatical, and nothing is easier than the application of such epithets of vague malice - it affects not the question of your duty - nor does it wash a single shade from the crimson of your guilt. Whatever may have been the desert of the individual, the constitution of your country surely deserved not such a wound at your hands.

Strange was it, even if no feeling of patriotism, or regard for the right moved within you, that you should have been so blind to considerations of self-interest. How could you look on and see a fellow citizen sacrificed, and not read in the atrocious transaction a warning of your own impending danger? Strange, that you could behold the triumph of brute force over law in this instance, and not feel you were witnessing the creation of a tyranny whose gory hand would be over you all. Did you not feel the cold shiver of the chain fastening around your souls? Infatuated men! how could you see an individual murdered for the expression of unpopular sentiments, and not feel you were hopelessly binding yourselves and your posterity to popular opinions, popular measures, popular prejudices, and popular crimes - in short, never to act or speak but with the permission of the populace, however degraded or guilt-stained it might be! Did you suppose that Abolitionism was to be the last object of popular hatred? How could you see liberty of speech smothered in blood in one instance, and not perceive you were creating a censorship over yourselves more jealous, fanatical, and intolerable, than that of the Chinese or Austrian, or the Romish despotism - that your own souls, the aspirations of your own hopes, your own reason and love of truth must henceforth whisper wizard-like from the dust? How could you fail to perceive that you were called upon to witness the obsequies of your own honor, and the consummation of your own shame - to set your seal to the act of your own enslavement, and of your deep and enduring disgrace? How could you, in retiring to your homes, look your wives and children in the face? Did you not feel that you had betrayed them - that the same red-handed power that had broken the heart of the wife, and made the child fatherless, might visit your own hearths with widowhood and orphanage; or, at least, that they could be secured against such a visitation, only by your becoming passive and pliant slaves, and that to the most despicable and brutal of masters? Should the violent and bloody spirit of the times, which you have at least tacitly countenanced, permit you to see old age, will this be a tale you will be proud to rehearse to your children? When the frenzy and infatuation of the day have had their ensanguined hour, and passion and party are silent in the grave, and impartial history shall take up the transaction; will your descendants, think you, be proud to read your names in connection with the disgraceful story? Aye, with the present indications of public feeling, and the expressions of indignant reprobation coming in upon you from all parts of our land, from every sect and party who have a regard for even their intellectual reputation, and who do not wish to rank with ruffians in morals, you may well tremble, lest the day be not far distant when a man will blush to have been on the night of the *seventh of November* a passive looker-on in Alton. You will pardon my plainness of speech. Had this out-breaking of popular violence come upon you with sudden and whirlwind fury, giving no warning of its approach, and admitting of no resistance in its explosive and desolating development, the case would have been widely different. But no. The approaches of the evil were gradual, and were foreseen - time was given for all counteracting and preventive influences, and for all requisite precautionary arrangements. The opportunity given for overawing the spirit of violence, by the solemn rebuke of public sentiment, was abused to its exasperation - the resolution that you would hold yourselves at the disposal of the Mayor was rejected - no plan was formed, no measure was adopted, no precautions were taken by the civil authorities. The whole matter was left to chance and impulse; and as the consequence, chance, and impulse, and misrule, and murder ruled the hour. The transaction seems to bear all the marks of systematic, deliberate, premeditated neglect or connivance. Therefore it is that my feelings and language are strong.

My remarks, thus far, apply to all who claim to be lovers of order and civil liberty, without distinction. But there is a class among you professing a higher morality, a more purifying hope, and a more scrupulous and abiding sense of right than other men - a faith stronger than expediency and holier than patriotism, and which eternally forbids that human fear or favor, or any power in the universe, should make them swerve from duty, or wink at iniquity. Where, let me ask of this class, were you during the progressive scenes of this shameful drama? Did you, in view of higher motives, and more solemn obligations of a mightier power, and more glorious example, stand by the right, when others, under the influence of interest, or fear, or worldliness, gave way before the tempest of wrong? or did you yield to the seductions of pecuniary interest or worldly hope? Did you succumb to a corrupt public sentiment, and truckle to the fanaticism of the mob?

Did you, in a Christian spirit, rebuke the spreading iniquity, or did you abet, or flatter, or palliate the spirit of lawless violence? Did you fear God or man? In short are you conscious of having done all that Christian duty, your awful vows, and your everlasting self-consecration to the God of truth and right, demanded? What course private individuals may have taken I know not; but I feel assured, that in no community where the church possesses the numerical strength, and wealth, and weight of character, she is reputed to embrace in her various branches in Alton, could such a series of progressive, and finally triumphant, acts of violence take place, without a gross dereliction of Christian duty - and it may be safely assumed, that had her professing members in that place, generally, acted worthily of the name they bear, these disgraceful outrages might have been prevented. But there are some of you, whose names from either peculiar influence, or office, or activity, have been painfully conspicuous in these transactions. Is it not a fact, that a professed preacher of the gospel in canvassing for a political office, publicly stated that he was for protecting the liberty of the press, but this was a case of its licentiousness - as if, forsooth, the mob, and not the laws, were to take cognizance of such licentiousness. Is it not a fact that clergymen of different denominations attended the first meeting called for tranquilizing your city; and why was it, when resolutions embracing principles, fundamental to freedom of speech and civil liberty were brought forward, that no voice was heard from these in their behalf? Is it not a fact, that one of the committee to draft resolutions, and one of the most prominent speakers at the second meeting, was a minister of Jesus Christ, and that that individual, instead of standing forth the fearless advocate of law and civil right, gravely recommended to an American citizen, in the exercise of constitutional rights, in a Christian country, and in a community claiming to be governed by law, the example of Paul, in a strange city, amid a dark-minded and pagan population, and under the dissolute, bloody, and venal despotism of Nero? and that before it was ascertained that the civil authority could not protect him, and when the only necessity for the adoption of that advice grew out of the fact, that the adviser and those like him, would not, or dared not defend the constitution under which they lived? This advice, too, we are to remember, which, if given at all, should have been whispered in secret, was in the presence of the mob who stood ready to overcome the contumacy that should dare reject it. What a spectacle was this to angels and to men! Why was that sacred man there? I know it could not have been to cover with the sanctity of his office the flagitiousness of the proceedings: but why was he there? To defend the right? Why then did he not defend it? Intimidated, seduced, or deluded, he presents the darkest and saddest of enigmas. By his sacred calling, as an ambassador of that Savior, who exhibited pureness amid the impure, benevolence amid the malignant, and an uncompromising rebuke of iniquity even unto death - by the mighty salvation he preached - by the souls of those dark-minded men around him, who were rushing: on to madness and murder, he was bound to be right, though all the millions of mankind, and of created orders, had been with the wrong - he was bound to know that, as a representative and teacher of the Christian faith, a slight lapse in him would give to others a license wide as the firmament - he was bound to know, that to him, in no small degree was committed the honor of that faith in that community, and that in prostituting its influence, or dishonoring its character, his would be a guilt no secular or infernal power could share - the guilt of sacrificing the only element of moral renovation among mankind. He was bound to remember, that he was to meet those misguided and guilty men, who he had full reason to know were verging on to crime, and, as the result proved, to murder, in a mighty assemblage, and before a more awful tribunal. To all this he was bound by obligations strong as immortality. But, alas! the evil passions which should have been rebuked, were exasperated. The prejudices, he should have enlightened, were abetted, the consciences which he should have aroused, were lulled to a fatal torpor. And here, then, let me ask, in view of these facts, (and to him it is a question of thrilling fear,) at whom, when the murderers shall be arraigned at the bar of the irreversible doom, will the *bloody fingers he pointed*? Strange was it, when he actually withdrew the protection of law, and gave up the victim to his fanatical haters - strange was it, he did not perceive, he was sacrificing the principles upon which his own religious liberty was based, and that that hatred and that triumph derived no small measure of their keenness, from the fact, that their prey was of his own order - a preacher of the gospel - and that that triumph would have been immeasurably enhanced, could the individual and his religion have been prostrated at the same blow? Whatever applause may have been rendered him, it must, in view of such facts, have arisen in his nostrils like the fumes of the pit - nor can it shut out forever the tones of that last, touching, solemn appeal and remonstrance, uttered by his slain brother, ere he was abandoned as the mark of a lawless and most iniquitous persecution: these, I am sure, will sometimes steal upon his hours of solitude and reflection, and the "voice within," I am told, cannot be entirely bribed to falsehood; and its decisions, it must be remembered, are but the anticipated sentence of the power that gave it commission. With reference to the actual perpetrators of the outrage, most of them, we are bound for the honor of the American name to presume, were of that refuse of society, which are wont to cluster around a commercial emporium, kenneling un-regarded in the grog-shop, and the gambling hell, till some demagogue or agitator calls them forth to personate the people, supersede the law, and take care of the public conscience and public morals. Many of them, in charity to the national character we may assume, are beneath the reach of an enlightened public sentiment, either from an ignorance that cannot, or a prejudice that will not read; or belong to those desperadoes in society to whom the whip, the axe, and the halter are the only arguments. Others there probably were, of slender intelligence and weak moral purpose, but of inflammable passions, who under the influence of evil men, and mistaken opinions, knew not what they did. Such are indeed objects of pity, and upon evidence of repentance are not to be excluded from forgiveness, confidence and kindness. But such, alas, were not all. We have reason to believe, that amid the immediate instigators or actual perpetrators of the felony were some, whose titled names, education enjoyed, profession in life and pride of standing in society, we should have hoped, would have kept them from such self-degradation - that there were those of enlightened conscience and cultivated intellect, who not only polluted themselves with the foul iniquity, but deliberately seduced others into it. With reference to such, whether with utter recklessness of character, appearing openly in the transaction, or skulking in concealment, and instigating the wretches, they had not courage to lead - it matters not - language is inadequate to the flagitiousness and wickedness of their character. That your malignity was too strong for your regard to the right, or your love of your country, is perhaps no matter of surprise; but I am surprised that it took no counsel of ultimate consequences. The act you were committing, by the interpretation of all courts and all codes, was murder. Why, in that guilty hour did not your good or your evil angel whisper you that, by the act you were perpetrating, you were putting yourselves and the laws of your country at an eternal issue? Yes, between them and yourselves there is, and ever must be, war to the knife, a war of extermination, in which one or the other must perish. Public anarchy and ruin are your only safety. Can you expect, can you be so impious as to hope, to conquer in such a warfare? But should you prevail, have you yet to learn from the admonitions of history, that the instigators and leaders of popular frenzy, however they may triumph for a while, sooner or later feed the Brazen Bull their own hands have reared? Sooner or later, themselves are gorged by the Anaconda which they are wont to caress, and whose hissing they pronounce excellent music. Did Robespierre and his compeers dream they were erecting the guillotine for themselves? But did he, or Danton, or Marat, sleep in bloodless graves? Have you yet to learn, that there is an avenging Providence, which often forbids that bloody and violent men should make their last bed in peace? But should you be left to the course of nature, are there no furies of the guilty mind, which the fugitive from human law can never escape, and which often make the guilty envy his victim the repose of the sepulcher? An American citizen murdered, a home desolated, a wife widowed, a child made fatherless - these are recollections which will not fade with the fading excitements of the hour. From these you can never flee - no bars can protect, no concealments hide you from them, no .flight can leave them behind - they are become a part of your own souls. The dreadful truth that you are murderers will follow you through all your future existence: in whatever scenes you may mingle - beneath whatever sky you may repose, the grisly accuser will dog you. Though you essay to drown its voice in the madness of intoxication, or in the excitements of deeper and still deeper crime - vain will be the attempt, it will await you in the grave. Yea, in the last great CONGREGATION the gory phantom will start forth, and arraign you at the bar of eternal justice. Much do I misjudge, if the hours do not frequently come, when you would gladly hide yourselves in the grave, were it not, that secret "dread of something after death," which God has left as his witness and prophet in the souls of the guiltiest, will warn you that the tortures you experience are but the faint and shadowy earnest of an immortal REMORSE. By the act you have committed you have also chained yourselves to the necessity of an unending war with virtuous public sentiment. Public opinion must be permanently vitiated, or you will become objects from which men will shrink as from something polluted, venomous, deadly. The dire and fixed necessity seems laid upon you of perpetually corrupting society, or of becoming the objects of its deep and lasting abhorrence.

And what have you gained by all this dreadful and guilty self-sacrifice? Whatever may have been the faults of your victim, you have embalmed and canonized them. Whatever may have been the defects of his cause, or of his advocacy of it, you have done much, by your mad act, to identify that cause with that of freedom of speech and American liberty, and you have given its advocate rank among the apostles of humanity and martyrs to the rights of man; among the Vanes and Sydneys of other times you have ensured his name a record, while the traducer and the murderer are forgotten in the grave. Instead of checking the cause, for which he labored, you have made the sympathies of this whole nation react upon you like an earthquake. You have virtually surrendered the field of argument, by a resort to force - you have made the name of the object of your hate a talisman and a power, worth more to him, and his cause, than a hundred years of life. You cannot bury his shed blood in the earth - it will have voice - it will plead louder than a thousand presses. From its every drop wall spring an army of living antagonists. Did you dream that at this age you could muzzle free discussion? You might as well attempt to muzzle Ætna. Did you hope to chain liberty of speech? You might as well lay grasp upon Niagara. Did you think to oppose yourselves to the progress of free opinion? You might as well throw yourselves across the path of the lightning or the whirlwind. The nation, or conspiracy of nations, that opposes itself to the course of free inquiry, opposes itself to the Providence of God and the destiny of the race, and might as well think to suspend the laws of nature, or stay the earth in her orbit. But that you, at the head of a drunken and swinish mob, with the force of an ignorant and brutish rabble, should hope to withstand the onward march of opinion, would provoke only contempt, did not the atrociousness of the attempt entitle it to indignation - it emulates only the sagacity of the animal that sometimes takes its stand upon the railroad track, and challenges battle with the locomotive.

In reflecting upon your infamous course, you have not even the poor satisfaction of successful villainy. Unhappy, infatuated men! whose only safety lies in the dissolution of social order, the corruption of public sentiment, and the ruin of your country: or who, should the promptings of reviving virtue and patriotism be ever again felt, must find your highest duty, and the sole act of magnanimity and patriotism left you - an ignominious death. Nevertheless, to that duty, and that act, I must commend you. Surrender yourselves to the justice of your country. Atone for your great wickedness by furnishing to your country the only use of which you are longer susceptible, a practical and fearful warning. Commending you to this, and to deep repentance before that Power which can pardon the penitent, and still maintain the majesty of law, I take my leave of you in commiseration and sorrow.

Citizens of Alton! If, in any respect, I may seem to have put myself in the unamiable and most undesirable attitude of a public accuser, it is that I may stimulate to sober inquiry into the causes of past outrage, and the means of future prevention. This means, melancholy experience demonstrates, is to be found only in the firm, fearless, impartial and universal maintenance of law. Abolition is not the last of unpopular doctrines; nor do we know who, or what may next become obnoxious to popular odium. Nothing less than the stern enforcement of law irrespective of persons, or opinions, or circumstances, will prevent persecution, proscription, and murder without end. This enforcement implies infliction of penalties, as well as promulgation of commands, and involves in your case a melancholy duty with reference to the past. The laws have been repeatedly, openly, and flagrantly violated among you - a public, premeditated, atrocious murder has been perpetrated. The course you may take with the offenders, will settle the question in the eye of mankind, whether you have moral energy and political virtue enough remaining, to retrieve your disgrace, and recover your lost position. God forbid that I should cherish towards the unhappy wretches implicated, any other than feelings of Christian kindness, and a desire for their repentance. God forbid that revenge should claim a bloody oblation for the shade of the murdered Lovejoy. Vengeance belongs to another hour, and a mightier hand. But the spirit of slain justice does walk your streets, and clamor for expiation. Until that be given, no charm can lay her unquiet shade. She will wander up and down your city, she will whisper you in the darkness of the night - her sorrowing tones will steal upon the solitude of your repose, and her gory apparition will affright your slumbers. Ages to come, her moan will resound among your cliffs, and rise upon the roar of the Mississippi. Unless atonement be made to violated law, order and security can never be restored among you - not, at least, until a generation unstained by this transaction have taken your places, and the offenders are beyond the reach of human justice.

AN AMERICAN CITIZEN

Remarks made at Rochester, at a meeting of the Western Convention of New York, January 10th, 11th, and 12th, 1838.

17. *Resolved*, That in the murder of the Rev. E. P. Lovejoy, in Alton, Illinois, by an uncontrolled and unrebuked mob, we feel that our country has lost a noble-hearted citizen, and an able and uncompromising defender of the liberty of the press - the cause of humanity a faithful friend; and, while we acquiesce in the dispensations of Providence, we deeply lament his untimely end.

January 10th, 1838
Alvan Stewart, Esq.

I am much pleased with this resolution. I can sympathize with the mover of it in all that he has expressed in admiration of the martyred Lovejoy. I am glad to see this resolution brought in. There would have been a chasm in the proceedings of this convention without it. This subject, painful as it is, deserves our careful consideration. Nothing has happened in many years which has produced so electric an effect upon the public mind as this. Such a feeling so broad and deep, was scarcely excited when the great and enlightened Hamilton, the patriot and statesman, fell. Even when the father of his country slept the sleep of death, there was not a much greater sensation produced than now, when our brother Lovejoy has fallen. The gradual lapse of years brings with it decay and death, so that when our own Washington in his turn was swept away by the great destroyer, we all looked upon it as an event, mournful it is true, but still expected and unavoidable. But Lovejoy, in the prime of life, in the full career of extensive usefulness, was struck down by the assassin's steel. But he fell in the cause of liberty, and the true sons of liberty are aroused in his behalf. He fell, but the length and breadth of the land was agitated by the blow. Where is the newspaper that has not cast its censure upon the murderers? What editor has failed to record his condemnation of the bloody deed?

But I want to comment for a moment on the facts and circumstances which led to this disastrous event. And when we look at them we may well thank God that there have been no more martyrs to this cause. But, indeed, there are many sacrificed at the bloody altar of oppression, martyrs who daily pour out their blood at the shrine of Slavery. Let us not forget that the life of the slave is one continued scene of martyrdom, equal in anguish and horror to that of Lovejoy. Sometimes it is a martyrdom of all life's holiest affections - of conjugal fidelity - of filial love - rudely broken and inhumanly sundered. But again, there are others who are as real martyrs to the system, and who as freely pour out their blood before it as ever Lovejoy could do. Let us not forget that thousands of human beings are annually sacrificed on the altar of this Moloch of our country, and that each one of them has been crushed by the same spirit that laid our brother in the grave.

The blind and perverse mob at Alton were only acting out public sentiment. They knew that the mobs at Boston, and New York, and Utica, were never called to account, and the sufferers never received redress, and why should not they escape with the same impunity?

Then when McIntosh was burned alive, and no one dared to publish the facts lest the wrath of the foul fiend of Slavery should be wreaked on their heads, this was the signal for Lovejoy. The groans of the dying McIntosh were ringing in his ears, and he braved the wrath of Slavery's minions, that he might plead against injustice. He published the facts and told the world of what had been done by Satan's power. But by so doing he incurred the wrath of the friend of Slavery, and his life was placed in danger. So loud, at length, became the clamors against him, that he thought it not safe to remain at St. Louis, and therefore removed with his paper to Alton, and published the "Alton Observer." Again, on the 2d of October, at St. Charles, the house in which he was, being attacked by a mob, he was only saved by the self-devotion of his wife from being torn in pieces by the infuriated mob. And afterwards, when his three presses were successively destroyed, it was only the gradual approach toward the final consummation of the tragedy. But he felt that it was in the cause of liberty he had been engaged, and he had no right to withdraw from the contest. He took his life in his hand, and went forward, resolved to sacrifice himself rather than surrender to oppression. And now we come to that last dreadful night, that laid him in the dust, and I weep for my country when I look upon the scene. The workmanship of God was destroyed. We saw a man of talents and of enterprise, of religious zeal and of ardent piety, the servant of God, and working in his master's cause, laying a poor corpse. I see what was done. Come with me and let us go into Mr. Oilman's warehouse on the night of the 7th of November. There we see a man, who, from the first attack had remained on his knees crying to God for help and for direction. He saw that human aid was gone, none but the arm of the Almighty could reach them, and he plead for mercy, and he did not lose his reward. How soon did he hear the invitation, well done thou good and faithful servant, enter thou into the joys of thy Lord. Yes, I can see the Savior bending over the walls of paradise, and, from amidst the glory of his own home, calling to his faithful minister in accents of love and approbation, cheering him through his struggle, and as soon as his spirit escaped from its prison house of clay, affectionately receiving it into his own bosom. Perhaps the first saint to whom he was introduced on entering the spirit world was St. Mark, or St. Stephen the proto-martyr, and who can imagine the joy with which those kindred spirits mingle with each other in that blest abode.

But let us return to this earthly scene a little longer. Come with me to Alton, and we will look at the scene after the mob had passed away. It is night: - all things around are wrapped in silence. The stars are reflected from the rolling Mississippi with their wonted luster, and seem to shrink from beholding the awful events which have just transpired. But who can describe the object lying in yonder silent chamber. Never did the moon go down behind the Rocky Mountains looking back on so dreadful a scene. In that still chamber in the warehouse lays the stiffening corpse; no friend is watching its repose, no taper gleams about his head, he rests in silence and darkness, alone and unguarded in the dead of night. Fresh and gory from the murderous shot, he rests in death. Those eyes shall no more weep for human woe; no more shall they look with pain upon the crushed and suffering slave. Those lips now rigid and unmoving shall no more pour consolation in the afflicted soul or plead for the slave's relief from the oppressor's rod. That noble right hand, the faithful servant of its master's mind, lies motionless by his side. Oh save that right hand from pollution, it is the best friend the poor slave ever had - but it shall never stir again till the resurrection morn shall awake the dead. Never again shall that pure heart be pained by the dying groans of the murdered McIntosh - never again shall his soul be sickened with report of northern minister's recreant to the cause of the poor and oppressed, sacrificing truth and duty on the altar of popularity. But let us leave his cause with God. But let us forget not, that his wife and child have no protection but our charity - then our homes shall be theirs, our kindness shall support them, our care shall guard them, our friends shall befriend them - and so shall we commend them to the God of grace, who is the widow's God, and the Father of the orphan.

G. R. Parburt,

Mr. President - Allow me to lay my small tribute on the altar where freedom bled. And though I may add nothing new 'to what has been said, I may at least repeat what should be kept in everlasting remembrance. But perhaps, floods of tears would best express the feelings of my heart on this solemn occasion. I may mourn, indeed, since Lovejoy is no more. Since Lovejoy, the amiable, the pious, has fallen by the hands of assassins, American assassins. Christian American assassins, nature unreproved may drop a tear. He fell the victim of pro-slavery influence - he fell in a manly defense of the dearest rights of humanity - the rights of mind. Deprive me of property, of reputation, of friends, and the loss may admit of reparation. But when I am deprived of the free expression of thought, then my noble nature is enchained - I am a free man no more. It was for the security of this right Lovejoy bled. Noble martyr! While thought is free to scan the universe of God, thy name shall live in sweet remembrance in the hearts of the freest of the free! Thy name shall be an amulet from which, in all coming time, tyranny shall instinctively shrink. Not for himself, sir, but for you, for me, for us all, for this great nation, for the friends of universal freedom throughout the world - he poured out his patriot blood. Had he abandoned the honorable post to which the Providence of God had called him, he would have acted unworthy his birth, his education, the land of the pilgrim fathers, the cause he had espoused, and that Christian heroine who rescued him from the mob at St. Charles, and who now lies bleeding on freedom's altar, the victim of Slavery, the continued expiation of this nation. But he did not abandon that post, environed as it was with reckless foes. He stood like a strong pillar, firm as the rock of truth on which he stood. The waves of popular commotion and of pro-slavery violence, dashed furiously around him, but every successive billow, as it broke in foaming rage, only proved that Lovejoy was there. Calmly and self-possessed he breasted the storm at St. Louis, and then planted himself at Alton, where he rationally expected the omnipotent protection of law and public sentiment. But the demon of Slavery pursued him. Its heated breath swept over the elements of oppression, and kindled a pro-slavery conflagration. Again was the press consumed, and again met a like disastrous fate - but still the form of its protecting angel was seen walking amidst the flame, unscathed - serene as the heaven which sustained him, - fast maturing for its holier enjoyments, and more unfading glories. But now the hour of his departure was at hand. He bared his bosom to the sword - all was still - 'twas the silence of death. Illinois trembled - Alton fell to the ground; its glory was departed.

Come now, ye ministers of Jesus, and behold an ambassador of your Lord, sealing the doctrines of humanity with his blood. Sublime spectacle! Gaze on it till your spirit catch the mantle of your ascended brother, and your hearts expand with a martyr's love for your crushed brethren in chains. Weep, weep bitterly, not for the departed, but for the heaven-forsaken people who have imbued their hands in the blood of an innocent, unoffending minister of Jesus. Lift up your voice, eloquent through grief, and demand, with the authority of your divine commission, that the church cleanse herself of this guilt, by ceasing to shield a system prolific of deeds of which this is one, marked with odious and horrid peculiarities.

Ye sentinels on the watch-tower of liberty, turn aside for one moment and contemplate this tragic scene. Like you, Lovejoy was stationed on the ramparts of freedom. But his was a dangerous post - a post of glory. He finished his work - now there he lies. Pale is that lofty brow, but not with coward fear. Mute is that tongue; but it plead for universal liberty till death. Sealed are those lips; but they ever scorned to kiss a tyrant's hand. Yonder lies the pen, that true Damascus blade of mind, which was wielded so skillfully and effectually against tyranny by that cold hand now paralyzed by the assassin's steel. And there are the fragments of the press, your own mighty engine of mental warfare, the palladium of liberty's self, stained with his blood so fresh and warm. And forget not his un-expiated shade yet hovers among you. But return, now, resume your pens, arouse the great and guilty nation from its extreme and passive torpidity, till it shake off that inexplicable stupor of oppression which has fallen upon it - or prepare yourselves to be slaves. Nay, rather let your bodies, like that of Lovejoy's, be laid among the fragments of the press, than that the dark spirit of Slavery should be permitted to enter the sacred precincts of the temple of liberty.

And ye American mothers, ye daughters of the revolutionary worthies, come and weep over the untimely fate of the son of that New England mother who, when she learned that her son had been slain for the cause of truth, nobly exclaimed: It is well; I had rather my son should have fallen a martyr to his cause than that he should have proved recreant to his principles. A mother well worthy of such a son! Mingle your tears with those of that mother, and those of the bereaved widow and the orphan. Press more closely to your hearts those babes you so much love; but, remember, God only knows whether they shall be such orphans, and yourselves such widows. But, still with their daily nourishment let them receive the elements of purest patriotism, of holiest freedom. Let their infant lips early learn to whisper Lovejoy - Lovejoy and the freedom of the press. Tell them full oft the horrid tragedy of Alton. And when they go forth into the world bid them return, having valiantly maintained the liberty of thought, or with a mother's blessing lay their bodies beside the illustrious Lovejoy.

But, ye slaveholders of the south, go now, and see a noble-hearted American slain at your bidding! Who will restore to your country another Lovejoy, the meek, the dignified, the unyielding friends of the liberties of your nation? Why did you command it? What was his fault? Was it not the defense of those principles, ye degenerate sons of noble fathers, for which your own Henry and your own Jefferson eloquently plead, and your own Marion and your own Washington exposed their bosoms to the Briton's bayonet? See now the legitimate fruits of the damnable tree of involuntary servitude planted by your ancestry, and which your own hands have so long, and so assiduously cultivated. You have brought innocent blood upon this nation. See your own hands red with a brother's gore; fratricides that ye are. Hasten now to the city of refuge ere the avenger of blood overtake you. Let your penitential tears timely evince your sorrow, that your murderous stain may be blotted out. Bring forth fruits meet for repentance, by breaking every yoke and letting the oppressed go free.

And thou city of destruction- for henceforth, Alton, shalt thou thus be known - come, come and behold the victim of your murderous spite. Look, ye men of Alton, on that gory form. See, ye cruel ministers of death, the uncompromising, the illustrious defender of freedom of thought stretched at your feet, yet noble in death, and your unhallowed hands dripping with his blood. What was your price, ye mercenaries in murder, that ye stained the American soil with blood as rich, as pure, as ever traitorous British steel caused to flow on Bunker Hill? What was your price, that ye wounded liberty in the house of her friends; that ye plunged your dagger to the heart of the incarnation of the rights of mind? Affect not to despise this deed; ye have done it, and the civilized world will hold you responsible for the assassination of Elijah P. Lovejoy. The sword of human justice, drunk with the innocent blood shed in your streets, may slumber over you, but eternal justice only delays awhile to make your damnation surer. Aye, even now, barbarous men that ye are, the lightning of your own reason consume you. Wherever ye go, in whatever ye engage, the avenger of blood haunts your guilty souls. Not the hoarse laugh of your forced jests, not the gloom of sullen silence, not the darkness of the midnight hour can shut out from your sight the murdered Lovejoy:

> "An inward day that never sets,
> Glares round your souls and mocks your closing eyelids,"

ever revealing the form of the man of God ye slew.

THE END

NOTE

We take this note from an account of the trials, now in press, of those defending-, and those who attacked the warehouse on the night of the 7th of November. John M. Krum, Mayor, was called and sworn. He was requested to give a connected account of all the disturbances, from the formation of the city government. After detailing the events which transpired on the evening of the 30th of October, at which time President Beecher preached, he proceeds:

Subsequently to this, I was frequently called upon by Mr. Lovejoy, (now deceased.) Mr. Tanner, Roff, and others, and my opinion asked in regard to the propriety and expediency of organizing an armed force. I remarked that at present there was no organized militia force in the city, and no force upon which I could depend upon in an emergency. They thought of forming a military company, and they asked me, if in case they did, I would head it. I told them I could not, that my official situation was such as would render it impossible. Mr. Lovejoy, in particular, called repeatedly upon me, and said, that I ought to command a military force. I told him I could not consent to do so: that I never should do so unless it became necessary for the protection of the laws. We had repeated conversations upon this subject, I repeatedly and I believe always told Mr. Lovejoy that it was within the province of any citizens to organize such force, if they deemed it necessary they could do it, if they pleased, at any time. Mr. Lovejoy stated to me, that they wished to organize their company under my sanction in an official capacity, and asked me, if I would give such sanction. I told him that I could not; and explained to him the reason why I should feel bound to withhold it. I told him what the provisions of the law, in regard to the formation of such companies, were: explained to him the mode of proceeding, necessary to be followed in the organization of their company.

Subsequently to this, I loaned my law books to someone who I understood was to join the company.

Mr. Gilman, in an interview shortly after, told me that they had organized a company, and had put themselves under the command of Wm. Harned; he tendered me the services of the company, and said, that they would at all times hold themselves in readiness to obey any command I might issue. I replied, again thanking him for his readiness to act, so often expressed, and told him whenever the time should come, in which I should think the occasion would warrant me to call for their services, I should unhesitatingly do it.

On the night of the sixth, or rather on the morning of the seventh of November last, at about three o'clock, Mr. Gilman and Mr. Roff came to my room and called me up. They stated that the press was coming - that the boat was in sight, coming up the river, and that Mr. Moore was upon the boat and had charge of the press; that arrangements had been made to have it safely landed and stored that right, and they requested me to go down, and be present at its landing; so that, in case of difficulty or disturbance, I might be there to suppress it. I got up, dressed as- quickly as I could, and went down to the river. I stood at Mr. Gilman's warehouse while the boat was Hearing, and till she landed. I did not go on board, I think. The hands of the boat put the press on shore, and removed it into the warehouse. I think I did not have conversation with anyone but Mr. Gilman at this time. After the press was stored, I went up into the warehouse. I found some twenty or thirty people assembled: they were all armed, and again offered me their services in aid of the laws. I told them, as I had repeatedly before, that at the time I did not see any occasion for their services, but that if occasion should arise, when their services should be needed by me, I should not only call for but should expect to receive their assistance. On the sixth, Mr. Gilman called upon me at my office, he introduced, as matter of consideration, the subject of the rights of citizens to defend their property. We had a long conversation, I gave him my opinion upon the subject, I think I read the law, and explained to him its principles, I do not know whether he asked my advice as mayor, as lawyer, or as a friend and citizen. I did not consider that I was then advising him as Mayor. In the course of our conversation we spoke of our municipal regulations, I told him I thought they were exceedingly deficient, and I believe I mentioned in what particulars. He asked me if I would appoint special constables, said he apprehended danger to his property. I told him that I had no authority to make any such appointment, that I would cheerfully do all I could, - that the Council would meet that day, and that at their meeting I would lay the whole matter before them. When the Council met, I did make the application, but I did not recommend in terms the appointment of such officers. I left the whole matter to the action of the Board. I was absent at the next meeting of the Council, when the records were read or I should have noticed the mistake in the record, and had it corrected.

On the evening of the 7th of November last, Mr. Oilman and Mr. Chappell called at my office. They told me they apprehended an attack would be made upon the warehouse, as they had understood the mob were determined to destroy the press; that a number of armed men had assembled and were then in the building for the purpose of defending it; and that they had come to the resolution of remaining there, and defending it at all hazards. They asked me what I thought of their determination. They spoke of the rumors they had heard in regard to the determination of the mob to destroy the press. At that time, all was quiet in the city, so far as I know, and I had but a little while before been in the streets, and observed nothing which led me to suppose an attack was meditated. I did not believe an attack would be made. I had exerted myself that day, as much as I was able, and had endeavored to get all the information which was possible. People seemed to shun me, and were very reluctant to communicate with me at all, and I could succeed in getting no information, which should have induced me to believe any design to destroy the press was meditated. Mr. Gilman asked me what I thought of the armed men who were in the building, remaining there for the purpose of defending their property. I told him, in my opinion they had an undoubted right to be there; that they might rightfully remain there, and that they would be justified in defending" their property, I did not understand them as making this application for advice to me, as Mayor. Mr. Gilman stated to me that they were well prepared with arms, - that they should remain there during the night, - that they were fully determined to defend the press, and the building, - and that if the attack, which they apprehended, was made, they wished it to be understood that their services would be ready to execute any order they might receive from any civil officer. I replied to them, that, if the emergency should require the aid of armed men, I should not hesitate a moment in commanding the men who were assembled there to suppress the riot, but that I should be the sole judge of such an emergency. He repeatedly asked me what I thought of their being there. I never ordered any man to repair to the warehouse; but in every instance, I was informed that they had already repaired there. Mr. Oilman repeatedly told me, that all he desired was to act under the authority of law, and the civil officers. After Mr. Oilman left, I remained in my office till between nine and ten o'clock. I stepped in to Dr. Hart's office at that time, and while I was there, I heard a number of people passing by. There were from fifteen to twenty. Immediately came down stairs. I recognized two of the crowd; one of them had a gun. I got my overcoat, prepared myself, returned to the street, but saw no one. I came down to Mr. Robbins' office, - sent for Judge Martin and other civil officers, and waited some time for them to come - Mr. Robbins and myself finally started together. As I was going down the stairs I heard two reports from fire-arms, - from the sound, I thought they were pistols, - the reports seemed to be low, I soon heard another which I took to be a gun. I hastened up, and soon saw people carrying a man, - it was Bishop. I stepped up to them and asked if any one was hurt, - they replied yes, one of our men was shot - I asked if he was much hurt, - they said they thought not. They seemed much excited, - I endeavored to persuade them to disperse - a crowd gathered round me; I addressed them, and used all the means in my power to induce them to disperse. I asked them what they intended to do. They said they were determined to have the press. Some one proposed that I should let those inside the warehouse know that they wanted the press; that they would have it at all events, and said, they would retire while I went in and communicated their determination. I acceded, supposing that if we could once get them scattered, the excitement would subside and we could then control them. They retired, and I went to the warehouse. Mr. Gilman opened the door, and let me (with Mr. Robbins and I believe Mr. West also,) in. He, Mr. Gilman, asked me how many outside were injured, if any. I told him there was but one injured, so far as I knew, - that there were but few outside. I then told Mr. Gilman what the mob said they wanted, and the determination they had expressed; and I also stated my impression, that, when I went out, we could control them. I staid in the warehouse some time purposely, longer than I otherwise should, in order that the excitement should subside, as I had no doubt it would.

While in the warehouse, I went up on to the second floor. I saw there, Gilman, Lovejoy, Walworth, Long, and (I think, but am not positive,) Hurlbut, and some others. I think I saw some arms about the walls. Gilman, Long, and Lovejoy, had guns in their hands. Gilman told me that two or three guns had been fired from the house. Deacon Long asked me if they were justified. I replied most certainly, I thought they were. My impression was that we should be able to quell any further disturbance, when we went out; and I so expressed myself. I had no idea any further attack would be made.

Question by W. S. Gilman: On the night of the 6th when I called you up, and you went down to the warehouse, did you not go into the building before the press was landed?

Answer: Yes, I believe I did, I think I did.

Question: Did you not ask me to go out, and did I not go out and stand by your side on the wharf at the time the press was landed?

Answer: Yes, you did.

Question: When the press was landing, did I not ask you to go down and receive it, and did you not say that as I was the owner, I had better go down and receive it, and you would be by my side?

Answer: There was a proposition of that kind made, and I believe I made it. I thought as you owned it, you ought to be there to receive it when it was landed.

Question: Did you not tell us we had better not leave the warehouse, not even to go to our meals, without some being there to guard it?

Answer: I think I told you, you had better keep a guard there, or something to that effect.

Question: Did I not seem anxious to know what to do?

Answer: You did: you appeared anxious that whatever was done should be done under the sanction of the civil authority.

Question: What course did you say you should take in case the press should be attacked?

Answer: I told you that if there was any danger that the people should attack the press, I should order them to desist, and should warn them of the serious consequences which would follow any attempt on their part to disturb or destroy the press.

Question: Did you not say that if the press was attacked, you should first order the mob to desist, and that if they persisted you should then order us to fire?

Answer: I believe I did, I said I should if it became necessary.

Question: Did you not at this time consider you appeared there as Mayor.

Answer: I did. I once agreed in one of the interviews I had with Mr. Oilman, to appoint Captain Harned a special constable at his (Mr. Gilman's) request; but afterwards, upon examination, I found I had no authority to make such appointment. I did not consider the armed force at the church, or at the landing of the press, as organized under my authority.

I have lived in the city for nearly five years. Godfrey and Oilman built the warehouse which was attacked; it has been in their possession ever since I have known the place.

I heard no noise in the warehouse, on the night of the 7th. I saw but few persons there, I saw Mr. Oilman first, on the lower floor; I saw Mr. Long, Lovejoy, and Hurlbut, and I presume others, but do not recollect who.

I know Mr. Oilman to be an orderly citizen. I gave no orders while I was in the building, either to Oilman or anyone else restraining them from firing, or doing anything else.

I saw no occasion for doing so. I thought they had a right to do as they were doing. When I went out I commanded the people assembled there to disperse. Had I seen anything riotous on the part of those in the warehouse, I should have ordered them to desist, I should have commanded them to disperse. When I first went up, the front of the store had been broken in. Some shot struck my hat while I was addressing the crowd. The guns were fired outside the building, and I thought from the southeast corner of the warehouse; there were three guns fired at the people who were raising the ladder to the warehouse. I supposed the shot which reached me was fired at them; and I afterwards ascertained that I stood about in the direction.

The two first discharges were from the outside, and they were the first which were fired, I think.

Question by Defendant's Counsel: From all the circumstances in the case, have you any doubt that Mr. Oilman in what he did, supposed he had your sanction?

Answer: From all the circumstances, I am induced to believe that Mr. Oilman supposed he was acting under my authority. While I was in the storehouse some conversation took place about the right which a man had to defend his property. I uniformly told them that they had a right to be there.

I told them they were justified in defending their property, but I told them so as a lawyer. "While I was in the warehouse, I told them if they were out of doors, I should command their aid in suppressing the riot, but that I could not command them while they remained there.

Cross examined: While I was in the building, I gave no directions to those inside as to the mode of resistance they should adopt. I considered that they acted upon their own responsibility, but I gave them my legal opinion. I took the message which the mob requested me to take, and communicated it to those inside. I told them that the mob swore they would have the press at all hazards. Oilman replied, that they had resolved to defend the press at the risk of their lives, and that they could not give it up. I saw Oilman, Lovejoy, Hurlbut, and Long, and I recollect of no others now whom I saw with guns.

In my remarks to the mob, I returned the language of Gilman; I spoke to them of the dangers they were in, the laws they were violating, and the penalties they were incurring by the breach of those laws.

Question by Linder for Government: Did Mr. Gilman ever tell you what principles that press was intended to advocate?

Answer: I do not think he ever did. He once told me that it was not determined whether the press should be established here, or at some other place.

I do not know that I ever heard Gilman say anything about keeping Mr. Lovejoy here, or persuading him to go off.

I never did confer upon those who were inside any authority to assemble; or give them any order to fire upon the people outside. I endeavored in the interviews I had with Mr. Gilman to explain to him the law.

Question by Linder for Government: Did you ever state to Mr. Gilman that he could not resort to violence, unless under the direction of an officer of the law?

Answer: I do not think I ever did. I told him that every man had a right to defend his person and property, and to use violence if it was necessary, and that each man must judge of his extremity. I repeatedly stated to him, that whenever a case presented itself, when I thought the emergency required it, I should not hesitate to call upon those men, or any other, to aid me in maintaining order; but, I thought it must be an extreme case which would justify such a course. I advised Mr. Gilman, in case of any disturbance, to address the crowd in the first place; I thought he took a correct view of the matter. I told him what course I should probably take if I was placed in a similar situation; but in all instances I advised him as a friend, and a citizen, and not as an officer. I might have been desired to remain in the building, at the time I went in. I think I was, and that I replied that I could have more influence with the crowd out of doors. At the time I addressed the crowd, after I came out of the warehouse, I think I stated to them, that unless they dispersed they would be fired upon by those in the budding. If I recollect right, the mob made no reply. They advised me to get out of the way and go home.

Question by Defendant's Counsel: At the time you stated to Mr. Oilman and others, that if they were outside you should command them to aid you, was any proposition made by any one for them to go out?

Answer: There was no proposition made by them, or to them, to go out of doors. They expressed their readiness to obey any orders I might give them.

Question by hinder for Government: Did you give them any orders?
Answer: I did not.

Made in the USA
Middletown, DE
02 December 2016